Chronology of Prophetic Events

Fazlur Rehman Shaikh

Ta-Ha Publishers Ltd.
1 Wynne Road,
London SW9 0BB
UK

Copyright © Fazlur Rehman Shaikh/Ramadan 1422-Shawwal/November 2001

Published by:
Ta-Ha Publishers Ltd.
1 Wynne Road
London SW9 0BB
Website: http://www.taha.co.uk
Email: sales@taha.co.uk

All rights reserved. No part of this publication may be reproduced, stored in any retrieval system, or transmitted in any form or by any means, electronic or otherwise, without written permission of the publishers.

By: Fazlur Rehman Shaikh
General Editor: Afsar Siddiqui
Edited by: Abdassamad Clarke

British Library Cataloguing in Publication Data
Shaikh, Fazlur Rehman
Chronology of Prophetic Events
I. Title

ISBN 1 842000 34 9

Typeset by: Bookwright
Website: http://www.bogvaerker.dk/Bookwright
Email: bookwright@bogvaerker.dk

Printed and bound by: Deluxe Printers, London NW10 7NR
Website: http://www.de-luxe.com
Email: de-luxe@Talk21.com

Preface

For centuries the Muslim world has been in confusion about the nature of the Arab calendar operating during the time of the Prophet ﷺ. Consequently no one has been able to locate any of the prophetic events correctly in the Christian calendar for a comparative historical study.

The presently used Hijrah calendar was instituted six years after the Prophet ﷺ with retrospective effect from his emigration to Madinah. Although from the tenth year of Hijrah, the people had abandoned intercalation and since then the years had regularly consisted of twelve months, the first nine years of the Muslim era were intercalary and consisted of 111 months. But in later centuries people erroneously held that it consisted of 108 months and considered the epochal day of the era from a point three months after the true date. Unfortunately this frame with the wrong epochal day had soon become a frame of reference for retelling the prophetic events for some of the early narrators.

In the second, third and fourth centuries of Islam when the classical biographers were collecting the materials for their work these narrators, ignorant of the disastrous effect it might create later, had innocently changed the names of the months in which the events occurred from those of the pagan calendar to those of the Hijrah. For example while the change of Qiblah in the second year of emigration took place in Sha'ban of the intercalary system they had changed it to Jumada al-Ula, the corresponding month of the non-intercalary system and narrated it as such. Yet many of the narrators continued to narrate with reference to the old system. Unfortunately none of the narrators ever bothered to specify the frames to which they were referring. Thus the classical biographers encountered two sets of report. They however collected both and incorporated them in their works. Thus a host of apparently contradictory reports had been incorporated into the classical works. The result was chaos. The pages of history were strewn all over with impossible dates and months. In the later stages of history we could neither reconcile the apparent conflicts nor dismiss any of them boldly. Then we started casting doubts on the sources. Outwitted by the problem elsewhere, one of the researchers even recorded his painful conclusion in the following words:

> In the chronological analysis of almost all the important events, there are apparent contradictions and variations on such a vast scale that these narrations can hardly be regarded as history. Neither the days tally with the dates, nor the months coincide with the seasons; and one is simply left with the only conclusion that most probably all the details were simply fabrications or pious intellectual exercise on the part of the early preachers of Islam who were too innocent to visualise that their versions might be scientifically examined at some later stage of history. (Burhan, May 1964, p 266)

This succinctly sums up the type of chronological mess we are in and the complexity of the problem we face in dealing with the dates of the sources.

Apart from this, in the modern biographical works there was also an element that largely contributed to the chronological complications. There were scholars who had visualised that any realistic attempt to locate a prophetic event in the Julian framework for a comparative historical study must be necessarily linked to the true intercalary pagan calendar. These had made serious individual efforts to reconstruct it. But because of using wrong parameters they came up with imperfect models and ended up with a train of impossible dates in the Julian framework – thus bringing in another set of complications to the previously already confused affair. These individual efforts, though they had been undertaken with no ill motive, have made the historicity of the Prophet ﷺ dimmer. Take the birth of the Prophet ﷺ as an instance. Over the centuries nearly a dozen Julian dates had been suggested for it by different individuals – none of them however agreeing with the biographical data. The fate of other events was similar.

Thus presently we are thrown into a network of contradictions, errors and confusion with seemingly no way out. Unless we dig out the lost calendar from the debris of the past we shall be compelled to remain watching helplessly the historic personality of the Prophet ﷺ being gradually transformed into a myth. This compelled me to undertake this research.

As the traditional information on the subject was scanty and the message embedded therein somewhat cryptic, it was really trying and difficult for the researcher to make out sufficient of the calendar. Yet certain aspects of it were very clear. It was intercalary in nature and was in operation for about 450 years. Despite intercalation the annual pilgrimage, which was initially placed in autumn, had finally moved to the threshold of spring by the time intercalation was abandoned. In the tenth year of Hijrah the lunar months, which had been displaced by intercalation, had returned to their normal positions. Therefore any calendar we devise for the pagan days must necessarily fulfil all these criteria. Or else it will be a defective model and lead to misleading results.

Now to the problem I made a scientific approach by exploring mathematically the possible ways in which the calendar could be designed to meet these conditions. I found that it could be done in eleven different ways – each being one calendar. Then I reconstructed all these eleven for the lifetime of the Prophet ﷺ and subjected each of them individually to a critical test by screening them against the biographical data. Only one coinciding with the pagan calendar must be able to come up in perfect agreement with the biographical information as far as the weekdays of the prophetic events were concerned. My endeavour was rewarded. Amongst the eleven I could detect one which could successfully agree with the biographical data. This must be the very frame used by people then. Thus did I discover the lost calendar.

If the reader was looking for the historical Muhammad ﷺ and an authentic chronological account of his life and mission, I believe, this work will help him.

Fazlur Rehman Shaikh
Imphal,
September 22, 1998

SPECIAL ABBREVIATIONS

AF	'Am al-Fil – the Year of the Elephant
AH	Anno Hijrah (non-intercalated)
BF	Before 'Am al-Fil
bH	Before Hijrah (in intercalated style)
BH	Before Hijrah (in non-intercalated style)
DLH	Dhu'l-Hijjah
DLQ	Dhu'l-Qa'dah
H	Hijrah Era (intercalated)
JML	Jumada'l-Ula
JMR	Jumada'l-Akhirah
MHR	Muharram
RBL	Rabi' al-Awwal
RBR	Rabi' al-Akhir
RJB	Rajab
RMD	Ramadan
SFR	Safar
SHB	Sha'ban
SHW	Shawwal

Contents

1. Sources: Conflicts and Confusions 1
   Cases where the same events were assigned to different points of time ... 1
   Cases of conflicting weekdays and dates 2
   Cases of unacceptable dates 3
   Confusion on the Calendar 3
   Notes 8

2. Earlier Researches 10
   PERCEVAL'S THESIS 10
   Alvi's Calendars 17
   Amir Ali's Reconstruction 20
   Hamidullah's Work 22
   Notes 25

3. Parameters of the Lost Calendar 26
   Cycle of Intercalation 31
   Possible Calendars 33
   Notes 35

4. Elements of Reconstruction 36
   Phases of the Moon 36
   Conjunction and Commencement of a Lunar Month 39
   Placement of Intercalary Months 40
   Notes 42

5. The Hijrah Calendar 43
   Notes 45

6. The Chroniclers' Dates 46
   1) The Birthday of the Prophet 46
   2) The Abyssinian Attack on the Ka'bah 48
   3) First Revelation of the Qur'an 48
   4) The Mi'raj 51
   5) Emigration to Madinah 51
   6) Ghazwah Buwat 52
   7) Ghazwah Badr al-Ula 52
   8) Ghazwah Yanbu' 53
   9) The Change of Qiblah 54
   10) Battle of Badr 55
   11) Ghazwah Qararat al-Kudr 56

- 12) Sariyyah Ghalib ibn 'Abdallah al-Laythi 57
- 13) Ghazwah Bani Qaynuqa' 57
- 14) Ghazwah as-Sawiq 59
- 15) Ghazwah Dhu Amarr 59
- 16) Battle of Uhud 60
- 17) Ghazwah Hamra al-Asad 61
- 18) Sariyyah 'Abdallah ibn Unays 62
- 19) Ghazwah Bani an-Nadir 62
- 20) Ghazwah Dhat ar-Riqa' 63
- 21) Ghazwah Badr al-Maw'id 64
- 22) Document of Ahl Maqna 65
- 23) Battle of al-Khandaq (Battle of al-Ahzab) 65
- 24) Ghazwah Bani Quraydah 66
- 25) Prediction of the Murder of Chosroe 67
- 26) Ghazwah al-Muraysi' (Ghazwah Bani al-Mustaliq) 68
- 27) Truce of al-Hudaybiyyah 70
- The Murder of Chosroe 71
- 28) The Postponed 'Umrah 71
- 29) The Opening of Makkah (to Islam) 72
- 30) Ghazwah Hunayn 72
- 31) 'Umrah from al-Jiranah 73
- 32) Return to Madinah 74
- 33) Ghazwah Tabuk (Ghazwah al-'Usra) 74
- 34) The Death of Ibrahim 76
- 35) The Farewell Hajj 77
- 36) Passing Away of the Prophet 78
- Burial 79
- Notes 80

7. The Pagan Calendar 84
The Hijrah Era and the Madinan Decade 86
Notes 87

8. Other Events 88
Pre-Prophethood Events 88
- 1. Abu Bakr's birth 88
- 2. Aminah's death 88
- 3. 'Abd al-Muttalib's death 88
- 4. First trip Muraysi' 88
- 5. Battles of Fijar 89
- 6. Hilf al-Fudul 89
- 7. Marriage to Khadijah 89
- 8. Zaynab's birth 89
- 9. 'Ali's birth 89
- 10. Ruqayyah's birth 89
- 11. Fatimah's birth 90

- 12. Rebuilding the Ka'bah 90
- 13. A'ishah's birth 90

Pre-Hijrah events 92
- 14. Emigration of the Companions to Abyssinia 92
- 15. The Isra' 93
- 16. 'Umar's Islam 93
- 17. Blockade in the Shi'b 93
- 18. Khadijah's death 94
- 19. Abu Talib's death 94
- 20. Visit to Ta'if 95
- 21. Meeting the chiefs of Khazraj 95
- 22. The First Pledge of 'Aqabah 95
- 23. Engagement to A'ishah 95
- 24. The Second Pledge of 'Aqabah 96

Events of 1 H 96
- 25. Increase in the length of the prayer 96
- 26. Sariyyah Hamzah ibn 'Abd al-Muttalib to Sif al-Bahr 96
- 27. Sariyyah 'Ubaydah ibn al-Harith towards Batn Rabigh 97
- 28. Sariyyah Sa'd ibn Abi Waqqas towards al-Kharrar 97

Events of 2 H 97
- 29. Ghazwah Dhu'l-'Ushayrah 97
- 30. Ghazwah al-Abwa 97
- 31. Sariyyah 'Abdallah ibn Jahsh al-Asadi at Nakhlah 98
- 32. Command for the fast of Ramadan 99
- 33. Execution of Asma' bint Marwan 99
- 34. Celebrartion of the first 'Id al-Fitr 99
- 35. Elimination of Abu 'Afak 99
- 36. Cohabiting with A'ishah 100
- 37. Fatimah's marriage 100
- 38. Celebration of the first 'Id al-Adha 101

Events of 3 H 101
- 39. Ghazwah Buhran against Bani Sulaym 101
- 40. Sariyyah of Zayd ibn Harithah towards Kindah 101
- 41. The elimination of Ka'b ibn al-Ashraf 102
- 42. Umm Kulthum's marriage 102
- 43. Marriage to Hafsah 103
- 44. The birth of Hasan 103
- 45. Marriage to Zaynab bint Khuzaymah 103

Events of 4 H 103
- 46. Sariyyah of Abu Salamah ibn 'Abd al-Asad al-Makhzumi against Qatan 103
- 47. Betrayal at ar-Raji' 103
- 48. The massacre of Bi'r Ma'unah 104
- 49. The death of Zaynab bint Khuzaymah 105
- 50. The death of Abu Salamah 105
- 51. The lunar eclipse 105

52. The birth of Hussein 105
53. Marriage to Umm Salamah 105
Events of 5 H 106
54. Ghazwah Dumat al-Jandal 106
55. The deputation of Muzaynah 106
56. Marriage to Zaynab bint Jahsh 106
57. Deputation of Ashja' 106
Events of 6 H 106
58. Sariyyah of Muhammad ibn Maslamah against al-Qurata 106
59. The ghazwah of Bani Lihyan 106
60. Ghazwah al-Ghabah (Ghazwah Dhu Qarad) 107
61. The sariyyah of 'Ukkashah ibn Mihsan al-Asadi towards al-Ghamr 108
62. The sariyyah of Muhammad ibn Maslamah towards Dhu'l-Qassah 108
63. The sariyyah of Abu 'Ubaydah ibn al-Jarrah towards Dhu'l-Qassah 108
64. The sariyyah of Zayd ibn Harithah against Bani Sulaym at al-Jamum .. 109
65. The sariyyah of Zayd ibn Harithah against al-'Is 109
66. The sariyyahs of Zayd ibn Harithah to at-Taraf and al-Hisma 109
67. The sariyyah of Zayd ibn Harithah against Wadi al-Qura 109
68. The sariyyah of 'Abd ar-Rahman ibn 'Awf to Dumat al-Jandal 109
69. The sariyyah of 'Ali ibn Abi Talib against Bani Sa'd ibn Bakr 109
70. The elmination of Abu Rafi' 110
71. Marriage to Juwayriyyah 110
72. The sariyyah of Zayd ibn Harithah against Umm Qirfah 110
73. The sariyyah of 'Abdallah ibn Rawahah against Usayr ibn Razim 111
74. The sariyyah of Kurz ibn Jabir al-Fihri towards 'Uraniyin 111
75. A solar eclipse 112
Events of 7 H 112
76. Letters to rulers 112
77. The return of Zaynab 112
78. Ghazwah Khaybar 112
79. The deputation of Ash'aris 113
80. The sariyyahs of 'Umar ibn al-Khattab, Abu Bakr as-Siddiq and Bashir ibn Sa'd al-Ansari 113
81. The sariyyah of Ghalib ibn 'Abdallah al-Laythi towards Mayfa'ah 113
82. The sariyyah of Bashir ibn Sa'd al-Ansari 113
83. The sariyyah of Ibn Abi'l-Awja as-Sulami 114
Events of 8 H 114
84. Sariyyah of Ghalib ibn 'Abdallah al-Laythi 114
85. Sariyyahs of Shuja ibn Wahb al-Asadi and Ka'b ibn 'Umayr al-Ghifari 114
86. The sariyyah of Zayd ibn Harithah to Mu'tah 114
87. The sariyyah of 'Amr ibn al-'As towards Dhat as-Salasil 114
88. The sariyyah Sif al-Bahr 115
89. The sariyyah of Abu Qatadah ibn Rib'i al-Ansari towards Khudrah in the territory of Muharib 115
90. The sariyyahs of 'Amr ibn al-'As, Hisham ibn al-'As, Khalid ibn Sa'id, Abu Qatadah, Sa'd ibn Zayd al-Ashhali and Khalid ibn al-Walid 115

91. The sariyyahs of Khalid ibn al-Walid and Tufayl ibn 'Amr ad-Dawsi ... 116
92. The ghazwah of Ta'if 116
93. Marriage to Fatimah bint ad-Dahhak 116
94. The letter to Jayfar 116
95. The sariyyah of Qays ibn Sa'd 116

Events of 9 H 117
96. The first zakat collections 117
97. The sariyyah 'Uyaynah ibn Badr al-Fazari 117
98. The sariyyah of Qutbah ibn 'Amir 118
99. The sariyyahs of 'Ali ibn Abi Talib and ad-Dahhak ibn Sufyan al-Kilabi 118
100. The deputation of Bani Kilab 118
101. The sariyyahs of 'Alqamah ibn Mujjazziz, 'Ali ibn Abi Talib and 'Ukkashah ibn Mihsan 118
102. The death of the Negus and the sariyyah of Khalid ibn al-Walid 119
103. The death of Umm Kulthum 119
104. The death of 'Abdallah ibn Ubayy 119
105. Abu Bakr's Hajj 119
106. The deputation of Bani Asad 119

Events of 10 H 120
107. The sariyyah of Khalid ibn al-Walid against Bani al-Harith 120
108. The sariyyah of of 'Ali ibn Abi Talib against al-Yaman 120
109. Visit of the Christian delegation of Najran 120
110. The sariyyah of Jarir ibn 'Abdallah 121

Events of 11 H 121
111. The deputation of an-Nakha' 121
Notes 122

Postscript 126
1. Birth of the Prophet ﷺ (Monday, 2nd Rabi' al-Awwal 1st AF / June 23rd, 570) 126
2. First revelation of the Qur'an (Monday, 18th Ramadan 40 AF / December 22nd, 609) 127
3. Emigration to Madinah (Monday, 12th Rabi' al-Awwal 1 H / June 28th, 622) 129
4. The battle of Badr (Friday, 16th Ramadan 2 H / December 16th, 623) .. 131
5. The battle of Uhud (Saturday, 11th Shawwal 3 H / December 29th, 624) 131
6. The battle of al-Khandaq (Saturday, 1st Dhu'l-Qa'dah 5 H / January 24th, 627) 132
7. The treaty of al-Hudaybiyyah (Thursday, 1st Dhu'l-Qa'dah 6 H / January 14th, 628) 133
8. The Opening of Makkah [to Islam] (Monday, 18th Ramadan 8 H / December 11th, 629) 134
Notes 137

Appendices ... 137
Appendix 1: Locations of Intercalary Months ... 138
Appendix 2: Pagan and Hijrah Calendars ... 139
Appendix 3: Tsybulsky's Chart ... 162
Appendix 4: Hours of Sunset ... 163
Appendix 5: How to use this calendar: ... 167

Bibliography ... 168

1. Sources: Conflicts and Confusions

The calendrical conflicts in the biographical works on the Prophet ﷺ, may Allah bless him and grant him peace, were of multifarious nature. The same events were assigned to widely apart points of time, different weekdays were recorded of the same events and in certain cases scientifically or historically unacceptable dates were reported. A brief resume of the conflicting reports may be tabulated as follows:

Cases where the same events were assigned to different points of time

1.	Isra	RBL	45 AF	Ibn 'Abbas[1]
		RJB		Al-Biruni[2]
2.	Mi'raj	RJB		Al-Biruni[3]
		RMD	51 AF	Abu Bakr ibn 'Abdallah[4]
3.	Ghazwah Buwat	RBL	02 H	Ibn Ishaq[5]
		RBR	02 H	Ibn Habib[6]
4.	Ghazwah Badr al-Ula	RBL	02 H	al-Waqidi[7]
		JMR	02 H	Ibn Habib[8]
5.	Change of Qiblah	JML	02 H	Imam az-Zuhri[9]
		RJB	02 H	Ibn Sa'd[10]
		SHB	02 H	Ibn Ishaq[11]
6.	Ghazwah Qararat al-Kudr	SHW	02 H	Ibn Ishaq[12]
		MHR	03 H	al-Waqidi[13]
7.	Ghazwah Bani Qaynuqa'	SHW	02 H	Imam az-Zuhri[14]
		SFR	03 H	Ibn Habib[15]
8.	Ghazwah Dhu Amarr	DLH	02 H	Ibn Hisham[16]
		RBL	03 H	al-Waqidi[17]
9.	Elimination of Abu Rafi'	JMR	03 H	at-Tabari[18]
		DLH	04 H	al-Waqidi[19]
		RMD	06 H	Ibn Sa'd[20]
10.	Tragedy of ar-Raji'	SHW	03 H	Ibn Habib[21]
		SFR	04 H	Ibn Sa'd[22]
11.	Ghazwah Dhat ar-Riqa'	JML	04 H	Ibn Ishaq[23]
		MHR	05 H	al-Waqidi[24]
12.	Ghazwah Badr al-Maw'id	SHB	04 H	Ibn Ishaq[25]
		DLQ	04 H	al-Waqidi[26]
13.	Ghazwah al-Muraysi'	SHB	05 H	Ibn Sa'd[27]
		SHB	06 H	Ibn Ishaq[28]
14.	Battle of al-Khandaq	SHW	05 H	Ibn Habib[29]
		DLQ	05 H	Ibn Sa'd[30]
15.	Ghazwah Bani Qurayzah	DLQ	05 H	Ibn Sa'd[31]
		MHR	06 H	al-Waqidi[32]

Chronology of the Prophetic Events

16. Ghazwah Bani Lihyan	RBL	06 H	Ibn Sa'd[33]
	JML	06 H	Ibn Ishaq[34]
	SHB	06 H	Diyarbakri[35]
17. Ghazwah Dhu Qarad	RBL	06 H	Ibn Sa'd[36]
	DLH	06 H	Bukhari[37]
18. Prophet's ﷺ writing letters	DLH	06 H	at-Tabari[38]
to neighbouring rulers	MHR	07 H	Ibn Sa'd[39]
19. Ghazwah Khaybar	MHR	07 H	Ibn Ishaq[40]
	JML	07 H	Ibn Sa'd[41]

Cases of conflicting weekdays and dates

1. Birth of the Prophet ﷺ	02	RBL	01 AF	MON	Abu Ma'shar Nujayh[42]
	10	RBL	01 AF	MON	Abu Ja'far[43]
	12	RBL	01 AF	MON	Ibn Ishaq[44]
2. First revelation	17	RMD	40 AF	MON	Abu Ja'far[45]
of Qur'an	18	RMD		MON	'Abdallah ibn Zayd[46]
	24	RMD		MON	Abu al-Jild[47]
3. Ghazwah Buwat					
Start:	03	RBR	02 H	MON	Ibn Habib[48]
Return:	20	RBR	02 H	MON	Ibn Habib[49]

(The two weekdays do not conform to each other. If the 20th was a Monday, the 3rd must be a Friday).

4. Ghazwah Yanbu'	14	SHB	02 H	TUE	Ibn Habib[50]
5. Change of Qiblah	15	SHB	02 H	TUE	al-Waqidi[51]

(Both the 14th and 15th of the month could not be Tuesdays).

6. Battle of Badr	16/17	RMD	02 H	FRI	'Urwah[52]
	17	RMD	02 H	FRI	Muhammad ibn Salih[53]
	17	RMD	02 H	MON	'Amir ibn Rabi'ah al-Badri[54]
	19	RMD	02 H		'Abdallah[55]
7. Ghazwah as-Sawiq	05	DLH	02 H	SUN	al-Waqidi[56]
	22	DLH	02 H		Ibn Habib[57]
	22/23	DLH	02 H	SUN	at-Tabari[58]
	25	DLH	02 H	SUN	Ibn Sa'd[59]
8. Battle of Uhud	07	SHW	03 H	SAT	al-Waqidi[60]
	11	SHW	03 H	SAT	Qatadah[61]
	15	SHW	03 H	SAT	Ibn Ishaq[62]
	17	SHW	03 H	SAT	Al-Biruni[63]
9. Ghazwah Hamra	08	SHW	03 H	SUN	Ibn Sa'd[64]
al-Asad	16	SHW	03 H	SUN	'Ikrimah[65]
10. Ghazwah Dhat ar-Riqa'	10	JML	04 H	MON	Ibn Habib[66]
	10	MHR	05 H	SAT	Ibn Sa'd[67]
11. Ghazwah al Muraysi'	01	SHB	05 H	SAT	Ibn Habib[68]
	02	SHB	05 H		Mas'udi[69]
	22	SHB	05 H	MON	Ibn Sa'd[70]
12. Battle of al-Khandaq					
Start:	10	SHW	05 H	THU	Ibn Habib[71]
	08	DLQ	05 H	MON	Ibn Sa'd[72]
End:	01	DLQ	05 H	SAT	Ibn Habib[73]
	23	DLQ	05 H	WED	Ibn Sa'd[74]
13. Ghazwah Hudaybiyyah	01	DLQ	06 H	THU	Ibn Habib[75]

14. Opening of Makkah [to Islam]		01	DLQ	06 H	MON	Ibn Sa'd[76]
		10	RMD	08 H		Ibrahim[77]
		17/18	RMD	08 H		Abu Sa'id al Khudri[78]
		19	RMD	08 H	FRI	Ibn Sa'd[79]
		20	RMD	08 H		Ibn Ishaq[80]

(The recorded weekday is against the traditional information that the Prophet ﷺ opened Makkah to Islam on a Monday).[81]

15. Ghazwah Hunayn						
	Start:	06	SHW	08 H	SAT	Ibn Sa'd[82]
	Arrival:	10	SHW	08 H	TUE	Ibn Sa'd[83]

(If the 6th was a Saturday, the 10th must be a Wednesday).

16. 'Umrah from al Ji'ranah		28	SHW	08 H		'Utbah[84]
		18	DLQ	08 H	WED	Ibn Sa'd[85]
17. Return to Madinah						
	Leaving Makkah:	19	DLQ	08 H	THU	Ibn Sa'd[86]
	Arrival at Madinah:	24	DLQ	08 H		Abu 'Amr Madani[87]
		25	DLQ	08 H	FRI	Mirkhond[88]
18. Ghazwah Tabuk						
	Start:	01	RJB	09 H	MON	Ibn Habib[89]
					THU	Ka'b ibn Malik[90]
19. Passing away of the Prophet ﷺ						
	Falling sick:	19	SFR	11 H	WED	Muhammad ibn Qays[91]
		30	SFR	11 H	WED	'Ali ibn Abi Talib[92]
	Death:	02	RBL	11 H	MON	Muhammad ibn Qays[93]
		12	RBL	11 H	MON	'Ali ibn Abi Talib[94]

Cases of unacceptable dates

1. Murder of Chosroe		10	JML	07 H	TUE	Ibn Sa'd[95]
		13	JML	07 H		al-Waqidi[96]

(The recorded year is against the historical information that the Emperor was murdered in February 628[97] which corresponded to around the end of 6 H).

2. Death of Prophet's ﷺ son Ibrahim		10	RBL	10 H	TUE	Ibn Sa'd[98]

(The recorded date is against a copious stream of traditions that there was a solar eclipse on the day the infant breathed his last[99] and the scientific fact that no solar eclipse can occur except on the day of conjunction).

CONFUSION ON THE CALENDAR

The foregoing tables will give the reader a fair idea of the contradictions woven into the fabric of our sources. We shall be able to resolve these if we can reconstruct the lost calendar. But our confusion on its model is of no less magnitude either. Scholars over the ages who pondered on its probable features and tried to glean some real facts from the past hold different views about how it worked. One group holds that the then calendar was lunar in character while another group believes that it was lunisolar with occasional intercalation. Yet there is a third group who subscribes to a double calendar theory. Let us now discuss briefly the views available in this regard.

Dr. A. Sprenger, the German scholar, says that intercalation in the ordinary sense of the word was not practised at Makkah and the Arab year was purely a lunar one, performing its cycle regularly and losing one year in every thirty-three.[100] Mahmud Pasha Falaki, the Egyptian astronomer also holds this view. This is however contrary to the Quranic information that the pagan Arabs used to intercalate their years and is therefore misleading.

Ibn Ishaq stated that the Arabs intercalated their years every year.[101] Apparently following this view, Lane was of the opinion that the Arabs did not resort to the intercalation of the thirteenth month but regularly added eleven days at the end of every lunar year.[102]

Another block of classical authorities – Azraqi, Ibn Habib and Abu 'Ubayd – asserted that the Arabs intercalated their years every two years.[103] No modern scholar, however, supports this view.

Mas'udi, the classical historian, stated that the Arabs did intercalation every three years.[104] Relying on this report Caussin de Perceval even reconstructed a model of the calendar on the basis of such triennial embolism.

According to al-Biruni, nearly two hundred years before Islam Hudhayfah, the first Arab intercalator, had taken the system of intercalation from the Jews who intercalated nine months in twenty-four years and in consequence their months were fixed and always came at their proper times. That state continued till the Farewell Pilgrimage of the Prophet ﷺ.[105]

Both Tsybulsky, the Russian astronomer, and Muhammad Asad, the Qur'anic scholar, subscribed to this view.

Tsybulsky says that the pre-Islamic Arabs adopted a lunisolar system in which the year was counted according to the Sun, and the months – according to the Moon. The lunar year being shorter than the solar by nearly eleven days, they observed the lag between the two and added an additional month to the lunar year every time the difference amounted to a whole month. Consequently in a cycle of twenty four years there were nine intercalated years.[106]

Asad thinks that the Arabs synchronised the passage of the two years in a course of eight years. Commenting on a Qur'anic ayah he says: "In their endeavour to obviate certain disadvantages for their trade caused by the seasonal rotation of the lunar months, the pagan Arabs used to intercalate a thirteenth month in the third, sixth and eighth year of every eight year period, with a view to making the lunar calendar more or less stationary, and thus roughly corresponding to the solar year."[107] (This 8 year system is a segment of the 24 year cycle mentioned by al-Biruni and is therefore equivalent to it).

Hajji Khalifah maintained that the pagans followed the Jews' system of 19 year cycle of intercalation wherein seven intercalary months were added in the course of the cycle.[108]

Dr. Hashim Amir Ali, the eminent Qur'anic scholar was of the opinion that the Arabs made intercalation every two and three years. He even attempted to reconstruct the calendar for the Madinan decade. But he did not state which system he believed the Arabs followed – the 19 year or the 24 year cycle? (In both systems intercalation is made at the intervals of two and three years).

Far removed from these opinions, Dr. Hamidullah argues that the pagan Arabs adopted a 30 year cycle of intercalation and used to add an additional month at the end of every three lunar years up to the thirtieth year to be followed by one more external intercalation at the end of the thirty-first.[109]

The opinion of W. Montgomery Watt in this respect is: "The pre-Islamic Arabs observed the lunar months, but kept their calendar in line with the solar year by introducing intercalary months where necessary. The matter is referred to in a passage of the Qur'an." But in the system of intercalation he smelt an element of arbitrariness. He wrote: "… despite some of the accounts, the Arabs had no *fixed* system of intercalation."[110]

Regarding the question whether the Muslims did actually practise intercalation in the first ten years at Madinah and how the chroniclers recorded the events he charged the early Muslim historians of manipulation and stated: "Even if the Muslims observed intercalary months (presumably three) during the ten years, it is almost certain that statements in the sources are made on the basis of orthodox Muslim reckoning, with no intercalation, since scholars in the second Islamic century would overlook intercalation or deliberately reject it."[111]

Differing from such views there is another group of scholars who holds that there were two different calendars simultaneously operating in the Arabian peninsula. Winckler, D. Nelson, Ishaqun Nabi Alvi and Dr. Ilyas belong to this category. Apparently they relied heavily on Mas'udi according to whom Makkah and Madinah had two different calendars.[112]

The diversity of opinions discussed in the foregoing paragraphs clearly indicates that our knowledge on the calendrical practice of the Arabs of that age is not yet sufficient for anyone to say anything definite.

Second, though the early Muslims followed the pagan calendar and all their narrations were made with reference to it, with the retrospective promulgation of the Hijrah calendar during the caliphate of 'Umar from the emigration of the Prophet ﷺ some of the then surviving Companions had apparently started referring to the new system by converting the pagan months to the corresponding Hijrah ones while other Companions continued to refer to the old one. By the time when the Caliph instituted the new Islamic era, the majority of the Companions were still alive, and they continued to live many years more. It was during their lifetime that the reminiscences of their blessed association with the Prophet ﷺ, were passed on to the succeeding generations who were not lucky enough to have seen him in person. By then the old calendar which had been operative up to the Farewell Pilgrimage was in use no more. All references were then to the newly conceived Islamic calendar. The old system was being fast forgotten and buried in oblivion while the new one was encountered daily. Would the Companions continue to relate their stories to the old calendar which had been completely detached from the usage of the new generation in preference to the new one which had already established its identity and was to become a permanent frame of reference for all Muslims for all time to come? It appears that at least some of the Companions had switched over to the new system and started narrating the stories of their past in terms of the new calendar.

Adding further complications, the classical biographers too had made not wholly successful attempts to convert the pagan references to the Hijrah, and *vice-versa*, without fully knowing their inter-relationship. (Instances of this kind we shall come across in plenty in the course of this study). Unfortunately, no one, neither the Companions nor the biographers, specified the frames to which they were referring. Because of such innocent manipulations the names of all the twelve Arabian months ubiquitously show up here and there in the biographical works throwing the historical perspective in disarray. In subsequent works, people confused and mistook the reference to one frame for the other and arrived at erroneous concordances with the Christian calendar.

Thirdly, as shown in the beginning of this work, the classical biographers often incorporated alternative dates about the same events following the inaccurate narrations floating around the time of compilation of their works. The later-day scholar judges the worth of each report according to his own opinion, chooses what fits his own criterion and works out the concordance giving rise to various Julian dates for the same events in modern works.

Our confusion in the chronological analysis of the early days of Islam is thus generated from:
(a) inadequate information of the true form of the pagan calendar and its correct relation to the Hijrah calendar,
(b) narrators' mixing up the frames of references and later-day scholars' mistaking the months of the pagan calendar for those of the Hijrah and *vice-versa*, and
(c) incorporation in classical biographical works of many inaccurate traditions current in the days of their compilation.

The plight of any serious historian working towards an acceptable sequence of events can well be imagined. Hard will be the task and worse the confusion. For a rewarding endeavour the true form of the pagan calendar must first be ascertained, its relation to the Hijrah calendar established and the months appearing in the classical works be identified as to what frame they belong. Then only, the events can be located precisely in any frame of reference. All attempts before this will only yield misleading results.

Notes

[1] Ibn Sa'd: *At-Tabaqat*, Vol 1, p 247
[2] Sachau: Chronology, p 329
[3] Sachau: Chronology, p 329
[4] Ibn Sa'd: *At-Tabaqat*, Vol 1, p 246
[5] Ibn Hisham: *As-Sirah*, Vol 1, p 691
[6] Burhan, Sept 1964, p 140
[7] Burhan, May 1964, p 283
[8] Burhan, May 1964, p 271
[9] Burhan, Oct 1964, p 209
[10] Ibn Sa'd: *At-Tabaqat*, Vol 1, p 284
[11] At-Tabari: *At-Tarikh*, Vol 1, p 158
[12] At-Tabari: *At-Tarikh*, Vol 1, pp 208, 209
[13] At-Tabari: *At-Tarikh*, Vol 1, p 208
[14] At-Tabari: *At-Tarikh*, Vol 1, p 206
[15] Burhan, Aug 1964, p 94
[16] Ibn Hisham: *As-Sirah*, Vol 2, p 23
[17] Burhan, Aug 1964, p 80
[18] At-Tabari: *At-Tarikh*, Vol 1, p 217
[19] At-Tabari: *At-Tarikh*, Vol 1, p 218
[20] Ibn Sa'd: *At-Tabaqat*, Vol 2, p 112
[21] Burhan, Aug 1964, p 81
[22] Ibn Sa'd: *At-Tabaqat*, Vol 2, p 66
[23] Ibn Hisham: *As-Sirah*, Vol 2, p 235
[24] At-Tabari: *At-Tarikh*, Vol 1, p 268
[25] Ibn Hisham: *As-Sirah*, Vol 2, p 242
[26] Burhan, Aug 1964, p 81
[27] Ibn Sa'd: *At-Tabaqat*, Vol 2, p 77
[28] Ibn Hisham: *As-Sirah*, Vol 2, p 345
[29] Burhan, Sept 1964, p 141
[30] Ibn Sa'd: *At-Tabaqat*, Vol 2, p 80
[31] Ibn Sa'd: *At-Tabaqat*, Vol 2, p 91
[32] Mirkhond: Rawzatus Safa, Pt II, p 777
[33] Ibn Sa'd: *At-Tabaqat*, Vol 2, p 97
[34] Burhan, Sept 1964, p 142
[35] Burhan, Sept 1964, p 142
[36] Ibn Sa'd: *At-Tabaqat*, Vol 2, p 99
[37] Bukhari, Vol 5, p 355
[38] At-Tabari: *At-Tarikh*, Vol 1, p 345
[39] Ibn Sa'd: *At-Tabaqat*, Vol 1, p 305
[40] Ibn Hisham: *As-Sirah*, Vol 2, p 392
[41] Ibn Sa'd: *At-Tabaqat*, Vol 2, p 131
[42] Ibn Sa'd: *At-Tabaqat*, Vol 1, pp 109, 110
[43] Ibn Sa'd: *At-Tabaqat*, Vol 1, p 109
[44] Ibn Hisham: *As-Sirah*, Vol 1, p 182
[45] Ibn Sa'd: *At-Tabaqat*, Vol 1, pp 223, 224
[46] At-Tabari: *At-Tarikh*, Vol 1, p 70
[47] At-Tabari: *At-Tarikh*, Vol 1, p 70
[48] Burhan, Sept 1964, p 140
[49] Burhan, Sept 1964, p 140
[50] Burhan, May 1964, p 268
[51] At-Tabari: *At-Tarikh*, Vol 1, p 158
[52] Burhan, May 1964, p 269
[53] At-Tabari: *At-Tarikh*, Vol 1, p 159
[54] Ibn Sa'd: *At-Tabaqat*, Vol 2, p 21
[55] At-Tabari: *At-Tarikh*, Vol 1, p 159
[56] Burhan, May 1964, p 270
[57] Burhan, Sept 1964, p 139
[58] At-Tabari: *At-Tarikh*, Vol 1, p 209
[59] Ibn Sa'd: *At-Tabaqat*, Vol 2, p 33
[60] Burhan, Nov 1964, p 268
[61] Burhan, Nov 1964, p 267
[62] Ibn Hisham: *As-Sirah*, Vol 2, p 84
[63] Sachau: Chronology, p 332
[64] Ibn Sa'd: *At-Tabaqat*, Vol 2, pp 57, 58
[65] At-Tabari: *At-Tarikh*, Vol 1, p 249
[66] Burhan, Nov 1964, pp 272, 275
[67] Ibn Sa'd: *At-Tabaqat*, Vol 2, p 74

[68] Burhan, Nov 1964, p 273
[69] Burhan, Nov 1964, p 273
[70] Ibn Sa'd: *At-Tabaqat*, Vol 2, p 77
[71] Burhan, Sept 1964, p 141
[72] Ibn Sa'd: *At-Tabaqat*, Vol 2, pp 81, 82
[73] Burhan, Sept 1964, p 141
[74] Ibn Sa'd: *At-Tabaqat*, Vol 2, p 86
[75] Burhan, Nov 1964, p 280
[76] Ibn Sa'd: *At-Tabaqat*, Vol 2, p 117
[77] Ibn Sa'd: *At-Tabaqat*, Vol 2, p 172
[78] Ibn Sa'd: *At-Tabaqat*, Vol 2, p 171
[79] Ibn Sa'd: *At-Tabaqat*, Vol 2, p 170
[80] Ibn Hisham: *As-Sirah*, Vol 2, p 522
[81] Bashiruddin: Holy Qur'an, p clxxiii
[82] Ibn Sa'd: *At-Tabaqat*, Vol 2, p 185
[83] Ibn Sa'd: *At-Tabaqat*, Vol 2, p 185
[84] Ibn Sa'd: *At-Tabaqat*, Vol 2, p 212
[85] Ibn Sa'd: *At-Tabaqat*, Vol 2, p 191
[86] Ibn Sa'd: *At-Tabaqat*, Vol 2, p 191
[87] Ibn Hisham: *As-Sirah*, Vol 2, p 604
[88] Mirkhond: Rawzatus Safa, Pt II, p 640
[89] Burhan, Dec 1964, p 358
[90] Bukhari, Vol 4, p 126
[91] Ibn Sa'd: *At-Tabaqat*, Vol 2, p 340
[92] Ibn Sa'd: *At-Tabaqat*, Vol 2, p 340
[93] Ibn Sa'd: *At-Tabaqat*, Vol 2, p 340
[94] Ibn Sa'd: *At-Tabaqat*, Vol 2, p 340
[95] Ibn Sa'd: *At-Tabaqat*, Vol 1, p 307
[96] Burhan, Nov 1964, p 281 f
[97] Burhan, Nov 1964, p 283
[98] Ibn Sa'd: *At-Tabaqat*, Vol 1, p 163
[99] Bukhari, Vol 2, p 84
[100] Hughes: Dictionary, p 214
[101] Islamic Review, Feb 1969, p 11
[102] Islamic Review, Jun 1956, p 36
[103] Islamic Review, Feb 1969, p 11
[104] Islamic Review, Feb 1969, p 11
[105] Sachau: Chronology, p 14
[106] Tsybulsky: Calendars, p 13
[107] Asad: Message, p 264 f
[108] Islamic Culture, Apr 1947, p 145
[109] Islamic Review, Feb 1969, p 10
[110] Watt: Muhammad at Madinah, pp 299, 300
[111] Watt: Muhammad at Madinah, p 339
[112] Bedar: Arab Calendar, p 13

2. Earlier Researches

Of those who attempted reconstruction of the lost calendar special mention may be made of Caussin de Perceval, Ishaqun Nabi Alvi and Dr. Hashim Amir Ali.

Perceval was an authority whose dates had been heavily drawn upon by the later-day writers and scholars. He published his thesis in French in the *Journal Asiatique* of Paris in April 1843. This was translated into English and flashed in *Islamic Culture* of Hyderabad in April 1947 under the title *Notes on Arab calendar before Islam*. Alvi published his works in the form of articles from May to December 1964 in the monthly Urdu magazine *Burhan*. These were later edited and translated into English by Dr. A.R. Bedar and published in 1968 under the title *The Arab calendar prevalent during the lifetime of Muhammad*. Amir Ali published his works in 1977 under the title *Upstream Downstream Reconstruction of Islamic Chronology*.

Notwithstanding serious flaws and shortcomings their theories were in themselves interesting. It will be worthwhile to discuss them in a nut-shell as it will bring the reader face to face with the practical aspects of calendar-framing and acquaint him more with the ideas involved in it.

PERCEVAL'S THESIS

Perceval's thesis and the supporting arguments were fairly lengthy. The following is an attempt to summarise it in a few paragraphs.

It is apparent, says Perceval, that in ancient times the year of the Arabs was primarily the vague lunar year. Their months had no permanent connection with the weather; and their names were different from those current in the time of the Prophet ﷺ. The beginnings of their year and the dates of their pilgrimage, being brought forward eleven days every year, revolved round the seasons in successive years.

About two centuries before Islam, the Arabs, being inconvenienced by the pilgrimage falling due in seasons of scarcity, had adopted the lunisolar calendar involving intercalation of a thirteenth month with a view to placing their pilgrimage in or about autumn when provisions were abundant; for the season of harvesting fruits, the staple food of the Arabs, ends in their country at the beginning of September. They, at the same time, gave to their months a series of names — some representing the seasons and others their religious gatherings.

But receding through the past fourteen centuries in regular succession of the current lunar months one finds that the Prophet ﷺ's pilgrimage at the end of 10 H fell not in autumn but about the approach of spring in the beginning of March 632. If the intercalation practised by the Arabs was the 19 or 24 year system, argues Perceval, this change would not have come about. But this can be explained away as natural acceleration of the lunar year if it is assumed that the Arabs regularly intercalated one month every three years.

So concording the Farewell Pilgrimage of Dhu'l-Hijjah 10 H to March 632 and placing one *nasi'* at the end of 7 H and thereafter at the gap of every three years Perceval worked out a calendrical table for the preceding 220 years and arrived at 413 when the pilgrimage, according to his formula, corresponded to October 21 — the first year of intercalation starting by November 21, 412 with the first *nasi'* at the end of the year falling against (November 10 - December 8, 413). The process incorporated 70 *nasi's* before the *Hijrah* and three in the Madinan decade. He also asserted that 10 H should have been an intercalary year but for abolition of the system by the Prophet ﷺ.

Discussing about the probable meanings of the Arab months as tied to them by the ancient people, he says that initially when the people adopted those names there was some link between some of them and the seasons tracing out etymologically that the word *Rabi* means verdure and the vernal rain, *Jumada* implies cessation of rain and setting in of drought and *Ramadan* conveys intense heat. When the Arabs switched over to the lunisolar system in 412, asserted Perceval, they located these in the appropriate seasons of the year. Therefore in his reconstruction, in the first year (412 - 413) he corresponded *Rabi' al-Awwal* to January-February, the months of rain in Arabia, *Rabi' al-*

Akhir to February-March, the months of vegetation, *Jumada al-Ula* to March-April, the months when rain becomes rare, *Jumada al-Akhirah* to April-May, the months when drought begins to be felt, *Ramadan* to July-August, the months of intense heat of summer and *Dhu'l-Hijjah* to October-November, the months of equable weather for pilgrimage.

For the triennial embolism he advocated, he quoted the authority of Mas'udi and Abu al Fida' and alleged that these historians seemed to have naively accepted and transmitted whatever tradition handed over to them. In examining the results accruing from the triennial intercalation, says Perceval, one may surmise that very probably such was the practice followed by the Arab intercalators.

He was also aware that this simple and rough system could not exactly synchronise the passage of the lunar year to that of the solar but would create a lag of a little more than 3 days in every three years. Therefore the relation between the two would go on diverging year after year. Although for about 30 years, the space of one generation, the divergence would not be so wide as to render ridiculous the designations of the months with respect to the seasons, finally the connection between them was bound to disappear.

As a corroboration of his thesis Perceval points out to a historical reference of 541 when in *a meeting of Roman Generals convened at Dara by Belisarius to discuss a plan of campaign two officers who commanded a corps formed of Syrian troops declared that they could not march with the main army against the town of Nisibius, alleging that their absence would leave Syria and Phoenicia an easy prey to the raids of the Almondar Arabs (al Mundhir III). Belisarius showed these two officers that their fears were groundless, because they were nearing the summer solstice, a time when the pagan Arabs used to devote two whole months to the practice of their religion, abstaining from any bellicose act whatsoever.*

Perceval believed that this was evidently the time of pilgrimage wherein the pagans completely abstained from warfare. His calendar could match with this by giving the date of pilgrimage in 541 around the summer solstice.

Perceval found still further corroboration in two more biographical references of weather conditions in the time of the Prophet ﷺ. The first, in the year of *Hijrah*, the Prophet ﷺ arrived at Madinah in the middle of Rabi' al-Awwal; the heat was then *very inconvenient*. Agreeing with this the middle of Rabi' al-Awwal in his calendar in 622 coincided with the first days of July which were the hottest days of the year. The second, in the 5th year of *Hijrah* while besieging Madinah in the battle of al-Khandaq, the allies faced in Shawwal extreme cold and inclemency of weather. His calendar could throw up in 627 the month of Shawwal against January-February which were the months of rain in Arabia.

Supported by this dual historical corroboration to his calendrical hypothesis, Perceval assumed the latter to be a proved fact.

After a synopsis of Perceval's thesis we may now proceed to examine its validity.

The first objection to his thesis was his assertion that the Arabs adopted intercalation as well as the new designations of their lunar months about 200 years before Islam.

Dr. Hamidullah's article shows that the practice of intercalation in Arabia could not be less old than 450 years before Islam as we shall discuss later in more detail. Here it will suffice to say that of the Arabs Malik ibn Kinanah was the first to hold the office of the intercalator while, however, Perceval maintains on the authority of Muhammad Jarkasi that the first was 'Amir ibn Tha'labah, the grandson of Malik ibn Kinanah. From Abu Thumamah, the last to hold this office to 'Amir ibn Tha'labah there were eleven generations according to al-Biruni. Considering thirty years for a generation, intercalation appears to be in operation at least for 330 years before its abandonment in 632. How could then Perceval contend that it was more than one century later?

Secondly, while the Arab memory could preserve even the names of all their intercalators why did not they transmit the old names of their months, if at all Mas'udi's assertion was correct? Was discarding of centuries-old names and adoption of new ones which affected not only the few holding the office of the *Nas'at* but the entire Arab people such an insignificant event that the vast traditional and historical records did not merit it mention anywhere? Mas'udi's – and therefore Perceval's – assertion is devoid of foundation.

Being satisfied with the performance of his calendar under the regular triennial embolism Perceval wrote: *In the 51st year of the nasi' it* [- the pilgrimage] *fell very near autumn at the beginning of September, which is the fruit season in Arabia. The object in view had thus been attained during at least half a century.* Here it must be remembered that desiring to place their pilgrimage in or about autumn, the Arabs had adopted embolism while according to him in the very first year (413) it turned up on 21st October, they had to wait for nearly 50 years to get it in the autumnal equinox. Only in the 50th year of *nasi'* (462) it fell on the 21st September never to return again but to drift away gradually - ultimately to arrive in March in 10 H (632). Had they wanted the pilgrimage around the autumnal equinox, they could continue with their non-intercalary system for another four years (for in 416 the pilgrimage would fall on September 18) and *then* adopt a system of intercalation which could fix the pilgrimage around this point. One cannot but wonder: Were the Arabs so ignorant as to wait for 50 years which they could easily achieve in 4 years? Perceval silently passed over this question.

In his Farewell Pilgrimage in Dhu'l-Hijjah 10 H the Prophet ﷺ stated that the lunar months displaced by intercalation had *by then* returned to the normal positions clearly indicating that the intercalary and non-intercalary months had coincided from that year and the position of Muharram (April 8 – May 9, 631) in 10 H was correct. From November 21, 412 whence Perceval starts the first year of intercalation to April 8, 631 there were exactly 2701 lunar months (225 lunar years and 1 month). Therefore by placing a Muharram against (April 8 - May 9, 631) and receding backwards in the non-intercalary style one gets a Dhu'l-Hijjah against (November 21 - December 21, 412) in the non-intercalary epoch. But in his calendar Perceval placed a Muharram there. He did not explain how that Dhu'l-Hijjah had been transformed to a Muharram in the intercalary epoch. (The reader must remember that Perceval's theory of adoption of new designations of the lunar months was not supported by historical or traditional evidences).

Secondly, when it was clear and decisive from the statement of the Prophet ﷺ that the courses of intercalary and non-intercalary years had coincided from the beginning of 10 H which was not possible unless there was an intercalation at the end of 9 H Perceval did not place a *nasi'* at its end by merely saying *it does not seem likely that the 9th or the 8th were embolismic years.*

Perceval picked up one historical reference of 541 and two weather references in the Madinan decade to corroborate his calendar with historical and biographical evidences.

Inferring from the statement of Belisarius he says that there was a pilgrimage on June 22 of that year. But he did not care to see that Belisarius could be speaking from hearsay. The words "a time when the pagan Arabs used to devote *two whole months* to the practice of their religion" showed Belisarius' ignorance of Arab custom; for the Arabs had three months of truce in succession, not two. Only if Balisarius was speaking from mere information passed on to him, could the discrepancy have been given room. In the true calendar, as we shall see in the course of this study, it was Safar and not Dhu'l-Hijjah that turned up in the summer solstice of 541. Two years before, in 539, the two months of truce, Dhu'l-Hijjah and Muharram turned up against April-May and May-June – a little before the summer solstice. Perhaps Belisarius meant that they were nearing the summer solstice *and were in* a time when the pagan Arabs used to devote their time to the practice of their religion, abstaining from all sorts of violence. Locating the pilgrimage here or there inferring from the mere statement of one not acquainted with the native custom is like catching at straws which seemingly support one's views.

Of the weather references in the biographical works he picked up the mention of *inconvenient heat* during the month of emigration and *inclement weather* during the siege of al-Khandaq apparently because his calendar could throw up the reported weather conditions against them. But he ignored two other references available in 8 and 9 H – the expedition of 'Amr ibn al-'As to Dhat as-Salasil in Jumada al-Akhirah 8 H when he experienced the severe cold of winter and Ghazwah Tabuk which took place in Rajab 9 H in an intensely hot season when the fruits had ripened. His calendar throws up September-October against the former and October-November against the latter – which were not periods of extreme cold, and the season of ripening fruits and intense heat. He himself says, quoting Buckhardt, that harvesting season of fruits in Arabia ends in the beginning of September. For obvious reasons Perceval avoided mention of these two references.

Apart from these loopholes and shortcomings, of 24 events covering up to 8 H his calendar could agree with the biographical reports on the weekdays only in two cases *viz.* the Emigration and Ghazwah Badr al-Maw'id as will be shown by the following table worked out with reference to his own calendar.

	TRADITIONAL DATES	**JULIAN DATES**
1. Abrahah's attack upon the Ka'bah	17 MHR 1 AF, SU	Jul 7, 570, MO
2. Birth of the Prophet ﷺ	2 RBL 1 AF, MO	Aug 20, 570, WE
3. First revelation of the Qur'an	18 RMD 40 AF, MO	Jan 21, 610, WE
4. Mi'raj	27 RMD 51 AF, SA	Jan 28, 621, WE
5. Emigration	12 RBL 1 H, MO	Jun 28, 622, MO
6. Ghazwah Buwat	20 RBR 2 H, MO	Aug 23, 623, TU
7. Ghazwah Yanbu'	2 SHB 2 H, TH	Dec 2, 623, FR
	14 SHB 2 H, TU	Dec 14, 623, WE
8. Change of Qiblah	15 SHB 2 H, TU	Dec 15, 623, TH
9. Ghazwah Badr	16 RMD 2 H, FR	Jan 14, 624, SA
	22 RMD 2 H, WE	Jan 20, 624, FR
10. Ghazwah Qararat al-Kudr	1 SHW 2 H, FR	Jan 29, 624, SU
11. Sariyyah Ghalib ibn 'Abdallah al-Laythi	10 SHW 2 H, SU	Feb 7, 624, TU
	16 SHW 2 H, SA	Feb 13, 624, MO
12. Ghazwah al-Sawiq	22 DLH 2 H, SU	Apr 18, 624, WE
13. Ghazwah Uhud	11 SHW 3 H, SA	Jan 28, 625, MO
14. Sariyyah 'Abdallah ibn Unays	5 MHR 4 H, MO	Apr 20, 625, SA
	23 MHR 4 H, SA	May 8, 625, WE
15. Ghazwah Dhat al-Riqa'	10 JML 4 H, MO	Aug 20, 625, TU
16. Ghazwah Badr al-Maw'id	1 SHB 4 H, TH	Nov 8, 625, FR
	20 SHB 4 H, WE	Nov 27, 625, WE
17. Document of Ahl-i Maqna	3 RMD 5 H, FR	Dec 29, 626, MO
18. Ghazwah al-Khandaq	1 DLQ 5 H, SA	Feb 24, 627, TU
19. Ghazwah al-Hudaybiyah	1 DLQ 6 H, TH	Feb 13, 628, SA
20. Postponed pilgrimage	6 DLQ 7 H, MO	Feb 7, 629, TU
21. Capture of Makkah	18 RMD 8 H, MO	Jan 10, 630, WE
22. Ghazwah Hunayn	10 SHW 8 H, TU	Jan 31, 630, WE
23. 'Umrah from al-Ji'ranah	5 DLQ 8 H, TH	Feb 25, 630, SU
	18 DLQ 8 H, WE	Mar 10, 630, SA
24. Return to Madinah	19 DLQ 8 H, TH	Mar 11, 630, SU
	25 DLQ 8 H, FR	Mar 17, 630, SA

The table indicates that acceptance of Perceval's calendar will be hazardous unless one dismisses as nonsense all the biographical information on the weekdays.

ALVI'S CALENDARS

Alvi did extensive work and covered nearly all the major events of the lifetime of the Prophet ﷺ. He asserts that there were two parallel calendars – one with occasional intercalation operating in Makkah and the other without intercalation operating in Madinah, both however using common names of the months. The Muhajirun referred to the Makkan calendar and the Ansars to the Madinan, giving rise to the apparent conflicts in the reports. In his analysis Alvi attempted to reconcile such conflicts, with a major thrust to corroborate the placement of the events to the reported weather conditions of the days and assigned a Muharram in the Makkan and a Rabi' al-Awwal in the Madinan calendar against (13 September – 12 October 622). The Madinan calendar continued in the normal sequence of the months without intercalation while the Makkan incorporated four intercalary months during the ten Madinan years – one each at the ends of 1 H and 4 H and one each between Safar and Muharram of 6 H and 9 H.

When the biographers reported more than one month for a particular event, Alvi maintains that one was with reference to the Makkan calendar and the other to the Madinan. As for instance, the change of Qiblah from Jerusalem to Makkah took place in 2 H – in Jumada al-Ula according to Imam az-Zuhri[1] but in Sha'ban according to al-Waqidi.[2] Alvi believes that both were correct; the former was with reference to the Makkan calendar and the latter to the Madinan – both concording with January-February 624.

His placement of some important events are shown in the table below. In the majority of cases he did not work out the corresponding Julian dates. Even in the few cases in which he did so, where his calendars revealed weekdays one or two days away from the biographers' weekdays, he ignored the departure by holding that one or two days' discrepancy does not make any difference. Therefore we have shown in the table only the dates in respect of which his calendars could agree with the biographical reports regarding the weekdays.

Chronology of Prophetic Events

		Makkan Calendar	Madinan Calendar	Corresponding Julian Dates
1.	Hijrah – Emigration	RBL 1 H (12 RBL, MO	(JML 1 H)	Nov 11 - Dec 10, 622 Nov 22, MO)
2.	Ghazwah Badr al Ula	RBL 2 H	JMR 2 H	Nov 30 - Dec 28, 623
3.	Ghazwah Buwat	RBR 2 H	(RJB 2 H)	Dec 29 - Jan 27, 624
4.	Change of Qiblah	JML 2 H	SHB 2 H	Jan 28 - Feb 25, 624
5.	Sariyyah 'Abdallah ibn Jahsh al Asadi	RJB 2 H	(SHW 2 H)	Mar 27 - Apr 24, 624
6.	Ghazwah Yanbu'	SHB 2 H (2 SHB, TH 14 SHB, TU	(DLQ 2 H)	Apr 25 - May 24, 624 Apr 26, TH May 8, TU)
7.	Ghazwah Badr	RMD 2 H	(DLH 2 H)	May 25 - Jun 23, 624
8.	Ghazwah Qararat al-Kudr	SHW 2 H	MHR 3 H	Jun 24 - Jul 23, 624
9.	Sariyyah Ghalib ibn 'Abdallah al Laythi	SHW 2 H	(MHR 3 H)	Jun 24 - Jul 23, 624
10.	Ghazwah Dhu Amarr	DLH 2 H	RBL 3 H	Aug 22 - Sep 20, 624
11.	Ghazwah Uhud	SHW 3 H	MHR 4 H	Jun 13 - Jul 12, 625
12.	Ghazwah Bani Nadir	RBL 4 H (12 RBL, TU	(JMR 4 H)	Nov 8 - Dec 6, 625 Nov 19, TU)
13.	Ghazwah Badr al-Maw'id	SHB 4 H	DLQ 4 H	Apr 4 - May 3, 626
14.	Ghazwah Dhat al Riqa'[3]	MHR 5 H	JML 5 H	Sep 28 - Oct 27, 626
15.	Ghazwah al Muraysi'	(RBR 5 H)	SHB 5 H	Dec 26 - Jan 23, 627
16.	Ghazwah al Khandaq	(JMR 5 H)	SHW 5 H	Feb 23 - Mar 23, 627
17.	Ghazwah Bani Qurayzah	(RJB 5 H)	DLQ 5 H (23 DLQ, WE	Mar 24 - Apr 22, 627 Apr 15, WE)
18.	Ghazwah al-Hudaybiyah	JMR 6 H	DLQ 6 H	Mar 13 - Apr 11, 628
19.	Postponed 'Umrah	JMR 7 H	DLQ 7 H	Mar 2 - Mar 31, 629
20.	Opening of Makkah to Islam	RMD 8 H	(SFR 9 H)	May 20 - Jun 17, 630
21.	Ghazwah Hunayn	SHW 8 H (6 SHW, SA	(RBL 9 H)	Jun 18 - Jul 17, 630 Jun 23, SA)
22.	Return to Madinah	DLQ 8 H	(RBR 9 H)	Jul 18 - Aug 15, 630
23.	Abu Bakr's Hajj	(JMR 9 H)	DLH 9 H	Mar 11 - Apr 8, 631
24.	Ghazwah Tabuk	RJB 9 H	MHR 10 H	Apr 9 - May 8, 631
25.	Farewell Pilgrimage	(JMR 10 H)	DLH 10 H (4 DLH, MO	Feb 28 - Mar 28, 632 Mar 2, MO)
26.	Issue of orders for an expedition against Byzantium	(SHB 10 H)	SFR 11 H	Apr 28 - May 26, 632
27.	Passing away of the Prophet ﷺ	(RMD 10 H)	RBL 11 H (12 RBL, MO	May 27 - Jun 25, 632 Jun 8, MO)

The foregoing table indicates that Alvi related the dates of Sariyyah 'Abdallah ibn Jahsh al-Asadi (the Nakhlah incident) and the Opening of Makkah to the months of the Makkan calendar and those of Abu

Bakr's Hajj and the Farewell Pilgrimage to those of the Madinan. Such treatment will raise the following questions.

Now, when 'Abdallah attacked the Makkans at Nakhlah in Rajab, the Prophet ﷺ expressed his serious displeasure for violating the sanctity of the sacred month;[4] and in setting forth for the capture of Makkah, he and the Companions maintained the obligatory fast of Ramadan which they broke at al-Kadid.[5] These show that the Prophet ﷺ was regulating the religious affairs with reference to the Makkan calendar at least up until 8 H. Celebration of 'Id al-Fitr and 'Id al-Adha introduced in the second year of migration[6] must also surely have been regulated according to this calendar at least up to this point of time. Then, how did the Prophet ﷺ send out Abu Bakr for a Hajj in Madinan Dhu'l-Hijjah 9 H which corresponded to Makkan Jumada al-Akhirah – only six months after the last Hajj observed in Makkan Dhu'l-Hijjah 8 H? Was there a divine commandment in the meantime to shift the location of the annual pilgrimage so abruptly? If so, how did the entire block of the Companions miss reporting such an important change? When did the Prophet ﷺ and the Muslims fast and celebrate 'Ids in the next two years of 9 and 10 AH?

Secondly, why did the Prophet ﷺ send 'Ali on the occasion of Abu Bakr's Hajj to declare the latest divine commandment about Immunity (Qur'an 9:1-6) which only concerned the polytheists and the pagans on an occasion when none but a few Muslims would attend? Although the following month was Rajab in the Makkan calendar and the Arabs would throng Makkah for the lesser pilgrimage which had always been performed in this month the question remains: When was the declaration supposed to be made? The Qur'an dictated that it should be on the day of the Greater Pilgrimage (Qur'an 9:3). Could the Prophet ﷺ cause it to be declared on any other days in contravention to the commandment? Certainly not. Did his sending 'Ali in Jumada al-Akhirah of the Makkan calendar carry any meaning? These questions remain unanswered if we assign Abu Bakr's pilgrimage in the Madinan Dhu'l-Hijjah.

In respect of three events, *viz.* Ghazwah as-Sawiq, Sariyyah 'Abdallah ibn Unays and document of Ahl-i Maqna, Alvi could not say to which calendar – Makkan or Madinan – the reported months related.

Apart from these, Alvi's calendars do not reveal weekdays in agreement with the biographical reports. Of twenty-five events for which weekdays were available to him, his calendars could agree with the biographical reports only in respect of seven events. In his zeal to corroborate the placing of events with the reported weather conditions of the days, Alvi sacrificed the need to corroborate his weekdays with those laboriously collected by the classical biographers.

Amir Ali's Reconstruction

Dr. Hashim Amir Ali holds that the pagan calendar was lunisolar in nature and maintains that their new year began with the new moon of Muharram more or less around the autumnal equinox. Consequently the two annual pilgrimages of *Hajj Akbar* and *Hajj Asghar* invariably fell around August-September and March-April; and the four sacred months of the Arabs always oscillated over the following Julian months:

Rajab	the month of lesser pilgrimage:	March-April
Dhu'l-Qa'dah	the month preceding the greater pilgrimage:	July-August
Dhu'l-Hijjah	the month of greater pilgrimage:	August-September
Muharram	the first month of the year:	September-October

Conforming to such assignment and presuming that the Prophet ﷺ, peace be upon him, in his sagacity actually left the city of Makkah only in a sacred month in order to avoid possible clashes, he placed the emigration in Muharram of the pagan calendar which he prefers to call the *Downstream calendar*, against Rabi' al-Awwal of the retrospectively reconstructed Hijrah calendar which he calls the *Upstream calendar* – both being concorded against September-October 622. He counted the Hijrah era from the first of this pagan Muharram and inserted three intercalary months in the Madinan decade in the *Downstream calendar* one each at the ends of 2 H, 5 H and 7 H.

He further believes that the fourth intercalation due at the end of the tenth year against (24 August – 22 September 632 CE) had been abandoned following the Prophet ﷺ's abolition of intercalation.

In his reconstruction, Amir Ali places the Hijrah, change of Qiblah, the Khandaq, Hudaybiyyah, the postponed 'Umrah and the death of the Prophet ﷺ in the *Upstream calendar* and Badr, Uhud, the Opening of Makkah [to Islam] and Abu Bakr's Hajj in the *Downstream*.[7]

About the Farewell Pilgrimage he maintains that the Prophet ﷺ actually did an lesser pilgrimage in Rajab 10 H (*downstream*) which corresponded to Dhu'l-Hijjah 10 AH (*upstream*).[8] In view of the supreme importance which this occasion had acquired after the demise of the Prophet ﷺ the people had later given this the status of a Hajj and changed the name of the month from Rajab to Dhu'l-Hijjah. This was partly to justify the enhancement of the status of the lesser pilgrimage to that of a Hajj and mainly to obliterate the existence of intercalary months in the Hijrah calendar. He says that if we go back in the *Downstream calendar* from this Rajab-turned-Dhu'l-Hijjah by naming the months retrogressively without allowing intercalation, the procedure will efface the three intercalary months interposing in the Madinan decade; the remaining two months of Muharram and Safar will recede behind the horizon of the *Hijrah* and be lost in the darkness of the pre-*Hijrah* Makkan period overlapped by the last two months of Dhu'l-Qa'dah and Dhu'l-Hijjah of the intercalary epoch. With the passage of time, the annihilation of these two months also would be effaced from the Muslim memory even as the other three intercalary months would have been effaced from the first decade of the newly introduced Muslim era.[9]

Amir Ali imagines that the second Caliph, being beset with the problem of reconciling the actual existence of the intercalary months and their desired elimination in the very first decade of the Muslim era and feeling it imperative to restore some order in the accumulating chaos of months and years, had commandeered the services of a member of the *Kalamas* clan to provide a solution. A shrewd representative of this calendar-manipulating clan had solved this problem in the way narrated above.[10]

Anticipating the question as to how it was that such a vital chronological manipulation, like the one he presumes, was not mentioned in all the copious traditional and biographical literature, he asserts that as the very purpose of the manipulation had been to obliterate the intercalary month – not only its stem and branches but its roots as well, the effacement had been totally suppressed in the historical records too.[11]

Despite the interesting but too audacious assumptions, the dismal feature of his calendar and placement of events is that out of ten events only the dates of the Farewell Pilgrimage and the death of the Prophet ﷺ could agree with the biographical reports regarding the weekdays on which they fell, as the following table will exhibit.

		Downstream Calendar	**Upstream Calendar**	**Corresponding Julian Dates**
1.	Commencement of the Hijrah era	DLQ	MHR 1 AH	Jul 16 - Aug14, 622
2.	Emigration	MHR 1 H	RBL 1 AH (12 RBL, MO	Sep 13 - Oct 12, 622 Sep 24, FR)[12]
3.	Change of Qiblah	JMR 2 H	SHB 2 AH (15 SHB, TU	Jan 28 - Feb 25, 624 Feb 11, SA)
4.	Badr	RMD 2 H (16 RMD, FR	(DLQ 2 AH)	Apr 25 - May 24, 624 May 10, TH)
5.	Uhud	SHW 3 H (11 SHW, SA	(MHR 4 AH)	Jun 13 - Jul 12, 625 Jun 23, SU)
6.	Al-Khandaq	(SHB 5 H)	DLQ 5 AH (1 DLQ, SA	Mar 24 - Apr 22, 627 Mar 24, TU)
7.	Hudaybiyyah	(RJB 6 H)	DLQ 6 AH (1 DLQ, TH	Mar 13 - Apr 11, 628 Mar 13, SU)
8.	Postponed 'Umrah	(RJB 7 H)	DLQ 7 AH (6 DLQ, MO	Mar 2 - Mar 31, 629 Mar 7, TU)
9.	Opening of Makkah	RMD 8 H (18 RMD, MO	(SFR 9 AH)	May 20 - Jun 17, 630 Jun 6, WE)
10.	Abu Bakr's Hajj	DLH 9 H	(JML 10 AH)	Aug 5 - Sep 3, 631
11.	Farewell Hajj	RJB 10 H	DLH 10 AH (4 DLH, MO 9 DLH, FR	Feb 28 - Mar 28, 632 Mar 3, SU Mar 8, FR)
12.	Passing away of the Prophet ﷺ	(SHW 10 H)	RBL 11 AH (12 RBL, MO	May 27 - Jun 25, 632 Jun 8, MO)

Hamidullah's Work

The review of the earlier works will not be complete without discussing the views of Dr. Hamidullah who was perhaps the first ever to have come near to the truth of the pagan calendar.

In his article on *Nasi'*,[13] Hamidullah argues that the presently available non-intercalary Hijrah calendar of the Madinan decade must not be relied upon as it does not consider *nasi's* while the period was intercalary in the time of the Prophet ﷺ. For representing the true state of affairs, the calendar must be reconstructed afresh by inter-stitching *nasi's*. As to the charges of the Orientalists, when they could not get the biographical weekdays in the Hijrah calendar, that the classical Muslim historians lacked a sense of historical accuracy, Hamidullah says that such charges are ridiculous and undeserved as the calendar drawn up without *nasi's* will never be in a position to agree with the traditional information. Instead the Orientalists should have considered that they might be looking up in the wrong frame of reference.

Of the system of intercalation used by the Arabs, Hamidullah was strongly inclined towards the Babylonian method in which the courses of the lunar and solar years were reconciled in 30 years by adding eleven extra months. But these eleven months could be inter-stitched within the span of the 30 years itself by intercalating at the ends of the 3rd, 6th, 9th, 11th, 14th, 17th, 20th, 22nd, 25th, 28th and 30th years or at the ends of every third year up to the 30th year and one at the end of the 31st.

Of the two methods Hamidullah prefers the second and says that after intercalating the eleventh *nasi'* externally at the end of the 31st year, the first *nasi'* of the second cycle must be placed after two years and thereafter the others regularly at the ends of every three years – for in that case the divergent reports about intercalation at the ends of every three years, every two years and every single year can be reconciled. He believes that all the reporters were partially correct but did not know the whole truth. Each reporter witnessing the occasion of intercalation once had generalised about it.

Recommending the system, he says that this was practised in the time of Hammurabi, the Nimrod of the time of the prophet Ibrahim, peace be upon him, and the Arabs being Isma'ilites must have adopted this system of their ancient forefathers.

About the location of *nasi'* in the Madinan decade, Hamidullah was of the opinion that because there was an intercalation at the end of the 9 AH, the sixth and third years of *Hijrah* and the year before *Hijrah* must have been intercalary years.

Based on this scheme he worked out the dates of seven major events of the lifetime of the Prophet ﷺ in the Julian calendar and the results could agree with the biographical reports in respect of the weekdays as shown below.

	Traditional dates	**Julian dates**
Birth of the Prophet ﷺ	12 RBL 53 bH, MO	Jun 17, 569, MO
First revelation of the Qur'an	17 RMD 13 bH, MO	Dec 22, 609, MO
Arrival at Madinah	12 RBL 1 H, MO	May 31, 622, MO
Badr	17 RMD 2 H, FR	Nov 18, 623, FR
Al-Khandaq	29 SHW 5 H, SA	Jan 24, 627, SA
Farewell Hajj	9 DLH 10 H, FR	Mar 6, 632, FR
Passing away of the Prophet ﷺ	2 RBL 11 H, MO	May 25, 632, MO

While doing so, he took it for granted that the day of Farewell Hajj was a Friday and worked out arithmetically the number of days separating two successive events and ascertained the weekdays by counting the number of days left over the complete sets of the week. In spite of the initial success in the seven events he did not proceed further to cover the remaining events of the lifetime of the Prophet ﷺ. Of the seven events shown above, despite agreement in weekdays, only the Julian dates of the first revelation of the Qur'an and the end of the siege of Khandaq were truly correct as we shall see in the course of this study.

Between the birth of the Prophet ﷺ and the Farewell Hajj he considered altogether 23 *nasi's*, while there were actually only 22 *nasi's* as this study will shortly disclose; but except for the Madinan decade he could not specify their locations.

The idea of probable sub-systems in the Babylonian method, which we shall discuss later, perhaps did not occur to him. That's why in search of the true location of the *nasi's* he drifted from idea to idea and went farther away from the true solution, at least of the Madinan decade after coming to it once. This is transparent from an excerpt of his letter addressed to Dr. Hashim Amir Ali in 1972. It read: "Then I had thought that the intercalation took place regularly every third year. Now in the article on *Nasi'* (1968) I hesitated ... in my present stage of research, intercalation were made at the end of the 3rd, 4th, 6th and 9th years of the Hijrah ..."[14]

Notes

[1] Burhan, Oct 1964, p 209

[2] At-Tabari: *Tarikh*, Vol 1, p 158

[3] Actually the event occurred in 4 AH; but in his calendars Alvi placed it in 5 AH.

[4] Ibn Hisham: *as-Sirah*, Vol 1, p 696

[5] Ibn Hisham: *as-Sirah*, Vol 2, p 473; Ibn Sa'd: *at-Tabaqat*, Vol 2, p 167

[6] At-Tabari: *Tarikh*, Vol 1, pp 159, 208

[7] Ali: *Upstream*, pp 34, 35

[8] Ali: *Upstream*, p 46

[9] Ali: *Upstream*, p 46

[10] Ali: *Upstream*, pp 45, 46

[11] Ali: *Upstream*, p 50

[12] Following al-Biruni, Amir Ali maintained that the Prophet ﷺ reached Madinah on the 8th of the month which corresponded to Monday, September 20, 622 (– Ali: *Upstream*, pp 17, 18). But here we consider the true date of arrival at Madinah.

[13] Islamic Review, Feb 1969, p 6

[14] Ali: *Upstream*, p 23

3. Parameters of the Lost Calendar

The foregoing discussion discloses that though the majority of the authorities agreed that the pagans occasionally intercalated an additional month in their years, yet they differed about the actual location of such intercalary months. Since their location will definitely affect any calendar that may be reconstructed and ultimately the placement of events it is of prime importance to dig out the exact locations where they actually placed them in their calendar. It is, therefore, essential that we equip ourselves with a thorough knowledge of the ways of intercalation in order to avoid the possible pitfalls in the reconstruction.

The Glorious Qur'an says: "**There have been twelve months with Allah in the Book of Allah, from the day He first created the heavens and earth; …Deferring a sacred month (intercalation) is an increase in kufr… One year they make it profane and another sacred…**" (9: 36-37) informing us that the pagans intercalated their years by occasionally increasing the number of months beyond the decreed twelve and the practice was an addition to kufr.

But why did the Arabs do intercalation and how did their calendar work? In the ancient days, the Arabs used a purely lunar system of reckoning years in which the year consisted of twelve lunations. As seasons work out in accordance with the revolution of the planet around the sun, they do not move through the months in the solar calendar. But in the pure lunar calendar they go on moving from month to month in successive years as the lunar year is shorter than the solar by about 11 days. This resulted in the continual movement of the Arab pilgrimage from season to season and often it fell on days of scarcity and inconvenient weather.

The pagan pilgrimage was a big event associated with annual fairs and festivals, lyrical competitions and trade activities, which type of activities normally demands equable weather conducive to social intermingling. Scarcity and inconvenient weather would certainly handicap people. Faced by the inconvenience, they started thinking of a solution to the problem by which they could still continue celebrating the pilgrimage in the month of Dhu'l-Hijjah but in equable weather and a season of abundance. They were also aware that occasional intercalation of an extra month in the lunar year could hold the pilgrimage more or less stationary in the same season. Therefore, at some point when their pilgrimage was in the natural course in the season they wanted, they had adopted intercalation. This is what transpires from the writings of al-Biruni, the fifth century astronomer-mathematician. He said:

"At the time of paganism the Arabs used their months in a similar way to the Muslims; their pilgrimage wandered around the four seasons of the year. But then they desired to perform the pilgrimage at such time as their merchandise (hides, skins, fruits etc.) was ready for the market and to fix it according to an invariable rule so that it should occur in the most agreeable and abundant season of the year.[1*] They learned the system of intercalation ... And they used intercalation ... adding the difference between their year and the solar year, when it had summed up to one complete month, to the months of their year. Then their intercalators themselves, the so-called Kalamas of the Kinanah tribe rose, after the pilgrimage have been finished, delivered a speech to the people at the fair and intercalated the month, calling the next following month by the name of the month in which they were. The Arabs consented to this arrangement and adopted the decision of the Kalamas. This proceeding they called '*nasi*' i.e. postponement, because in every second or third year they postponed the beginning of the year for a month, as it was required by the progression of the year ..."

Regarding the method of the practice, he stated:

"The first intercalation applied to Muharram; in consequence Safar was called Muharram, Rabi' al-Awwal was called Safar, and so on; and in this way all the names of all the months were changed. The second intercalation applied to Safar, and in consequence the next following month (Rabi' al-Awwal) was called Safar. And this went on till intercalation had passed through all the twelve months of the year and returned to Muharram. Then they commenced anew what they had done the first time.

"... This went on till the time when the Prophet ﷺ fled from Makkah to Madinah when the turn of intercalation, as we have mentioned, had come to Sha'ban."

"... then the Prophet ﷺ waited till the Farewell Hajj, on which occasion he addressed the people and said: 'The seasons, the time has gone round as it was on the day of Allah's creating the heavens and the earth' by which he meant that the months had returned to their original places[2] and they had been freed from what the Arabs used to do with them. Thereupon intercalation was prohibited and altogether neglected."[3]

But about when the Arabs started intercalation opinions differed amongst the authorities. Al-Biruni, Maqrizi and Muhammad Jarkasi maintained that they had adopted it about 200 years before the preaching of the Prophet[4] ﷺ while Dr. Hamidullah was of the view that it could be much earlier than that.

Quoting very old sources, such as Azraqi (d. 223 AH), Hamidullah says that the affair of intercalation was first in the hands of the Kindah tribe of Yemen who in their expansion of power had even captured parts of Syria and Iraq at the cost of the Byzantines and the Persians, and later it passed on to the family of Kalamas of Kinanah tribe of Makkah. He further informs us that the marriage of Malik ibn Kinanah to the daughter of Mu'awiyyah ibn Thawr al-Kindi was the real cause for the transfer of the function of intercalation from the Kindah tribe to the Kinanah tribe. According to Wustenfeld's *Genealogische Tabellen* there were thirteen generations between Malik ibn Kinanah and Islam and seventeen generations between Mu'awiyyah al-Kindi and Islam. Reckoning thirty years for a generation, says Hamidullah, the matrimonial alliance must have taken place between 390 to 510 years previously and the Kinanah tribe may have taken over the function not later than 450 years (average of the two) before Islam. However he cautions us that nobody knows how long the Kindites had practised intercalation in Makkah before the final transfer of the function to the tribe of Kinanah.[5]

These studies lead us to the following conclusions:

(a)   The Arabs started intercalation more than 450 years before the advent of Islam with a view to placing their pilgrimage around the time of the autumn equinox and they abandoned it after 9 H, when they did it for the last time;

(b)   The intercalary month was appended at the end of the year after the normal Dhu'l-Hijjah, the month of annual pilgrimage, and was also called Dhu'l-Hijjah;

(c)   The intercalation which was carried out immediately before the Prophet ﷺ's flight was against Shaʿban,[6] that is, had there been no intercalation at all the name of that month would have been Shaʿban; and

(d)   Intercalation against the remaining months of the year was successively carried out in due course in the next ten years of the Prophet ﷺ's lifetime at Madinah and when the course of intercalation through all twelve lunar months was complete with an intercalation against Dhu'l-Hijjah the intercalary and the non-intercalary courses of the months coincided; that is, the months in the pagan calendar had returned to the position where they should have been had there been no intercalation.

The Prophet ﷺ was waiting for this juncture and could not afford to miss this first available chance. Firstly, because indications had been given to him that he was approaching the last phase of his life[7] and might perhaps not live to the next occasion of Hajj; and secondly, the innovation of intercalation, commandments for the abolition of which had already descended, could best be abolished at this time without causing any dislocation to the system. If he did the correct pilgrimage in the month of Dhu'l-Hijjah of the tenth year of Hijrah, the months had already come to the normal positions from Muharram of that year. From this, we can with certainty infer that the intercalation which restored the months to the correct positions was done against Dhu'l-Hijjah at the end of the ninth year and that was the last in the history of Arab intercalation.

Deviating a bit from our theme, we may ask: Why did the Prophet ﷺ forbid continuance of intercalation under which system he had spent almost his entire life?

In this regard we may quote an illuminating passage from Montgomery Watt. He wrote: "There are so many obscurities in the whole question of intercalary months that it is difficult to say what were the underlying reasons for the adoption of a lunar year. The Qur'an implies that the intercalation was in some respect a human activity infringing God's law, ... As reason for the prohibition of intercalation there are two main possibilities. The method of settling when a month was to be intercalated may have been connected with paganism in some way of which we are not aware; it was certainly linked with the observance of the sacred months. Or else there may have been a risk that the uncertainty about which months were sacred would cause disputes and endanger the *Pax Islamica*."[8]

The Arabs were a people who were easily provoked and highly revengeful among whom forays against peaceful habitations and solitary trade caravans were not infrequent and armed retaliation was a tribal duty. Amidst such raids and counter-raids, enforcement of non-violence during some part of the year, preferably during some periods of equable weather, conducive to economic activity and social intermingling would serve as an effective restraint over their impetuous nature. Therefore there prevailed amongst them an unwritten taboo against violence during the four months of the year, namely Rajab, Dhu'l-Qa'dah, Dhu'l-Hijjah and Muharram. Initially so scrupulously did they observe the sanctity of these months that even if a man were to be faced with his own father's murderer, he did not dare to unsheathe his sword if this encounter happened to be during these sacred months. The survival of this community was delicately balanced on the maintenance of these months of peace, for otherwise it would have perished in the mists of history.

Nevertheless with the passage of time the system was later seriously abused by the intercalating clan of the *Kalamas*. When an additional month was interposed between Dhu'l-Hijjah and Muharram the question arose whether it should be treated as sacred or secular. The *Kalamas* at his whims or under the influence of others often declared it secular wherein fighting and retaliation were permissible. Innocent pilgrims were not allowed the time to return to their hearth and home and were often exposed to retaliatory bloodshed. When the sanctity of the sacred month was violated so frequently to the disadvantage of the pilgrims and traders, its peaceful effect remained no more; and the need to root out this evil became imperative and so the divine command for the abolition of intercalation descended.

Secondly, Islam was meant for the whole of mankind and not only for the Arabs. Religious laws and regulations should not be oblivious of the people inhabiting other parts of the globe. By fixing the months, the performance of obligatory duties would become either too exacting or too easy in certain cases. It would impose upon people elsewhere the hardship of the month-long fasting of Ramadan in the longest and hottest part of the year. Only a Ramadan which moves through the seasons would relieve them of such hardship.

Also, the Almighty Allah had revealed elsewhere that He measures out the phases of the moon that mankind might know the number of years and the count of time (Qur'an 10: 5) indicating that we should base our reckoning of the years only on the waxing and waning phases of the moon.

These considerations may be a part of the wisdom in the Prophet ﷺ who, in obedience to the revelation of Allah, abolished the much abused system of intercalation.

CYCLE OF INTERCALATION

Now reverting to our theme, let us endeavour to ascertain the last intercalation. It must be borne in mind that the identity of this *nasi'* is extremely important. Because not only will it affect the calendar of the preceding period in a unique way but it will also disclose the exact time when the pagans had adopted intercalation. To find this out we must necessarily know: in the course of how many years did the Arabs attempt to synchronise the passage of the two years and at what intervals did they place the intercalary months?

On this too, again the authorities differed in views – 19 years according to Hajji Khalifah with intercalation at the ends of the 2nd, 5th, 7th, 10th, 13th, 16th and 18th years;[9] 24 years according to al-Biruni with intercalation at the ends of the 3rd, 6th, 8th, 11th, 14th, 16th, 19th, 22nd and 24th years[10] and 30 years according to Dr. Hamidullah.[11]

Against such conflicting views, before we make a critical analysis of the respective merits of the systems it would be hazardous to take a decision as to what the cycle was and what the intervals of intercalation were.

We understand that the period the lunar year gains over the solar is precisely 10.875139 days (=365.242199-354.36706). Therefore the total gain accumulated in the aforementioned courses can be arrested by adding seven, nine or eleven extra months – some of 29 days and some of 30 as shown in the following table:

	19 YEARS	**24** YEARS	**30** YEARS
Lead of the lunar year (in days):	207	261	326
Adjustment by intercalation:			
Months of 29 days –	3	9	4
Months of 30 days –	4	–	7

We see that adjustments under these systems are perfect completely neutralising the gain in days and leaving no fraction to cause any seasonal shift of the lunar festivals, while we know that despite intercalation the pagan pilgrimage, which was initially placed some time in the autumn at the time of adoption of intercalation, had gradually moved and arrived at the threshold of spring at the time of the Prophet ﷺ. How could such slippage be possible if the gain had been totally absorbed in the cycle as it is in the above mentioned systems? The natural inference is that the Arabs could not have used any of these methods. We shall have to look deeper.

The initial aim of the pagans being to fix their pilgrimage in the season they wanted, if the pilgrimage moved despite intercalation it must have been due to a factor they did not perceive. For they could not knowingly adopt a defective system which would frustrate their aim. The slippage could arise only because of an inadvertent mistake. We may now think about how such an error could have arisen in the system.

Let us examine Hamidullah's preference as to the intervals of intercalation and see whether it could give rise to a factor which may cause gradual slippage of the pilgrimage. He stated that intercalations were to be made every three years up to the thirtieth year to be followed by one more external intercalation at the end of the thirty-first. Then the first intercalation of the second cycle must be made after a lapse of only two years from the preceding one and the rest as usual after every three years. If this is so, the gain of the first cycle would be fully absorbed by the 11 intercalations (326 days = 4 months of 29 days and 7 of 30 days) and not carried over – again disabling the system to drag the pilgrimage. Clearly therefore, this also could not have been the interval adopted by them. How then could an element of imperfection creep into the system to cause a seasonal shift of the pilgrimage?

In our view, understanding inadequately the requirements of the system, the Kalamas had initially made a mistake in the beginning of the second cycle – a mistake unwittingly repeated throughout the intercalary epoch. Instead of placing the first intercalation of the second cycle at the end of the 33rd year (three years from the end of the first cycle) he had placed it at the end of the 34th year (three years from the external intercalation of the 31st year) as shown below:

| Method intended | ... | <u>27</u> | 28 | 29 | <u>30</u> | <u>31</u> | 32 | <u>33</u> | 34 | 35 | <u>36</u> | 37 | ... |
| Method adopted | ... | <u>27</u> | 28 | 29 | <u>30</u> | <u>31</u> | 32 | 33 | <u>34</u> | 35 | 36 | <u>37</u> | ... |

(intercalary years represented by underlined figures)

In consequence, while all the time the Kalamas remained under the illusion that the system he was following was a 30 year cycle, it had in fact, without his being aware of the same, become a 31 year cycle, each cycle becoming independent of the other but imperfect in itself and leaving a gain of about 12 days in each cycle as shown below:

31 solar years	11,322.5 days
31 lunar years	10,985.3 days
Total gain:	337.2 days
Adjustment by 11 intercalations	325.0 days
(5 of 29 days and 6 of 30 days):	
Gain left over:	12.2 days

Despite the intercalation this unadjusted balance would drag the pilgrimage by two days in a little more than five years. This is the only possible way in which an element of imperfection could occur in the system.

Possible Calendars

Let us for the time-being assume that this was the system actually used by the Arabs and later check whether this assumption is truly correct. Then the first intercalation at the end of the third year will be against

Muharram, the second at the end of the sixth year will be against Safar, the third at the end of the ninth year will be against Rabi' al-Awwal, and so on. The last intercalation of the first cycle, that is, the one at the end of the thirty-first year will be against Dhu'l-Qa'dah. Thereafter the second cycle will start, of which the first intercalation will be against Dhu'l-Hijjah, the second against Muharram and so on. The following table indicates the plan of intercalation as well as what *nasi'* arrives against Dhu'l-Hijjah.

YEARS OF THE CYCLE INTERCALATED AGAINST THE MONTHS OF											*NASI'* AGAINST
MHR	SFR	RBL	RBR	JML	JMR	RJB	SHB	RMD	SHW	DLQ	DLH	Dhu'l-Hijjah
3	6	9	12	15	18	21	24	27	30	31	3	12N34
6	9	12	15	18	21	24	27	30	31	3	6	24N68
9	12	15	18	21	24	27	30	31	3	6	9	36N102
12	15	18	21	24	27	30	31	3	6	9	12	48N136
15	18	21	24	27	30	31	3	6	9	12	15	60N170
18	21	24	27	30	31	3	6	9	12	15	18	72N204
21	24	27	30	31	3	6	9	12	15	18	21	84N238
24	27	30	31	3	6	9	12	15	18	21	24	96N272
27	30	31	3	6	9	12	15	18	21	24	27	108N306
30	31	3	6	9	12	15	18	21	24	27	30	120N340
31	3	6	9	12	15	18	21	24	27	30	31	132N372

The penultimate column of the table shows that eleven different *nasi's* may arrive against Dhu'l-Hijjah – the twelfth intercalary month at the end of the thirty-fourth year (abbreviated as 12N34), the twenty-fourth intercalary month at the end of the sixty-eighth year (24N68), and so on. After the twelfth cycle, that is, after 372 years (=31x12) the whole sequence of intercalation shown in the table will repeat. This larger cycle may be called the *cycle of repetition*.

One of these eleven *nasi's* must necessarily turn up at the end of 9 H for the months to return to the normal positions at the beginning of 10 H. But as one particular *nasi'* at the end of 9 H will generate a peculiar calendar of the preceding period, the eleven possible *nasi's* will generate eleven different calendars. These may be identified by prefixing the length of the cycle to the abbreviated names of the *nasi's* themselves. That is, by 31.12N34 let us understand the calendar reconstructed by placing the 12N34 intercalary month as the last *nasi'* and so on. The eleven calendars may then be represented by the following abbreviations:

31.12N34,   31.24N68,   31.36N102,   31.48N136,   31.60N170,   31.72N204,

31.84N238,   31.96N272,   31.108N306,   31.120N340,   and   31.132N372

These were the sub-models of the system that could have arrived at the time of the Prophet ﷺ. If at all the Arabs were adopting the imperfect 31 year cycle of intercalation, the calendar operating during the lifetime of the Prophet ﷺ must have been one of these eleven.

These are the few parameters of the lost calendar that we can glean from the past.

Notes

[1] Interpreting the '*abundant season*' Perceval wrote that "the Arabs had adopted intercalation with a view to timing their pilgrimage to take place in that season when provisions were abundant, that is, in or about autumn, for the fruit harvest, staple food of the Arabs, ends in their country at the beginning of September." – *Islamic Culture*, Apr 1947, p 143

[2] The Companions were aware of this as is evident from one of the traditions of the rare kind. Mujahid reported: The pilgrimage of the Prophet ﷺ coincided with the month of Dhu'l-Hijjah. He therefore said: This day time has revolved to its state when Allah created the heavens and the earth.— Ibn Sa'd: *Tabaqat*, Vol 2, p 231

[3] Sachau: *Chronology*, pp 73, 74

[4] Sachau: *Chronology*, pp 14, 73; Islamic Culture, Apr 1947, pp 137, 146

[5] Islamic Review, Feb 1969, p 6

[6] This was an error of al-Biruni. The intercalation was in fact against Ramadan as the true calendar now reveals.

[7] Bukhari, Vol 6, p 485

[8] Watt: *Muhammad at Madinah*, p 300

[9] Islamic Culture, Apr 1947, p 145

[10] Sachau: *Chronology*, p 14

[11] Islamic Review, Feb 1969, p 10

4. Elements of Reconstruction

Now we shall discuss the phases of the moon, the age of the crescent moon which plays a vital role in deciding the starting point of the lunar month, the astronomical method of fixing the first date of the month and the placement of the intercalary months in the eleven possible calendars.

PHASES OF THE MOON

It is He who appointed the sun to give radiance, and the moon to give light, assigning it phases so you would know the number of years and the reckoning of time. Allah did not create these things except with truth.

Qur'an 10: 5

The moon does not emit light of its own. The light which we know as moonlight is the light from the sun reflected by it. The amount of sunlight reflected by its surface determines its phases. At conjunction earth, sun and moon are almost in one straight line; the moon, however, being placed between the earth and the sun, reflects no light although half of its surface is exposed to sunlight. Therefore the newly born moon can never be seen except during a solar eclipse. If the conjunction occurs at sunset on a particular day, no part of the moon will be seen that day. By the next sunset, the earth would have made one rotation on its own axis and twenty-four hours would have passed. During this period the moon would have moved in its orbit around the earth and would no longer be aligned with the earth and the sun. Then a small part of its surface, which is sunlit, reflects light towards the earth, and a crescent moon is born. It will appear in the western horizon for some time before it sets, due to the earth's eastward rotation. At the next sunset it is twenty-four hours older and will appear higher in the sky than the previous evening. A larger area of its surface will reflect sunlight; it will grow in size and will stay a longer period in the sky before it again sets. Each subsequent night a greater area of its surface will reflect light from the sun and it will also increase its altitude in the sky. These varying amounts of reflected light are referred to as the phases of the moon.

Approximately seven days after conjunction, the moon will be directly above us at sunset and a quarter of it will be illuminated. About seven days later, it will be full moon and the moon will seem to rise from the east and shine all night. It then appears gradually to lose its brightness and in another seven days, in the phase of the last quarter, only a part of its surface reflects light. After about another seven days, it would have returned to the position of the conjunction and a new cycle for another lunar month will start.

But the conjunction may occur any time during the twenty-four hours of the day; and the question is whether the crescent will be sighted at the following sunset for the lunar month to commence.

The faint crescent separated from the earth-sun alignment after the conjunction can only be seen when the sun has set and after its light has diminished. The last ray of sunlight leaving the sun at the time of sunset, when the sun goes goes down below the horizon, takes eight minutes to reach the earth. Furthermore, when the sun has set, there appears a ring of haze low on the western horizon, within which visibility is low and which takes sixteen minutes to subside. Therefore, only the crescent moon not setting within twenty-four minutes of sunset will be visible. In other words, for the crescent to be visible, it must have been born sufficiently early before sunset so as to remain above the horizon for more than twenty-four minutes after it.

The moon revolves around the earth through 360 degrees in 29.5 days from west to east [with respect to the sun], that is, through 12.2 degrees in twenty-four hours or 0.5 degree in one hour. Therefore every sunset it will be seen 12.2 degrees higher on the western horizon.

The time from the moment of conjunction up to the following sunset is called the age of the crescent. This (expressed in hours) may be converted into altitude (in degrees) by multiplying by 0.5. With the eastward rotation of the earth, the crescent will appear to set towards the western horizon at the rate of one degree for every four minutes as the earth rotates at the rate of 360 degrees per day. Therefore the altitude multiplied by four will give the time (in minutes) for which the crescent will remain in the sky after the sunset before disappearing under the western horizon. Let us handle some practical examples to understand these better.

(1) Suppose the conjunction occurred at 10 30 PM on a particular day and the following sunset at 6 10 PM of the next day. Then:

Age of the crescent at sunset	19 hours 40 minutes	19.66 hours
Altitude of the crescent at sunset	19.66 x 0.50	9.83 degrees
Time taken for disappearance after sunset	9.83 x 4	39.32 minutes

Subtracting the twenty-four minutes during which the crescent will not be visible, the visibility period works out at 15.32 minutes. That is, it will remain visible for 15.32 minutes.

(2) If the conjunction had occurred at 7.00 AM of the day and the following sunset was at 5 45 PM, then:

Age of the crescent at sunset	10 hours 45 minutes	10.75 hours
Altitude of the crescent at sunset	10.75 x 0.50	5.375 degrees
Time taken for disappearance after sunset	5.375 x 4	21.50 minutes

Since this is within the twenty-four minute period of invisibility, the crescent will set before it becomes visible.

Then how old a crescent is visible for practical purposes? The table below will give an insight as to how the age of the crescent determines its visibility.

Age at sunset (Hours)	Altitude at sunset (Degrees)	Setting time after sunset (Minutes)	Ysibility period (Minutes)
10	5.08	20.3	Nil
11	5.59	22.4	Nil
12	6.10	24.4	0.4
13	6.61	26.4	2.4
14	7.12	28.5	4.5
14.5	7.37	29.5	5.5
15	7.63	30.5	6.5
16	8.14	32.5	8.5
17	8.64	34.6	10.6
18	9.15	36.6	12.6
19	9.66	38.6	14.6
20	10.17	40.7	16.7
21	10.68	42.7	18.7
22	11.19	44.7	20.7
23	11.69	46.8	22.8
24	12.20	48.8	24.8

We gather from the table that when the new moon is only ten hours old, only a very faint crescent appears very low on the western horizon and that it would be obscured by the haze at twilight after sunset. The crescent will, therefore, not be visible. After twelve hours there is a very short period of visibility before the crescent sets.

The youngest crescent in astronomical records was of the age of 14.5 hours. To the unaided eye, a crescent 17 hours old was once reported sighted in Trinidad.[1] But this was a very rare phenomenon and cannot be held as a visibility criterion for all the time. Astronomers consider a criterion of 22±2 hours for sighting a crescent.[2] In our studies, therefore, we shall hold an age of 22 hours as the cut-off line. That is, if the age is below 22 hours it will not be sighted that sunset and the lunar month will commence from the next sunset. If it is 22 hours or more, the crescent will be sighted that sunset and the lunar month will commence.

Conjunction and Commencement of a Lunar Month

They will ask you about the crescent moons. Say, 'They are set times for mankind and for the hajj.' Qur'an 2: 189

With these preliminary concepts, we may now reach the stage of finding out the astronomical dates and hours of conjunction and commencement of the lunar months. The astronomical method involved is a complicated one and is beyond the scope of this book. Tsybulsky has given a very simple and fairly accurate method which is reproduced at the end of this book as Appendix 3 for reference. Using this chart we can easily find the dates of commencement of the lunar months at any point.

For assimilation of the method let us see how the dates are worked out practically using the aforementioned chart for the following months in 570 CE.

	January 570	February 570	March 570
Millennium	(0) 0.0	(0) 0.0	(0) 0.0
Century	(5) 21.7	(5) 21.7	(5) 21.7
Decade	(6) 26.2	(6) 26.2	(7) 6.0
Year	(9) 20.2	(9) 20.2	(0) 0.0
Month	(J) 13.4	(F) 11.9	(M) 24.2
Correction for calendar	0.2	0.2	0.5
Adjustment for Gregorian style	0.0	0.0	0.0
	81.7	80.2	52.4
	- 59.1	- 59.1	- 29.5
	22.6	21.1	22.9

Now the figure 22.6 must be interpreted as 0.6 day (14 hours 24 minutes) past 22nd day of the month i.e. 14 24th hour of the 23rd day. In this way the next two figures will stand for 02 24th hour of the 22nd and 21 36th hour of the 23rd of the month. Further calculations will be as follows:

	Date	Hour	Date	Hour	Date	Hour
Hour of conjunction (GMT)	23	14 24	22	02 24	23	21 36
add for change to Makkan time[3]		+02 38		+02 38		+02 38
Hour of conjunction (Makkan time)	23	17 02	22	05 02	24	00 14
Hour of sunset at Makka[4]	23	17 45	22	18 01	24	18 12
Age of crescent at sunset		00 43		12 59		17 58
Date of start of the lunar month		January 24		February 23		March 25

Although the pagan calendar might have evolved some centuries before Islam, we are not interested in its remote past but only in its last sixty-three years because of its intimate connection with the life of the Prophet ﷺ. Hence we shall limit our reconstruction work to this period only. The dates worked out using Tsybulsky's chart have been serially laid out in column 3 of Appendix 2.

A word of caution is here necessary. Weather conditions also play another role in determining the visibility of the crescent from the earth. As the crescent is placed between the earth and the sun on the days of the new moon, its phase is not in any way affected by weather conditions on the earth. However, our vision may be impaired by clouds, fog, smoke, dust and pollution. In those days, the Arabs counted the lunar months from the sunset the crescent was sighted. Since presently we go without considering the weather conditions that might have been actually present then, in certain cases our reckoning of the months may start one day earlier than the date the then people actually started it. There is no way of avoiding this discrepancy. Therefore an adjustment of one day may sometimes be necessary so as to make the reported dates agree with the weekdays in the chronological analysis that is to follow.

PLACEMENT OF INTERCALARY MONTHS

The next step in the reconstruction is the placement of the *nasi's* in their proper places. The last *nasi'* for each of the eleven calendars must be placed against March 10 – April 9, 631 CE, the location of the concluding month of 9 H, the last intercalary year. Thereafter the preceding *nasi's* may be laid out in the calendars at proper intervals as dictated by the identity of the last *nasi'*. (From May 3, 569 CE to March 19, 633 CE there are 790 lunar months. To facilitate location of the *nasi's* in our work these have been serially numbered counting from the beginning of the intercalary epoch).

Consider the 31.36N102 calendar as an example. The last *nasi'* i.e. 36N102, must be placed against month number 5856. Then going backwards by 36 months 35N99 must be placed against 5819 and 34N96 against 5782 after providing another gap of 36 months, and so on. The locations of the intercalary months for each of the eleven calendars are shown in Appendix 1.

Since we do not know the particular calendar used by them there is no shortcut and one has to reconstruct all of these and identify by trial and error the one which can give the weekdays in agreement with the biographical reports. We are informed that the ascension of the Prophet ﷺ to the Heavens, which is called Mi'raj in the traditional works, took place on the 27th Ramadan one and a half years before the Hijrah and that was on a Saturday.[5] The true calendar must be able to give a Saturday on that date. It must also be able to agree with the reported weekdays of the other events too. If we achieve one such calendar amongst the eleven we have solved the fourteen hundred years old mystery. That must have been the very calendar prevalent then. If not, we shall have to continue the search.

We have reconstructed these eleven calendars for the lifetime of the Prophet ﷺ and tested the worth of each one of them with the 36 events the dates and weekdays of whose occurrence the classical biographers collected from people's memories. The 31.36N102 calendar (shown in Appendix 2 as the pagan calendar) could agree with the biographical reports. Shortly we shall undertake to prove this claim. But before this, let us briefly discuss the origin of the Hijrah calendar to clear some misconceptions about it.

Notes

[1] Hydal & Hydal: *the Crescent*, p 20
[2] Ilyas: *Islamic Calendar*, p 101
[3] Makkan time is ahead of GMT by 02 38 hours.
[4] Refer Appendix 4.
[5] Ibn Sa'd: *Tabaqat*, Vol 1, p 246

5. The Hijrah Calendar

It will unfold as we proceed further that while locating the events in a historical time-frame latter-day biographers often confused and mistook the Hijrah calendar months for those of the pagan calendar and attempted to concord the same in the Julian calendar leading to irreconcilably misleading dates. Therefore a brief account of how and when the Hijrah calendar was evolved will not be out of place.

Elsewhere we have discussed that the Farewell Hajj was also called the Correct Hajj because by then the months had returned to the correct positions. This restoration was brought about by one intercalation at the end of 9 H. That is, the months had come back to the normal positions from the beginning of 10 H, whereupon the Prophet ﷺ abolished the system of intercalation. Since then the Arabs abandoned intercalation and the years without fail consisted of only twelve months. But the idea of recording the year numbers somehow did not occur to them until the caliphate of 'Umar (RA). In the sixteenth year of Hijrah, the Caliph received a cheque payable in Sha'ban and he could not make out which Sha'ban that was – Sha'ban of that year or Sha'ban of the following year?[1] Also he was apprised by his advisors that people of other countries used to record the number of the year in their letters and edicts.[2] Then for the first time, the utility of recording the year number occurred to the Caliph and his administrators, and they sat down to conceive an era of their own which later came to be known as the Hijrah era.

After a conference, the Companions decided to commence the era from the emigration of the Prophet ﷺ and to use Muharram as the first month of the year.[3] The previous years were not re-opened to make every year consist of twelve months. 'Umar ascertained only the number of years elapsed since the Hijrah and used it in his official dating.[4]

At some later stage when the historical need of precisely locating every event of the lifetime of the Prophet ﷺ was strongly felt, Muslims as well as non-Muslims started making serious effort to reconstruct the calendar of the first decade. (The first known reconstruction was dated 1609).[5] Unfortunately while doing so they ignored the last three *nasi's* intervening in the decade and reconstructed the calendar on a uniform scale of twelve months a year and wrongly fixed the epochal date as July 15, 622 CE – the termination point of the backward reconstruction. Lay people had to accept it without any reservation for the intricacies of calendar-making were beyond their grasp. Only at a fairly late stage, did it occur to serious historians that there had been something wrong somewhere in the work for the calendar miserably failed to agree with the weekdays available in the biographical works.

Because of elimination of *nasi's* in the reconstruction, the Hijrah months could not coincide with their pagan counterparts but rather lagged behind by one to three months in the first nine years of the calendar. Second, in the newly conceived calendar, the months of 30 and 29 days were alternated. Only in leapyears, had the last month of the year, which normally consists of 29 days, been made to consist of 30 days in order to cover leapdays. Thus the Hijrah calendar followed a pre-determined course irrespective of the visibility of the crescent. While in pagan days, only the sighting of the crescent heralded the commencement of the month, in the Hijrah calendar, whether the crescent was sighted or not, the month must start according to the fixed formulae – this again creating a lag of one day between the commencement of the months in the two calendars. The calendar could serve official purposes very well but not historical and religious needs. Should this be mistaken for the pagan calendar and the reported dates be located therein the resulting weekdays would not agree with those found in the biographical works. This is exactly what happened later. Historians and researchers were bewildered as they could not make any of the reported weekdays agree with those shown in the calendar. In their desperate attempts to reconcile the discrepancies, in frustration some had even said that the classical biographical information could not be lent much credence.

Nevertheless for our own satisfaction let us assess its worth ourselves by checking it against 19 incontrovertible dates spanning the first nine years of the Madinan decade. If the Arabs did not resort to intercalation and their calendar coincided with the Hijrah calendar, it must be able to agree with the biographical reports. The weekdays it reveals against these dates were as follows:

		Biographical weekdays		Hijrah weekdays	
1.	Emigration to Madinah	Monday	12 RBL 1 H	Friday	Sep 24, 622
2.	Ghazwah Buwat	Monday	20 RBR 2 H	Friday	Oct 21, 623
3.	Change of Qiblah	Tuesday	15 SHB 2 H	Monday	Mar 12, 624
4.	Battle of Badr	Friday	16 RMD 2 H	Tuesday	Mar 13, 624
5.	Ghazwah Qararat al-Kudr	Friday	1 SHW 2 H	Wednesday	Mar 28, 624
6.	Sariyyah Ghalib ibn 'Abdallah al-Laythi	Sunday	10 SHW 2 H	Friday	Apr 6, 624
7.	Ghazwah as-Sawiq	Sunday	22 DLH 2 H	Saturday	Jun 16, 624
8.	Battle of Uhud	Saturday	11 SHW 3 H	Wednesday	Mar 27, 625
9.	Sariyyah 'Abdallah ibn Unays	Saturday	23 MHR 4 H	Saturday	July 6, 625
10.	Ghazwah Bani Nadir	Tuesday	12 RBL 4 H	Thursday	Aug 22, 625
11.	Ghazwah Dhat ar-Riqa'	Monday	10 JML 4 H	Saturday	Oct 19, 625
12.	Ghazwah Badr al-Maw'id	Wednesday	20 SHB 4 H	Saturday	Jan 25, 626
13.	Document of Ahl-i Maqna	Friday	3 RMD 5 H	Tuesday	Jan 27, 627
14.	Battle of al-Khandaq	Saturday	1 DLQ 5 H	Thursday	Mar 26, 627
15.	Ghazwah Hudaybiyyah	Thursday	1 DLQ 6 H	Monday	Mar 14, 628
16.	Postponed 'Umrah	Monday	6 DLQ 7 H	Wednesday	Mar 8, 629
17.	Opening of Makkah	Monday	18 RMD 8 H	Wednesday	Jan 10, 630
18.	Ghazwah Hunayn	Tuesday	10 SHW 8 H	Wednesday	Jan 31, 630
19.	'Umrah from al-Ji'ranah	Wednesday	18 DLQ 8 H	Friday	Mar 9, 630

This table shows that for all practical purposes the Hijrah calendar was a completely useless frame of reference as far as the first nine years were concerned as nothing of the past related to it.

With this background we may now pass on to the stage of checking the weekdays and dates of the events with the pagan calendar for precisely locating them in the Julian framework. Since we shall often be referring to both calendars in the course of this work, in the following chapters let us differentiate the pagan calendar from the Hijrah by using H for the former and AH for the latter.

Notes

[1] Ali: *Upstream*, p 43

[2] Ali: *Upstream*, p 44

[3] *Islamic Review*, Feb 1969, p 8

[4] Tabari: *Tarikh*, Vol 3, p 55

[5] *Islamic Review*, Feb 1969, p 8

6. The Chroniclers' Dates

The chroniclers have passed on to us dates of thirty-six events from the life of the Prophet ﷺ with the mention of weekdays on which they happened. We may check these out one by one with the 31.36N102 calendar. This exercise will not only precisely locate the events in the Julian calendar but will also point out the inaccurate dates embodied in the classical works.

The dates have been collected mostly from the works of the earliest biographers such as Ibn Ishaq (d. 150 AH), al-Waqidi (d. 207 AH), Ibn Hisham (d. 213 AH), Ibn Sa'd (d. 230 AH), Ibn Habib (d. 245 AH), and at-Tabari (d. 310 AH) who were the first biographers of the Prophet ﷺ and compiled their works in the second, third and fourth centuries of Islam. Wherever available, dates furnished by the later biographers have also been used.

An important thing to note is that in the Hijrah and pagan reckoning the day is counted from sunset and therefore a lunar day extends over two days in the Julian calendar. That is, for example, 12 Rabi' al-Awwal in 632 is from sunset of June 7 to sunset of June 8. Therefore, an event occurring before midnight must be concorded with the first date and the one occurring after it with the second date of the Julian calendar.

From now on we shall often refer to the pagan calendar (Appendix 2) every time we make an attempt to locate an event. The weekdays may be ascertained using the Millennium calendar provided at the end of the book as Appendix 5.

1. The Birthday of the Prophet ﷺ

The classical biographers inform us that the Prophet ﷺ was born on a Monday, in the month of Rabi' al-Awwal in the year of the Elephant (Qays ibn Makhramah),[1] forty to fifty-five days after Abrahah's attack on the Ka'bah.[2] The dates provided are:

Abu Ma'shar Nujayh:	2[3]
Abu Ja'far Muhammad ibn 'Ali:	10[4]
Ibn Hisham:	12[5]

Now all historians agree that Abrahah attacked the Ka'bah in 570 CE. In this year Rabi' al-Awwal started at sunset on June 21 in the calendar (refer Appendix 2). Let us see what weekdays it throws up against the reported dates.

1 AF RBL	1	570 Jun 21 (SA)	–	22 (SU)
	2 (MO)	22 (SU)	–	**23 (MO)**
	10 (MO)	30 (MO)	–	Jul 1 (TU)
	12 (MO)	Jul 2 (WE)	–	3 (TH)

The calendar reveals a Monday on the 2nd of the month. But unfortunately it does not do so against the most popular date of the 12th calling us to discard it despite its age-long popularity. The Prophet ﷺ was born on Monday, June 23, 570.

Some authorities believed that the Prophet ﷺ was born in 569 while many contended that it was in 571. The reports on 571 may be rejected outright, for it was shortly after the Abyssinian ruler Abrahah's unsuccessful march upon the Ka'bah that the Prophet ﷺ was born, and we have the information that Abyssinian rule in Yemen had ended in 570 itself due to seizure of power by the Iranians[6] indicating that the march could not have been in 571.

In the calendar that we have re-discovered, we get a Rabi' al-Awwal against June-July in 570, the Year of the Elephant. In June, the conjunction occurred on the 20th at 9.50 AM Makkan time (7.12 AM GMT) according to Tsybulsky's calculation chart. The next Makkan sunset on the 21st occurred around 6.40 PM (vide Appendix 4) when the age of the crescent was about 32 hours which was more than sufficient for sighting. Therefore the lunar month commenced on the sunset of June 21st, and the 2nd of the month fell on June 23rd which was a Monday. Is not June 23rd, 570 then the best solution? It agrees with traditional information, fits well in the scheme of intercalation and accords with astronomical calculation.

This corresponded to Jumada al-Ula in the non-intercalary reckoning (refer month number 5105 in column 4 of Appendix 2). Therefore in relation to the Hijrah calendar we must celebrate his birth anniversary on the 2nd of Jumada al-Ula, or, if we choose to go by the Gregorian calendar, on the 23rd of June. Celebration in Rabi' al-Awwal falls neither on the first option nor on the second.

2. The Abyssinian Attack on the Ka'bah

After the establishment of the date of birth of the Prophet ﷺ we may attempt to locate the date when Abrahah launched his attack upon the Ka'bah.

On this Ibn Sa'd said that it was in the middle of Muharram[7] of the year in which the Prophet ﷺ was born, while al-Biruni pinpointed the date as 17th Muharram and Abu al-Fida' furnished the weekday as the Sunday.[8]

Let us now see whether the calendar can attest any of these dates.

1 AF MHR	1	570	Apr 23 (WE) – 24 (TH)
	15 (SU)		May 7 (WE) – 8 (TH)
	17 (SU)		May 9 (FR) – 10 (SA)

Al-Biruni's date misses the reported weekday by one day. If the crescent was sighted one day later, which was not an impossibility as we have discussed earlier, it will agree with the report. It appears that Abrahah launched the attack on Sunday, May 11th, 570 – forty-two days before the birth of the Prophet ﷺ.

From the month of Abrahah's attack upon the Ka'bah, the reminiscence of which we read in Surah al-Fil (5), the Makkans had started an era called the *'Am al-Fil* (the Year of the Elephant).[9] The epochal day of this era must be Wednesday, April 23, 570 as the said month started from this date.

3. First Revelation of the Qur'an

The biographers say that the Prophet ﷺ received his first revelation on one of the nights of Ramadan in the fortieth year of his life ('Urwah)[10] or after the fortieth year (Ibn 'Abbas, Anas ibn Malik).[11] While everyone agreed that it was on a Monday, the authorities differed about the date. It was the 17th according to Abu Ja'far,[12] the 18th to 'Abdallah ibn Zayd al-Hadrami and the 24th to Abu al-Jild.[13]

The Qur'an says that it was sent down on the blessed night (44:3) of

Laylat al-Qadr (97: 1) in the month of Ramadan (2: 185). Inferring from this, some scholars are inclined to believe that the first revelation was in Laylat al-Qadr and try to link up the date with this night. A bit of discussion in this regard will not, therefore, be out of place.

Initially the Prophet ﷺ sat for *i'tikaf* (seclusion in the Mosque) in the first ten days of Ramadan, but Jibril came and informed him that the night he was looking for was ahead of him. Therefore he continued sitting for it in the middle ten days. Again Jibril appeared to tell him that it was still ahead of him. Then he directed his Companions to sit for it in its last ten days with the disclosure that Laylat al-Qadr was in one of the odd nights of the last ten days.[14] Discussion ensued and some of the Companions, who had seen dreams about it, started narrating their dreams to one another whereupon the Prophet ﷺ said: "It seems that all your dreams agree that it is in the last seven nights, and whoever wants to search for it should search in the last seven."[15] Now if we consider only the odd nights in the last seven days the possible dates are the 23rd, 25th, 27th and 29th. Later the range was further narrowed down to the 25th, 27th and 29th as reported by 'Ubada ibn as-Samit. He said: "The Prophet ﷺ came out to inform us about the Laylat al-Qadr while two persons were quarrelling. So the Prophet ﷺ said: 'I came out to inform you about the Laylat al-Qadr but because of your quarrel the information about it had been taken away; yet that might be for your own good. Search for it on the 29th, 27th and 25th."[16]

Although some of his Companions speculated strongly that it was on the 21st (Abu Sa'id al-Khudri),[17] the 23rd ('Abdallah ibn Unays),[18] the 24th (Ibn 'Abbas)[19] and the 27th night (Ubayy ibn Ka'b),[20] these were their own opinions and Laylat al-Qadr still remains as elusive as ever.

While commenting upon ayah 2: 85, Ibn Kathir stated that the Prophet ﷺ was asked about what could be the meaning of the descent of the Glorious Qur'an in Ramadan, and that too in Laylat al-Qadr, when the revelation extended over a period of years. Thereupon the Prophet ﷺ said that the Qur'an in its entirety had been sent down to the first Heaven in Ramadan in the Night of Destiny (Ibn 'Abbas).[21] Elaborating on this, Jalaluddin as-Suyuti says that the Qur'an is said to have been extant in the highest Heaven from eternity, written on the

Preserved Tablet near the throne of Allah, and from thence to have been sent down to the lowest Heaven in the month of Ramadan in the night of al-Qadr and stored up there in the Temple of Majesty from whence it was revealed to Muhammad ﷺ in smaller or larger portions in the course of twenty to twenty-five years (*Itqan*).[22]

This makes it clear that the descent of the Qur'an from the Preserved Tablet and its first delivery to the Prophet ﷺ were on different dates. Were the first revelation in the night of al-Qadr, there could not arise the need for the Prophet ﷺ to search for it because he could never forget the date of his first divine experience. The natural inference is that the night for which he was searching must be the very night when the Glorious Qur'an was transferred to the lowest Heaven. When it was revealed that this night is better than a thousand months (Qur'an 97:3) he felt eager to locate it and therefore sat in *I'tikaf*. This possibly resolves the confusion that the first revelation was in the night of al-Qadr.

In the fortieth and forty-first years of the Prophet's ﷺ life the calendar threw up the following weekdays against the reported dates.

40 AF RMD	1	609 Dec	4 (TH) –	5 (FR)
	17 (MO)		20 (SA) –	21 (SU)
	18 (MO)		21 (SU) –	**22 (MO)**
	24 (MO)		27 (SA) –	28 (SU)
41 AF RMD	1	610 Nov	23 (MO) –	24 (TU)
	17 (MO)	Dec	9 (WE) –	10 (TH)
	18 (MO)		10 (TH) –	11 (FR)
	24 (MO)		16 (WE) –	17 (TH)

The calendar reveals a Monday against the 18th Ramadan in the 40th year but not against any of the other dates either in the 40th or in the 41st year. December 22nd, 609 may therefore have been the actual date on which the Prophet ﷺ received his first revelation. What a value Providence placed in the longest night of the year! (Read the hint in Qur'an at 76:26).

Now with certainty we have established the date of revelation of the first five ayat of Surah al-'Alaq (96) which were the first ayat ever revealed to the Prophet ﷺ.

4. The Mi'raj

Regarding the reputed events of the Prophet's ﷺ night journey to Masjid al-Aqsa in Jerusalem (*Isra*) and the ascent through the Heavens (*Mi'raj*), some scholars believe that these were on one and the same occasion while others maintain that these were on different occasions. Despite the general belief that the latter was in continuation of the former, the Qur'anic narration thereof was placed in two different surahs – the Mi'raj in an-Najm (53) and the Isra in Bani Israel (17) which are respectively classed as early and late Makkan surahs (Hashim Amir Ali). If judged by the order of revelation the Mi'raj must precede the Isra, but in the narrators' reports the latter preceded the former – the Isra occurring on the 17th Rabi' al-Awwal one year before the Prophet's ﷺ seeking refuge in the valley of Abu Talib (Ibn 'Abbas)[23] and the Mi'raj on a Saturday on the 27th Ramadan eighteen months before emigration to Madinah (Abu Bakr ibn 'Abdallah ibn Abi Sabrah).[24]

Eighteen months before the emigration Ramadan started on November 2nd, 620; and the calendar reveals weekdays as follows:

51 AF RMD	1	620 Nov	2 (SU) – 3 (MO)
	27 (SA)		28 (FR) – 29 (SA)

It throws up a Saturday against the reported date in complete agreement with the biographical report. The Prophet ﷺ made the heavenly visit on the night of November 29th, 620.

5. Emigration to Madinah

The dates reported about the various stages of the Prophet's ﷺ emigration to Madinah by the various authorities are as follows:

Conference of the Quraysh leaders:	1 H	RBL	1, TH	(Alvi)[25]
Leaving the cave of Thawr:		RBL	5, MO	(Ibn Sa'd)[26]
Arrival at Quba:		RBL	12, MO	(Abu Ja'far)[27]
Entry into Madinah:		RBL	16, FR	(Ibn Hisham)[28]

These reports are very consistent in themselves regarding the sequence of the weekdays and can be relied upon without any hesitation despite al-Biruni's contention that the Prophet ﷺ arrived at Quba on the 8th of Rabi' al-Awwal.

Let us see whether the calendar can attest the weekdays.

1 H RBL	1 (TH)	622	Jun	16 (WE) – **17 (TH)**
	5 (MO)			20 (SU) – **21 (MO)**
	12 (MO)			27 (SU) – **28 (MO)**
	16 (FR)		Jul	1 (TH) – **2 (FR)**

It reveals weekdays in complete agreement with the biographical reports establishing that the Prophet ﷺ left Makkah on June 21, landed at Quba on June 28 and entered the city on July 2, 622.

6. Ghazwah Buwat

There are contradictory reports about this expedition. Ibn Ishaq, al-Waqidi and Ibn Sa'd maintain that it occurred in Rabi' al-Awwal 2 H[29] while Ibn Habib and at-Tabari say that it was in Rabi' al-Akhir.[30] The presently available work of Ibn Habib furnishes the dates as follows:

| Start: | 2 H | RBR 3, MO |
| Return: | | RBR 20, MO |

There is an inconsistency in the report itself; if one of the dates falls on Monday, the other cannot. Alvi therefore holds that there had been an inadvertent error in copying the date of the start. It was the 13th which a careless copyist had taken down as the 3rd.[31] This appears to be a reasonable explanation. In our analysis we have, therefore, considered it to be the 13th. If the calendar can give a Monday on the 20th, it will not only establish the date in the Christian calendar but will also correct this error.

Now let us see what weekdays the calendar throws up against the aforementioned dates.

2 H RBR	1	623 Jul	5 (TU) – 6 (WE)
	3 (MO)		7 (TH) – 8 (FR)
	13 (MO)		17 (SU) – 18 (MO)
	20 (MO)		24 (SU) – **25 (MO)**

The calendar successfully reveals that the Prophet ﷺ returned from this ghazwah on Monday, July 25th. The date of the start must have been Monday, July 18th, 623.

7. Ghazwah Badr al-Ula

Ibn Habib furnished the date of start for this ghazwah as Monday, 12th

Jumada al-Akhirah 2 H.³² As against this Ibn Ishaq said: "Hardly a few nights had passed after the Prophet's ﷺ return from Dhu'l-'Ushayrah when Kurz ibn Jabir al-Fihri launched an attack in the pastures of Madinah and the Prophet ﷺ set out in his pursuit and reached as far as Safwan. Kurz escaped and the Prophet ﷺ returned in Jumada al-Akhirah."³³ At-Tabari also said that the return was in Jumada al-Akhirah.³⁴

We have the information that for Dhu al-'Ushayrah the Prophet ﷺ set out on the first of Jumada al-Ula.³⁵ Therefore it appears that in pursuit of Kurz the Prophet ﷺ set out in Jumada al-Ula and not in Jumada al-Akhirah. It calls us to speculate whether inadvertently Ibn Habib took down the month as Jumada al-Akhirah while it was Jumada al-Ula.

Let us see which one the calendar attests.

2 H	JML	1	623	Aug	3 (WE) – 4 (TH)
		12 (MO)			14 (SU) – **15 (MO)**
	JMR	1		Sep	2 (FR) – 3 (SA)
		12 (MO)			13 (TU) – 14 (WE)

The calendar discloses a Monday in Jumada al-Ula but not in Jumada al-Akhirah. It appears that the Prophet ﷺ set out for this expedition on Monday, August 15th, 623 (12th Jumada al-Ula 2 H).

Al-Waqidi and Ibn Sa'd dated this event in Rabi' al-Awwal.³⁶ In the second year, Rabi' al-Awwal of the Hijrah calendar corresponded to Jumada al-Akhirah of the pagan calendar. Perhaps these writers recorded the month of return in terms of the Hijrah calendar. This is an example of the biographers' conversion of pagan months into Hijrah months.

8. Ghazwah Yanbu'

Ibn Habib recorded that the Prophet ﷺ set out for this expedition on Thursday, 2nd Sha'ban and concluded an agreement with Bani Sulaym and Bani Ghifar on Tuesday, 14th Sha'ban 2 H.³⁷

The dates fall on the following weekdays.

2 H SHB	1	623	Oct	31 (MO) – Nov 1 (TU)
	2 (TH)		Nov	1 (TU) – 2 (WE)
	14 (TU)			13 (SU) – 14 (MO)

The dates miss the reported weekdays by one day. But al-Waqidi maintained that 15th Sha'ban was a Tuesday (refer to next event). If so, the weekdays of this event should have been more correctly Wednesday and Monday as also disclosed by the calendar. It appears that the Prophet ﷺ set out on Wednesday, November 2nd and concluded the treaty on Monday, November 14th, 623.

Nevertheless it remains to be seen whether the Prophet ﷺ could possibly have been back in Madinah the next day on the 15th Sha'ban when the commandment for the change of Qiblah descended during Dhuhr prayer.

9. The Change of Qiblah

After his emigration to Madinah, for sixteen or seventeen months the Prophet ﷺ used to offer prayers facing towards Bayt al-Muqaddas, the qiblah of the Jews. He wished that the direction be changed and therefore often he raised his face imploringly towards the heavens. Then one day in the middle of the afternoon prayer descended the ayah:

> We have seen you looking up into heaven, turning this way and that, so We will turn you towards a direction which will please you. Turn your face, therefore, towards the Masjid al-Haram. Wherever you all are, turn your faces towards it. (2:143)

During the prayer itself the Prophet ﷺ turned his face towards the Ka'bah. So did his followers.[38]

Imam az-Zuhri says that change of Qiblah occurred in Jumada al-Ula in 2 H[39] while Ibn Ishaq, al-Waqidi and at-Tabari believe that it was in Sha'ban. But Ibn Sa'd and al-Waqidi are more specific and furnish the dates and days as Monday, the middle of Rajab[40] and Tuesday, the middle of Sha'ban[41] respectively.

The calendar reveals the following weekdays against these dates.

2 H	RJB	1	623 Oct	1 (SA) – 2 (SU)
		15 (MO)		15 (SA) – 16 (SU)
	SHB	1		31 (MO) – Nov 1 (TU)
		15 (TU)	Nov	14 (MO) – **15 (TU)**

The calendar attests al-Waqidi's report. The change occurred on Tuesday, November 15th, 623 (15th Sha'ban 2 H). This corresponded to Jumada al-Ula of the Hijrah calendar. Imam az-Zuhri reported in terms of the Hijrah calendar.

Ibn Sa'd further informs us that following the change of Qiblah the adhan was ordained.[42]

10. Battle of Badr

The battle occurred in Ramadan 2H and, according to Ibn Sa'd, the Prophet ﷺ and his Companions set out on Saturday, 12th Ramadan.[43] About the day of the battle, the authorities provided the following dates.

'Urwah ibn az-Zubayr:	16/17, FR[44]
Muhammad ibn Salih, 'Abdallah ibn Mas'ud:	17, FR[45]
'Amir ibn Rabi'ah al-Badri:	17, MO[46]
'Abdallah:	19[47]

According to at-Tabari, the return was on a Wednesday when 8 nights of Ramadan were still left.[48]

The calendar reveals the weekdays as follows:

2 H RMD	1	623	Nov 30 (WE)	-	Dec 1 (TH)
	12 (SA)		Dec 11 (SU)	-	12 (MO)
	16 (FR)		Dec 15 (TH)	-	**16 (FR)**
	17 (FR/MO)		16 (FR)	-	17 (SA)
	19		18 (SU)	-	19 (MO)
	22 (WE)		**21 (WE)**	-	22 (TH)

Regarding the date of the battle Ibn Sa'd recorded that it was beyond doubt a Friday and the report about Monday was exceptional.[49] Also the calendar does not reveal any Monday against any of the dates. The report about Monday must be wrong. The battle was fought on Friday, December 16th and the return therefrom was on Wednesday, December 21st, 623.

At-Tabari narrates on the authority of Ibn 'Abbas that immediately before the beginning of the battle, the Makkan army had infested the wells of Badr depriving the Muslims of water, and under the influence of thirst, some of the latter fell prey to utter despair, when suddenly abundant rain fell and enabled them to satisfy their thirst[50] which the Qur'an describes in its inimitable style as:

And when He overcame you with sleep, making you feel secure, and sent you down water from heaven to purify you and remove the taint of Shaytan from you, and to fortify your hearts and make your feet firm. (8:11)

In his biography of the Prophet ﷺ, Muir says quoting Burton that in Arabia rains begin in October and last with considerable intervals through the winter.[51] Our finding that the battle was fought in December also agrees with such a report.

Ibn Ishaq stated that after the battle, the Prophet ﷺ sent 'Abdallah ibn Rawahah and Zayd ibn Harithah in advance to Madinah to announce the Muslim victory in Badr. Usamah ibn Zayd narrated: "We received this news when we were spreading earth on the grave of Ruqayyah, the daughter of the Prophet ﷺ and the wife of 'Uthman ibn 'Affan. The Prophet ﷺ left me and 'Uthman in Madinah to look after the ailing Ruqayyah."[52] As the Prophet ﷺ returned to Madinah on December 21st, 623 Ruqayyah must have died a few days before this.

'Ikrimah says the following ayah was revealed on the day of Badr.[53]
They will ask you about booty. Say: 'Booty belongs to Allah and the Messenger. So have taqwa of Allah and put things right between you. Obey Allah and His Messenger if you are muminun.' (8:1)

1.) Ghazwah Qararat al-Kudr

Ibn Ishaq, Ibn Habib and at-Tabari stated that it was in Shawwal 2 H[54] that the Prophet ﷺ started for this expedition while al-Waqidi and Ibn Sa'd recorded that it was in Muharram 3 H.[55]

The dates and days furnished by the biographers were as follows:

	Start	Return
Ibn Habib:	2 H SHW 1, FR	
At-Tabari:	3 H SHW 1, FR[56]	3 H SHW 10

Ibn Ishaq recorded in clear terms that the Prophet ﷺ had rested only for seven days after returning from Badr when he started for Kudr[57] indicating thereby that it was an event of 2 H. Tabari's 3 H could be a slip of the pen. We therefore consider it to be 2 H.

Let us see what weekdays the calendar shows up against these dates.

2 H SHW	**1 (FR)**	623 Dec 29 (TH) – **30 (FR)**
	10	624 Jan 7 (SA) – 8 (SU)

It reveals that the Prophet ﷺ started on Friday, December 30th, 623 and returned on Sunday, January 8th, 624.

On the contentions of al-Waqidi and Ibn Sa'd that the expedition took place in Muharram 3 H we may seek a suitable explanation through the Pagan-Hijrah concordance as follows:

			Pagan		Hijrah	
623	Dec 29 –	624 Jan 28	2 H	SHW	2 AH	RJB
624	Jan 28 –	Feb 26		DLQ		SHB
	Feb 26 –	Mar 27		DLH		RMD
	Mar 27–	Apr 25	3 H	MHR		SHW

Although the event occurred in Shawwal of the pagan calendar, perhaps al-Waqidi and Ibn Sa'd had erroneously considered it to be Shawwal of the Hijrah calendar. When converted to the pagan, it became Muharram 3 H. Then they reported it as such.

This shows that in their time the biographers had some workable information on the relation of the two calendars and they often converted the months of one calendar to those of the other. But the months carried forward by narration from one generation to another appear to pose a permanent problem in identification. In the process, serious errors were made giving rise to many misleading dates in the biographical works.

12. Sariyyah Ghalib ibn 'Abdallah al-Laythi

Ibn Habib says that this expedition set out on Sunday, 10th Shawwal 2 H[58] while at-Tabari gives the date as 11th Shawwal.[59] Regarding the return, both concur that it was on a Saturday, when fourteen nights of the month were still left.

As already seen in the previous event, the 10th Shawwal worked out to be a Sunday. The date of return will therefore work out to be a Saturday as shown below.

2 H SHW	1	623 Dec	29 (TH) – 30 (FR)
	10 (SU)	624 Jan	7 (SA) – **8 (SU)**
	11		8 (SU) – 9 (MO)
	16 (SA)		13 (FR) – **14 (SA)**

Ghalib started on Sunday, January 8th and the return was on Saturday, January 14th, 624.

13. Ghazwah Bani Qaynuqa'

Imam az-Zuhri maintained that this was an event of Shawwal 2 H[60] while other biographers furnished the following dates.

	Start	Return
Waqidi:	2 H SHW 15, SA[61]	
Ibn Sa'd:	2 H middle of SHW, SA[62]	
Ibn Habib:		3 H SFR 7, SU[63]
At-Tabari:		3 H SFR 9[64]

Although al-Waqidi stated the day of setting out to be Saturday, 15th Shawwal his secretary Ibn Sa'd avoided mention of any specific date but moderated it as the middle of Shawwal while however retaining the weekday. In the case of Sariyyah Ghalib ibn 'Abdallah al-Laythi, as seen in the previous event, 16th Shawwal (and not 15th Shawwal) worked out to be a Saturday. This was perhaps the reason for Ibn Sa'd's avoiding his master's specific date which, perhaps he knew, was not accurate. The actual date of setting out could be, therefore, Saturday, 16th Shawwal 2 H (January 14th, 624).

Was the return in Safar 3 H? It could not have been. First, because the Prophet ﷺ could not have taken such a long period from Shawwal to Safar for this expedition, and secondly we have the information that the Prophet ﷺ was very much present in Madinah in Dhu'l-Hijjah 2 H arranging the marriage of his daughter Fatimah, celebrating the first 'Id al-Adha in the life of the new nation and conducting Ghazwah as-Sawiq. The return could have been in Dhu'l-Qa'dah of the same year because according to Ibn Sa'd the siege continued up to 1st Dhu'l-Qa'dah.[65] Ibn Habib and at-Tabari apparently considered this to be a reference to the Hijrah calendar. Converting into the corresponding pagan month, they dated the return in Safar 3 H as the following Pagan-Hijrah concordance will show:

			Pagan		Hijrah
623	Dec 29	-	624 Jan 28	2 H SHW	2 AH RJB
624	Jan 28	-	Feb 26	DLQ	SHB
	Feb 26	-	Mar 27	DLH	RMD
	Mar 27	-	Apr 25	3 H MHR	SHW
	Apr 25	-	May 25	SFR	DLQ

Then the calendar speaks about the weekday of the return.

2 H DLQ	1	624 Jan	28 (SA)	–	29 (SU)
	7 (SU)	Feb	3 (FR)	–	4 (SA)
	9		5 (SU)	–	6 (MO)

Ibn Habib's weekday agrees with at-Tabari's date. It appears that the Prophet ﷺ returned from the locality of Bani Qaynuqa' after sunset on Sunday, February 5th, 624 (Monday, 9th Dhu'l-Qa'dah 2 H).

This is another glaring example of the biographers' confusion of the months of one calendar with those of the other and the resulting chaos in the chronology.

Ibn Sa'd stated that there was a pact between the Prophet ﷺ and Bani Qaynuqa'. On the day of Badr, out of jealousy they violated the pact. Yet they were the bravest of the Jews and the Muslims entertained some sort of fear for them. Thereupon descended the ayah:[66]

If you fear treachery on the part of a people, revoke your treaty with them mutually. Allah does not love treacherous people. (8:58)

Right away the Prophet ﷺ marched against them. This places the date of revelation of this ayah in January 624 (Shawwal 2 H).

14. Ghazwah as-Sawiq

Of this ghazwah the biographers concurred in saying that the start was on a Sunday in Dhu'l-Hijjah 2 H but differed about the date, indicating its uncertainty.

Waqidi:	5, SU[67]
Ibn Habib:	22[68]
Tabari:	23, SU[69]
Ibn Sa'd:	25, SU[70]

Against these dates the calendar shows the following weekdays:

2 H DLH	1	624	Feb 26 (SU)	-	27 (MO)
	5 (SU)		Mar 1 (TH)	-	2 (FR)
	22 (SU)		**18 (SU)**	-	19 (MO)
	23 (SU)		19 (MO)	-	20 (TU)
	25 (SU)		21 (WE)	-	22 (TH)

The Prophet ﷺ set out after sunset on Sunday, March 18th, 624 (22 Dhu'l-Hijjah 2 H).

15. Ghazwah Dhu Amarr

The reports of this ghazwah are in a highly confusing state. According to Ibn Ishaq the Prophet ﷺ started either at the end of Dhu'l-Hijjah 2 H or in the beginning of Muharram 3 H, halted almost the whole of Safar in Najd and returned in Rabi' al-Awwal.[71] At-Tabari also wrote that it was an event of either Safar or Rabi' al-Awwal 3 H.[72]

But al-Waqidi and Ibn Sa'd held a different view and maintained that the Prophet ﷺ set out for this expedition only in Rabi' al-Awwal 3 H and furnished the following dates.

| Waqidi: | RBL 12, TH[73] |
| Ibn Sa'd: | RBL 12[74] |

Let us see what the calendar says.

| 3 H RBL | 1 | 624 | May 25 (FR) | - | 26 (SA) |
| | 12 (TH) | | Jun 5 (TU) | - | 6 (WE) |

The date misses the reported weekday by one day. Ibn Sa'd when he re-wrote the Prophet's ﷺ biography, omitted mention of the weekday although al-Waqidi's weekday was available to him, presumably because he could not get a Thursday against the date. If the lunar month started one day later from the sunset of May 26th, the date will agree with the reported weekday. Perhaps the Prophet ﷺ set out after sunset on Wednesday, June 6th, 624 (Thursday, 13th Rabi' al-Awwal 3 H).

Ibn Ishaq's Dhu'l-Hijjah could be a reference to the Hijrah calendar for Rabi' al-Awwal 3 H corresponded to Dhu'l-Hijjah 2 AH.

According to Ibn Sa'd, on this occasion the Prophet ﷺ was absent from the city for 11 nights.[75] Therefore the return could have been on Sunday, June 17th, 624 (23 Rabi' al-Awwal 3 H).

16. Battle of Uhud

Every authority agreed that the battle was fought on a Saturday in Shawwal 3 H, but differed widely about the date as shown below.

Al-Waqidi, Ibn Sa'd, at-Tabari:	7[76]
Qatadah, Qastalani:	11[77]
Ibn Ishaq, at-Tabari:	15[78]
Al-Biruni:	17[79]

We have also the information that the Makkans arrived at Wadi al-'Aqiq (Jabl Uhud) on Wednesday, 3rd Shawwal (at-Tabari),[80] the Prophet ﷺ sent Anas and Munis (sons of Fadalah) to collect information on Thursday, 5th Shawwal (Ibn Sa'd)[81] and set out on Friday after saying the funeral prayer for Malik ibn 'Amr, an Ansari who died that day.[82]

Let us see which one of these dates is attested by the calendar.

3 H SHW	1	624 Dec	18 (TU) – 19 (WE)
	3 (WE)		20 (TH) – 21 (FR)
	5 (TH)		22 (SA) – 23 (SU)
	7 (SA)		24 (MO) – 25 (TU)
	11 (SA)		28 (FR) – **29 (SA)**
	15 (SA)	625 Jan	1 (TU) – 2 (WE)
	17 (SA)		3 (TH) – 4 (FR)

On 11 Shawwal we get a Saturday, establishing beyond all doubt that Qatadah's date was the actual date. The battle was fought on December 29th, 624.

The calendar shows that the dates of the Makkans' arrival and the spying mission of the Muslims, as furnished by at-Tabari and Ibn Sa'd, were not correct. This was because of placing the battle on a wrong date. Now with the establishment of the date of the battle, we can work out the dates of the sequel preceding it.

Arrival of the Makkans:	Wednesday	8 Shawwal	December 26, 624
Sending spies:	Thursday	9 Shawwal	December 27, 624
Prophet's ﷺ start:	Friday	10 Shawwal	December 28, 624

Ibn Sa'd says that the Prophet ﷺ returned to Madinah the very day of the battle before sunset.[83]

In the battle, the Prophet ﷺ was wounded – one of his incisors was knocked out, his forehead cleft and blood flowed over his face. For a moment, the rumour spread that the Prophet ﷺ had been killed, and the Muslims became gloomy and disheartened whereupon the ayah descended:[84]

Muhammad is only a Messenger and he has been preceded by other Messengers. If he were to die or be killed, would you turn on your heels? (3:144)

17. Ghazwah Hamra al-Asad

It is recorded that on Sunday, the day after Uhud, the Prophet ﷺ set out for Hamra al-Asad, eight miles distant from Madinah, in pursuit of Abu Sufyan's army, halted there for three days from Monday to Wednesday and returned to Madinah on Friday.

Following the confusion in regard to the day of Uhud, the biographers furnished the date of setting out on this ghazwah as follows:

| Ibn Sa'd: | | 3 H | SHW 8, SU[85] |
| Tabari: | | | SHW 16, SU ('Ikrimah)[86] |

For the previous event we have established the correct date of the battle of Uhud as Saturday, December 29, 624 (11 Shawwal). As it was on the next day that the Prophet ﷺ set out for Hamra al-Asad, the date must be beyond doubt Sunday, December 30, 624 whatever may be the dates furnished by the biographers.

18. Sariyyah 'Abdallah ibn Unays

Al-Waqidi says that the sariyyah started on Monday, 5th Muharram 4 H.[87] Ibn Sa'd also furnishes the same date but omits mention of the weekday.[88] He says that the return from it was on Saturday, 23rd Muharram.[89]

Now let us see what the calendar says.

4 H MHR	1	625 Apr	15 (MO)	–	16 (TU)
	5 (MO)		19 (FR)	–	20 (SA)
	23 (SA)	May	7 (TU)	–	8 (WE)

The pagan calendar does not attest the dates, hinting that these could not be pagan dates. Let us see whether the Hijrah calendar can do it.

4 AH MHR	1	625 Jun	13 (TH)	–	14 (FR)
	5 (MO)		**17 (MO)**	–	18 (TU)
	23 (SA)	Jul	5 (FR)	–	**6 (SA)**

It attests the weekdays, indicating that the reports were with reference to Hijrah calendar. It appears that at some later stage the Companions had converted the original pagan month to the corresponding Hijrah month and narrated it in terms of Hijrah.

The sariyyah party set out after sunset on Monday, June 17th and returned on Saturday, July 6th, 625.

19. Ghazwah Bani an-Nadir

Ibn Habib says that the Prophet ﷺ started for this ghazwah on Tuesday, 12th Rabi' al-Awwal and returned on 5th Rabi' al-Akhir 4 H.[90] Without giving any date, Ibn Sa'd, however, maintains that it was on a Saturday in Rabi' al-Awwal[91] that the Prophet ﷺ set out for this expedition.

Against these dates the calendar throws up the following weekdays.

4 H RBL		1		625 Jun	13 (TH)	–	14 (FR)
		12 (TU)			24 (MO)	–	**25 (TU)**
RBR		1		Jul	12 (FR)	–	13 (SA)
		5			16 (TU)	–	17 (WE)

The calendar discloses that the Prophet ﷺ set out on Tuesday, June 25th and returned on Wednesday, July 17th, 625.

Ibn Hisham says that it was in this occasion that the prohibition of liquor was revealed.[92]

20. Ghazwah Dhat ar-Riqa'

Ibn Ishaq and at-Tabari located this expedition in Jumada al-Ula 4 H[93], but al-Waqidi placed it in Muharram 5 H.[94] While enumerating the expeditions of the Prophet ﷺ, 'Abdallah ibn Abi Bakr placed this expedition between Ghazwah Bani Nadir and Ghazwah Badr al-Maw'id.[95] But some of the traditions place it in 7 H as discussed below.

When 'Abdallah ibn Qays (honorific: Abu Musa) of the tribe 'Ash'ar of Yemen heard of the Prophet's ﷺ emigration to Madinah, he set out in a boat with some people of his tribe to pay allegiance to the Prophet ﷺ. A gale caused their boat to drift to the Abyssinian coast where he found Ja'far and other Muslims who had migrated to this place on account of the atrocities of the Makkans. Ja'far informed him that the Prophet ﷺ had sent them to take refuge there and advised him to stay with them. So he stayed there for seven years after which they set forth for Madinah and reached there when the Muslim army was returning victoriously from Khaybar. As a special honour the Prophet ﷺ allowed him a share in the allocation of the booty from Khaybar.[96]

Traditions also say that the expedition of Dhat ar-Riqa' was undertaken after the fall of Khaybar[97] and that Abu Musa joined it [98] after he came from Abyssinia to Madinah in 7 H.[99] Of his participation in the ghazwah, Abu Musa is reported to have narrated: "We set out on the expedition with the Messenger of Allah. We were six in number and had only one camel which we rode in turn. Our feet were injured. My feet were so badly injured that my nails dropped off. We covered our feet with rags; so this expedition was called Dhat ar-Riqa' (i.e. the expedition of rags) because we bandaged our feet with rags."[100]

Yet there are other explanations for the name. Some say that it was so called after the name of a peculiar tree under which the people camped.[101] Others say that it originated from the texture of the hill where they camped. Some patches of it were white, some black and some red.[102]

Only the calendar can tell us when the expedition was actually undertaken. The biographers' dates are as follows:

	Start	Return
Ibn Habib:	4 H JML 10, MO[103]	
Ibn Sa'd:	5 H MHR 10, SA[104]	5 H MHR 25, SA[105]

Ibn Habib did not mention the date of return except for saying that the Prophet ﷺ returned on a Wednesday in the same month. Ibn Sa'd stated that on this occasion the Prophet ﷺ was absent from Madinah for 15 nights – placing the return on the 25th of the month.

Let us see whether the calendar confirms any of these dates or pushes down the event to 7 H.

4 H JML	1	625	Aug	10 (SA)	–	11 (SU)
	10 (MO)			**19 (MO)**	–	20 (TU)
	25 (WE)		Sep	3 (TU)	–	**4 (WE)**
5 H MHR	1	626	Apr	4 (TU)	–	5 (WE)
	10 (SA)			13 (SU)	–	14 (MO)
	25 (SA)			28 (MO)	–	29 (TU)

The calendar successfully attests Ibn Habib's dates, placing the event in 4 H. We are to reject Abu Musa's link with the report and dismiss the idea that it took place in 7 H. Perhaps the narrator of the above quoted tradition was not Abu Musa himself but some other companion of the Prophet ﷺ who took part in the expedition.

The Prophet ﷺ set out for this ghazwah after sunset on Monday, August 19th and returned on Wednesday, September 4th, 625 (25th Jumada al-Ula 4 H).

Abu Hurairah and Jabir ibn 'Abdallah say that it was in this expedition that the ayat of shortening prayers on the occasion of fear (4:102-104) descended and that *Salat al-Khawf* (Prayer of Fear) was performed for the first time.[106]

21. Ghazwah Badr al-Maw'id

Ibn Ishaq and at-Tabari say that this expedition was undertaken in Sha'ban 4 H[107] while according to al-Waqidi it was in Dhu'l-Qa'dah.[108]

Ibn Sa'd and Ibn Habib give the undermentioned dates.

	Start	Return
Ibn Habib:	SHB 1, TH	SHB 20, WE[109]
Ibn Sa'd:	DLQ 1[110]	

The calendar reveals weekdays as follows:

4 H	SHB	**1 (TH)**	625 Nov	**7 (TH)**	–	8 (FR)
		20 (WE)		26 (TU)	–	**27 (WE)**
	DLQ	1	626 Feb	4 (TU)	–	5 (WE)

The Prophet ﷺ started after sunset on Thursday, November 7th and returned on Wednesday, November 27th, 625.

22. Document of Ahl Maqna

Quoting the authority of Dr. Hamidullah, Alvi mentions a document of Ahl Maqna and furnishes the date as Friday, 3rd Ramadan 5 H.[111]

The calendar shows the following weekdays:

5 H	RMD	1	626 Nov	26 (WE)	–	27 (TH)
		3 (FR)		**28 (FR)**	–	29 (SA)

The date of the document was Friday, November 28th, 626.

23. Battle of al-Khandaq (Battle of al-Ahzab.

This battle was fought around the end of 5 H. Biographers furnished the following dates:

	Start	End
Ibn Habib:	SHW 10, TH	DLQ 1, SA[112]
Al-Waqidi, Ibn Sa'd:	DLQ 8, MO	DLQ 23, WE[113]

The calendar reveals the following weekdays against these dates.

5 H	SHW	1	626 Dec	26 (FR)	–	27 (SA)
		10 (TH)	627 Jan	4 (SU)	–	5 (MO)
	DLQ	**1 (SA)**		**24 (SA)**	–	25 (SU)
		8 (MO)	Jan	31 (SA)	–	Feb 1 (SU)
		23 (WE)	Feb	15 (SU)	–	16 (MO)

The calendar discloses that the battle ended on Saturday, January 24th, 627.

Bukhari recorded that the people dug the trench on a very cold morning[114] and at-Tabari added that the siege extended over severe winter nights.[115] If the siege lasted up to the fourth week of January, the

24. Ghazwah Bani Quraydah

Classical biographers maintain that this ghazwah was undertaken in Dhu'l-Qa'dah – Dhu'l-Hijjah.[116] According to Ibn Sa'd the people set out for this expedition on Wednesday, 23rd Dhu'l-Qa'dah and returned on Thursday, 7th Dhu'l-Hijjah 5 H.[117]

During the battle of al-Khandaq, the Quraydah tribe betrayed the Muslims. The biographers tell us that no sooner had the Prophet ﷺ reached Madinah on returning from Khandaq than Jibril brought the divine command for action against the traitorous Quraydah. The Prophet ﷺ forthwith passed orders that the people should immediately set out for Bani Quraydah and none should offer the ensuing 'Asr prayer but in the locality of the said tribe[118] – from which it is clear that the Prophet ﷺ set out for this ghazwah on the very day the battle of Khandaq was over.

Ibn Sa'd believed that the battle of Khandaq ended on 23rd Dhu'l-Qa'dah 5 H and therefore furnished the same date for the raid on Bani Quraydah. But we have already seen that his date is not attested by the calendar. If the battle of Khandaq ended on Saturday, January 24th, 627 (29th Shawwal 5 H) the raid on Quraydah must have also been on this very day.

The extent of the siege differs amongst the biographers – 14 nights or 15 days according to Ibn Sa'd,[119] 25 nights to Ibn Hisham,[120] and 1 month and 25 days to at-Tabari[121] making it difficult to work out the date of the return.

It was during this expedition that the Prophet ﷺ married Rayhanah bint 'Amr ibn Khunafah.[122] She was a women of Quraydah. According to al-Waqidi it was in Muharram 6 H that she became the wife of the Prophet ﷺ.[123] The capture of Bani Quraydah was an event in Dhu'l-Qa'dah 5 H. It appears that al-Waqidi considered it to be Dhu'l-Qa'dah 5 AH and worked out its corresponding month in the pagan calendar as the following concordance will show:

		Pagan		Hijrah	
627	Jan 24 – Feb 23	5 H	DLQ	5 AH	RMD
	Feb 23 – Mar 25		DLH		SHW
	Mar 25 – Apr 23	6 H	MHR		DLQ

This is another example of the biographers' conversion of the months of one calendar to those of the other.

25. Prediction of the Murder of Chosroe

Al-Waqidi and Ibn Sa'd stated that the Prophet ﷺ predicted that Chosroe, the then Persian Emperor, would be murdered on Tuesday, 10th Jumada al-Ula 7 H[124] (13th Jumada al-Ula according to another report of al-Waqidi).[125]

From historical records we understand that the Emperor was murdered in February 628 – on the 27th (Hamidullah)[126] or the 29th (Gibbon, Noldeke)[127] which corresponded to Dhu'l-Hijjah 6 H. This indicates that the month referred to must have been of 6 H and not of 7 H. Further it must be the month when the forecast was made and not the one when the murder was supposed to be committed as was believed by the biographers.

Considering this to be an event of 6 H, let us see whether the calendar can reveal a Tuesday against any one of these two dates.

6 H JML	1	627 Jul	20 (MO)	-	21 (TU)
	10 (TU)		29 (FR)	-	30 (SA)
	13 (TU)	Aug	1 (MO)	-	**2 (TU)**

In agreement with the report it reveals a Tuesday on August 2nd, 627 against 13th Jumada al-Ula 6 H. This must be the date on which the prediction was made.

The biographers wrote that the Emperor being enraged by the Prophet's ﷺ activities ordered his governor in Yemen to arrest and produce the Prophet ﷺ at his court.[128] A delegate deputed by the governor communicated the imperial order to the Prophet ﷺ and apprised him of the consequences threatened in the case of his refusal to obey such orders. It was to this delegate that the Prophet ﷺ made the prediction.

Some of our biographers believe that the Prophet ﷺ wrote a letter to Chosroe inviting him to accept Islam and that was the cause of his anger. They narrate that the Emperor tore up the letter[129] and issued orders for his arrest. But this does not appear to be correct. First, because Ibn Sa'd informs us that the Prophet ﷺ wrote letters to foreign rulers only in Muharram 7 H (April 628). This was after Chosroe had already been murdered. Second, the letter which was reported to have been torn into pieces has come down to us intact.[130] Perhaps the letter reached Persia after Chosroe had already been murdered and was received by his son Cyrus.

As the Emperor was murdered in February 628 (Dhu'l-Hijjah 6 H), the delegation and the prediction must necessarily precede the murder.

26. Ghazwah al-Muraysi' (Ghazwah Bani al-Mustaliq.

The biographers agreed that this expedition was undertaken in Sha'ban but differed about the year – 5 H according to al-Waqidi and Ibn Sa'd,[131] but 6 H to Ibn Ishaq and at-Tabari.[132] Examination of co-lateral evidence will be worthwhile for resolution of this conflict.

It was in this expedition that A'ishah (RA) was left out in the desert and was picked up by one Safwan ibn al-Mu'attal, and the scandal spread that she had spent one night with a stranger and could not have remained chaste. Revelation thereafter descended about slandering chaste women and the punishment thereof in Surat an-Nur (24). In A'ishah's own narration it was after the first command for the veil[133] and Hamnah (the sister of Zaynab, another wife of the Prophet ﷺ) took a leading role in spreading the slander because A'ishah was a rival of her sister[134] and the Prophet ﷺ took counsel from Sa'd ibn Mu'adh,[135] the chief of the clan of Aws.

Now the Prophet ﷺ married Zaynab in Dhu'l-Qa'dah after the battle of the Khandaq (Trench), and the first command for the veil (Qur'an 33:59) descended on the same day of the marriage[136] and Sa'd ibn Mu'adh, the chief of Aws had died shortly after this battle and was succeeded by Usayd ibn al-Hudayr. All these events took place in 5 H. Had the slander been in Sha'ban 5 H A'ishah could not have mentioned that it was after the first command for the veil and that Zaynab's sister Hamnah took part in spreading the slander. The report must therefore be wrong beyond doubt. The more correct year could be 6 H. Such reports arose only because in some traditions A'ishah was reported to have mentioned the name of Sa'd ibn Mu'adh. But this could be due to confusion of the sub-narrators and not attributable to A'ishah herself. We shall therefore consider it to be 6 H in our analysis.

The following were the dates furnished by the biographers for this ghazwah.

	Start	Return
Ibn Habib:	SHB 1, SA[137]	
Mas'udi:	SHB 2[138]	
Ibn Sa'd:	SHB 22, MO	RMD 1[139]

Against these dates the calendar reveals the following weekdays.

6 H SHB	1 (SA)	627	Oct	17 (SA)	–	18 (SU)
	2			18 (SU)	–	19 (MO)
	22 (MO)		Nov	7 (SA)	–	8 (SU)
RMD	1			15 (SU)	–	16 (MO)

Ibn Habib's date is attested by the calendar. The Prophet ﷺ appears to have started after sunset on Saturday, October 17th and returned on Monday, November 16th, 627.

Although Ibn Sa'd stated that the start was on 22nd Sha'ban, he also wrote a few lines after that the Prophet ﷺ returned on the first day of Ramadan after an absence of 28 days. If we consider the start from the 22nd, the absence would only be for 8 days including the period of travelling while the campaign could not possibly have been over in such a short period. For allowing 28 days' absence the start must have been in the beginning of Sha'ban. Perhaps while the information received by him was 2nd Sha'ban, inadvertently he took it down as 22nd Sha'ban.

The scandal and its after-effects must have been floating in the air for quite some time, because for some days the Prophet ﷺ was not speaking to A'ishah, and she was ill for one month[140] and took leave of the Prophet ﷺ to spend some days with her parents. She spent one month more[141] in anguish and weeping until Allah (SWT) revealed her innocence. If the Prophet ﷺ had returned from the expedition in the beginning of Ramadan which corresponded to the middle of November 627, the revelation about A'ishah's innocence must have descended some time in January 628. This is corroborated by a report of Bukhari who recorded that the revelation descended on a wintry day.[142]

It was while returning from this expedition that the Qur'anic ayah on Tayammum (5:6) and ayat 63:5 and 8 had been revealed.[143]

27. Truce of al-Hudaybiyyah

In Dhu'l-Qa'dah 6 H, the Prophet ﷺ set out for an 'Umrah. This was later abandoned due to Makkan obstruction and the Prophet ﷺ returned after concluding a treaty which later came to be known as the Treaty of al-Hudaybiyyah. Ibn Sa'd and Ibn Habib furnished the date of setting out as follows:

    Ibn Sa'd: DLQ 1, MO[144]
    Ibn Habib: DLQ 1, TH[145]

Now attesting Ibn Habib's report, the calendar reveals a Thursday – Friday against the first of Dhu'l-Qa'dah as shown below:

    6 H DLQ **1** (MO/**TH**)   628 Jan **14 (TH)** – 15 (FR)

It appears that the Prophet ﷺ set out after sunset on Thursday, January 14th, 628.

In the Hijrah calendar, the first of Dhu'l-Qa'dah was a Monday. Perhaps Ibn Sa'd believed that the report was with reference to the Hijrah calendar and apparently supplied the weekday from it. This is another example of the biographers' confusion of the months of one calendar for those of the other.

Although the biographers agree that it was in Dhu'l-Qa'dah, Abu Yusuf maintained that it was in Ramadan.[146] In the sixth year of the Hijrah, the pagan Dhu'l-Qa'dah corresponded to Hijrah Ramadan indicating that he stated that with reference to the Hijrah calendar.

Anas ibn Malik narrated that when the Prophet ﷺ was returning from al-Hudaybiyyah the following ayah was revealed.[147]

Truly We have granted you a clear victory, so that Allah may forgive you your earlier errors and any later ones and complete His blessing upon you, and guide you on a Straight Path, and so that Allah may help you with a mighty help. (48:1-3)

Ibn Sa'd adds that it was at a place called ad-Dajnan.[148] The Prophet ﷺ recited it to an assembly of his companions at Kura' al-Ghamim. A companion asked: "Messenger of Allah! Is it a victory?" He replied: By Him in whose hand is my soul! It is surely a victory."[149]

The Murder of Chosroe

Here a word about the murder of Chosroe, the Persian Emperor, of which the Prophet ﷺ made a prediction on August 2nd, 627 (13th Jumada al-Ula 6 H) will not be out of place, as the murder falls around this period.

In his work Ibn Sa'd recorded that the halt at al-Hudaybiyyah extended for more than 13 days but less than 20 days.[150] When the Prophet ﷺ hurriedly proceeded to Madinah in his emigration, the journey took at least 7 days to reach the suburbs of Madinah. On this occasion when he led the pilgrims numbering thousands by a longer route, it must have taken more than 10 days to reach the outskirts of Makkah.[151] Adding a 13 to 20 days' halt at al-Hudaybiyyah, almost the whole month of Dhu'l-Qa'dah must have been over when he turned back for Madinah. Ibn Sa'd and at-Tabari also stated that the Prophet ﷺ returned in Dhu'l-Hijjah.[152] Now when the Emperor was murdered on 27 or 29 February 628[153] (which corresponded to the middle of Dhu'l-Hijjah 6 H), the Prophet ﷺ must have been on the way back to Madinah. Therefore at-Tabari's report that a wave of joy and jubilation swept the people on the occasion of al-Hudaybiyyah when the news of the murder reached them[154] is truly correct. As the news could not have come to them so soon, it must have been more appropriately a disclosure through revelation.

28. The Postponed 'Umrah

Ibn Ishaq and Ibn Sa'd say that the Prophet ﷺ performed the postponed 'Umrah ('Umrah al-Qadiyyah) of the sixth year in Dhu'l-Qa'dah 7 H.[155] Ibn Habib provides the date as Monday, 6th Dhu'l-Qa'dah 7 H.[156]

The calendar reveals the weekday as follows:

7 H DLQ	1		629 Feb	1 (WE)	–	2 (TH)
	6 (MO)			**6 (MO)**	–	7 (TU)

The Prophet ﷺ appears to have performed the postponed 'Umrah after sunset on Monday, February 6th, 629.

The Prophet ﷺ halted only three days in Makkah during which time he married Maymunah daughter of al-Harith. He consummated the marriage at Sarif.[157]

29. The Opening of Makkah (to Islam.

The narrators concur in saying that the Prophet ﷺ conquered Makkah in Ramadan 8 H but furnish different dates as follows:

	Day of setting out	Day of Opening
Ibrahim:		10[158]
Abu Sa'id al-Khudri:	2	17/18[159]
Al-Hakam:	6[160]	
Ibn 'Abbas, Tabari:	10[161]	
Ibn Ishaq:		20[162]
Waqidi:	10, WE[163]	
Ibn Sa'd:	10, WE[164]	19, FR[165]

In disagreement with Ibn Sa'd, many traditions inform us that Makkah was opened on a Monday.[166]

Let us see what weekdays the calendar reveals against these dates.

8 H RMD	1	629 Nov	23 (TH)	–	24 (FR)
	2		24 (FR)	–	25 (SA)
	6		28 (TU)	–	29 (WE)
	10 (WE)	Dec	2 (SA)	–	3 (SU)
	17		9 (SA)	–	10 (SU)
	18 (MO)		10 (SU)	–	**11 (MO)**
	19 (FR)		11 (MO)	–	12 (TU)
	20		12 (TU)	–	13 (WE)

In agreement with the tradition, against the date of the Opening the calendar reveals a Monday. It does not attest Ibn Sa'd's Friday. The day of the Opening was Monday, December 11th, 629 (18th Ramadan). Ibn Sa'd's weekday of setting out agrees with al-Hakam's date of setting out. The Prophet ﷺ appears to have set out on Wednesday, November 29th, 629 (6th Ramadan).

Ibn Sa'd says that the opening of Makkah was in the 23rd month after the treaty of al-Hudaybiyah.[167] The said treaty was concluded in Dhu'l-Qa'dah 6 H. Counting 23 months from Dhu'l-Hijjah 6 H and considering one *nasi'* at the end of 6 H we arrive at Ramadan 8 H. This shows that Ibn Sa'd knew that 6 H was an intercalary year.

It is also recorded that while proceeding for this expedition the Prophet ﷺ was keeping the fast of Ramadan which he broke at al-Kadid.[168]

30. Ghazwah Hunayn

This expedition was a sequel to the opening of Makkah. Ibn Sa'd furnished the following dates.[169]

Setting out for Hunayn: SHW 6, SA
Arrival at Hunayn: SHW 10, TU

The weekdays suffer from inconsistency. If the tenth was a Tuesday, the sixth must have been a Friday. Let us see what weekdays the calendar reveals.

8 H SHW	1	629 Dec	23 (SA)	–	24 (SU)
	6 (SA)		28 (TH)	–	29 (FR)
	10 (TU)	630 Jan	1 (MO)	–	**2 (TU)**

The Prophet ﷺ appears to have started for Hunayn on Saturday, December 30th, 629 (7th Shawwal) and arrived there on Tuesday, January 2nd, 630 (10th Shawwal). Ibn 'Abbas says that in the occasion of the opening of Makkah the Prophet ﷺ halted in the city for 19 days.[170] If he left for Hunayn on 7th Shawwal, the halt must have extended from 18th Ramadan to 6th Shawwal – which was 19 days exactly, agreeing with the report.

31. 'Umrah from al-Jiranah

'Utbah reported that on returning from Ta'if the Prophet ﷺ halted at Ji'ranah, divided the booty there and performed an 'Umrah on 28th Shawwal. Mutarrish al-Ka'bi elaborated that the Prophet ﷺ came from Ji'ranah, performed the 'Umrah at night and returned forthwith as if he had come to pass the night and for that reason this 'Umrah remained unknown to many people.[171] Mutarrish' version is authenticated by the available reports. Sa'id ibn al-Jubayr, 'Ikrimah, Ibn Abi Mulaykah, 'Amir and 'Ata – all report that the Prophet ﷺ did not perform any 'Umrah except in Dhu'l-Qa'dah.[172] This 'Umrah remained unknown to many people. The only exception is A'ishah. She says: "The Prophet ﷺ performed three 'Umrahs in all – one in Shawwal and two in Dhu'l-Qa'dah."[173]

The dates reported about the 'Umrahs are as follows:

'Umrah:	8 H	SHW 8	('Utbah)[174]
Reaching Ji'ranah:		DLQ 5, TH	(Ibn Sa'd)[175]
Donning *Ihram*:		DLQ 12	(Mirkhond)[176]
Setting out for 'Umrah:		DLQ 18, WE	(Ibn Sa'd)[177]

We have already seen that the Prophet ﷺ performed the 'Umrah al-Qadiyyah (Postponed 'Umrah) in Dhu'l-Qa'dah 7 H. The other two remaining 'Umrahs must have been the two mentioned above. It appears that after returning from Ta'if, the Prophet ﷺ did two 'Umrahs in quick succession one after the other.

Let us check the weekdays with the calendar.

8 H	SHW	1	629	Dec	23	(SA)	–	24	(SU)
		28	630	Jan	19	(FR)	–	20	(SA)
	DLQ	1			21	(SU)	–	22	(MO)
		5 (TH)			**25 (TH)**		–	26	(FR)
		12		Feb	1	(TH)	–	2	(FR)
		18 (WE)			**7 (WE)**		–	8	(TH)

The Prophet ﷺ did the first 'Umrah after sunset on Friday, January 19th (concorded with the first date as the 'Umrah was performed at night, on Saturday, 28th Shawwal), arrived at Ji'ranah apparently after sunset on Thursday, January 25th (5 Dhu'l-Qa'dah), donned the *Ihram* on Friday, February 2nd (12th Dhu'l-Qa'dah) and did the second 'Umrah after sunset on Wednesday, February 7th, 630 (18th Dhu'l-Qa'dah).

32) RETURN TO MADINAH

About the Prophet ﷺ's return to Madinah, the authorities provide the following dates.

Leaving Makkah:	8 H	DLQ 19, TH	(Ibn Sa'd)[178]
Reaching Madinah:		DLQ 24	(Abu 'Amr Madani)[179]
		DLQ 25, FR	(Mirkhond)[180]

The calendar reveals weekdays as follows:

8 H	DLQ	1	630	Jan	21	(SU)	–	22	(MO)
		19 (TH)		Feb	**8 (TH)**		–	9	(FR)
		24			13	(TU)	–	14	(WE)
		25 (FR)			14	(WE)	–	15	(TH)

It appears that the Prophet ﷺ left Makkah after sunset on Thursday, February 8th (19th Dhu'l-Qa'dah) and arrived at Madinah after sunset on February 15th, 630 (Friday, 26th Dhu'l-Qa'dah).

33. Ghazwah Tabuk (Ghazwah al-'Usra)

Ibn Habib stated that the Prophet ﷺ set out for this expedition on Monday 1st Rajab 9 H[181] while Ka'b ibn Malik and Ibn Sa'd maintained, without however mentioning the date, that he set out on a Thursday.[182]

Creating a conflict to such reports 'Ikrimah narrated that while returning from Hajj, Abu Bakr met the Prophet ﷺ setting out for this ghazwah.[183] As Abu Bakr did the Hajj in Dhu'l-Hijjah 9 H[184] there appears to be a serious error in 'Ikrimah's report because Rajab preceded Dhu'l-Hijjah by five months. And also we have the information that Abu Bakr took part in this ghazwah.[185]

The pagan calendar throws up a Saturday against 1st Rajab in disagreement with Ibn Habib's information while, however, the Hijrah calendar reveals a Monday against the date as the following concordance will show.

	Pagan calendar	Hijrah calendar
9 H RJB 1 (MO/TH)	630 Sep 14 (FR) – 15 (SA)	630 Oct 14 (SU) – 15 (MO)

Did Ibn Habib report with reference to the Hijrah calendar and did the Prophet ﷺ actually set out on Monday, 1st Rajab 9 AH (October 15th, 630)? Is it attested by the climatic conditions stated to be prevalent during those days? We must find an answer to these questions.

Our sources inform us that it was during an intensely hot season[186] and was when the harvesting season of the fruits had just set in that the Prophet ﷺ started making preparation for this expedition; and therefore many were unwilling to leave their hearth and home. On the unwillingness of the lukewarm the following revelation descended:[187]

They did not want to do jihad with their wealth and themselves in the Way of Allah. They said, 'Do not go out to fight in the heat.' Say: 'The Fire of Hell is much hotter, if they only understood.' (9:81)

According to Bukhari also it was at a time when the fruits had ripened and the shade looked pleasant.[188] If the Prophet ﷺ started in Rajab (October), his preparations must have been made during Jumada al-Akhirah (September-October). It however remains to be seen whether September-October was the season of harvesting fruits in Arabia. Perceval tells us, quoting Buckhardt, that the season of harvesting fruits in Arabia ends at the beginning of September;[189] therefore the reported month cannot be correct.

Going back a few months, Jumada al-Ula of the pagan calendar commences on a Tuesday (Wednesday in the Muslim reckoning) on July

17th, 630 and the reported climatic condition prevails exactly during June-July. If the crescent was sighted one day later at the sunset on July 18th, the first day of the month would have been Thursday, agreeing with the report. Was it in the beginning of Jumada al-Ula that the Prophet ﷺ set out for this ghazwah? Was Rajab a reporting error? We shall have to ponder. Dinet and Sliman in their biography of the Prophet ﷺ furnished the month of the expedition as Jumada[190] without however quoting the source. There must be some basis for their saying so. It appears that the Prophet ﷺ started for this ghazwah after sunset on Wednesday, July 18th, 630.

Ibn Sa'd and at-Tabari stated that the Prophet ﷺ returned from this expedition to Madinah in Ramadan.[191] We cannot accept it as we have information from Umm 'Atiyyah that the Prophet ﷺ was present at the funeral of Umm Kulthum[192] who expired in Sha'ban 9 H. She narrated that she participated in washing the dead body and the Prophet ﷺ instructed them how to wash it.[193] Therefore the Prophet ﷺ was already back in Madinah in Sha'ban. Considering the transit periods and the long halt at Tabuk, the expedition must have engaged him from Jumada al-Ula to Rajab.

Unfortunately the date of this ghazwah had been most erroneously recorded.

34. The Death of Ibrahim

Traditions report that on the day the Prophet's ﷺ son Ibrahim died the sun was eclipsed[194] while Ibn Sa'd recorded the day as Tuesday, 10th Rabi' al-Awwal 10 H.[195]

Now, as no solar eclipse can occur except on the new moon, the report about 10th Rabi' al-Awwal cannot be correct. This must be rejected straight away.

Quoting the authority of Muhammad ibn 'Umar, Ibn Sa'd also recorded that Ibrahim was born in Dhu'l-Hijjah 8 H[196] (February 19th – March 21st, 630) while at the same time informing us that the infant died at the age of 18 months.[197] At-Tabari also furnished the same month of birth.[198] Counting 18 months from Dhu'l-Hijjah 8 H considering the *nasi'* at the end of 9 H we land in Rabi' al-Akhir 10 H. Now around the end of this month there was a solar eclipse on Saturday, August 3rd, 631 (28th Rabi' al-Akhir) according to a French work of reference.[199] This must be the real date on which the infant breathed its last.

As against this, some authorities maintained that there was a solar eclipse on January 27th, 632 and that could be the date on which the infant died.[200] But in that case it must be living for 24 months – a period which does not agree with the narrator's report.

35. The Farewell Hajj

A'ishah says that the Prophet ﷺ left Madinah for the Farewell Hajj when five nights were still left of Dhu'l-Qa'dah,[201] and Ibn Sa'd furnishes the dates as follows.[202]

Setting out from Madinah:	10 H	DLQ	25, SA
Reaching Marr az-Zahran:		DLH	4, MO
Landing at Mina:		DLH	8
Standing at 'Arafat:		DLH	9

There is also the report that the day of 'Arafat was a Friday.[203]

Now against these dates the calendar throws up the following weekdays.

10 H DLQ	1	632 Jan	29 (WE)	–	30 (TH)
	25 (SA)	Feb	**22 (SA)**	–	23 (SU)
DLH	1		28 (FR)	–	29 (SA)
	4 (MO)	Mar	**2 (MO)**	–	3 (TU)
	8		6 (FR)	–	7 (SA)
	9 (FR)		7 (SA)	–	8 (SU)

The calendar reveals that the Prophet ﷺ set out from Madinah on Saturday, February 22nd (25th Dhu'l-Qa'dah) after sunset, reached Marr az-Zahran on Monday, March 2nd (4th Dhu'l-Hijjah) after sunset, and stood at 'Arafat on Sunday, March 8th, 632 (9th Dhu'l-Hijjah).

Against the day of 'Arafat the calendar throws up a Sunday contrary to the popular belief of a Friday. The belief appears to spring up from a narration of 'Umar about ayah 3 of Surah al-Ma'idah (5). A certain Jew spoke to 'Umar that if the ayah, **"Today I have perfected your deen for you and completed My blessing upon you and I am pleased with Islam as a deen for you"** had been revealed in relation to them, they would have celebrated the day of its revelation. Thereupon 'Umar said: "I know the day when it was revealed and the place where it was revealed. It was revealed on the night of Friday and we were at 'Arafat with Allah's Messenger at that time."[204] Ash-Sha'bi also reported that this ayah was revealed to the Prophet ﷺ while standing at 'Arafat at the Mawqif Ibrahim.[205]

When thus the day of 'Arafat had been considered to be Friday and the ayah had been stated to have been revealed on the day of 'Arafat, Sufyan, a sub-narrator of the tradition expressed doubt about its revelation on a Friday[206] as the day of 'Arafat was not a Friday.

Correctly the day of the 'Arafat was a Sunday.

36. Passing Away of the Prophet ﷺ

The dates reported about the passing away of the Prophet ﷺ and the sequel preceding it were as follows:

Falling sick:	11 H SFR 19, WE	(Muhammad ibn Qays)[207]
	SFR 30, WE	(Ibn Sa'd)[208]
Issue of orders for an expedition against Byzantium:	SFR 26, MO	(Ibn Sa'd)[209]
Lecture on appointment of Usamah ibn Zayd:	RBL 10, SA	(Ibn Sa'd)[210]
Death:	RBL 2, MO	(Muhammad ibn Qays)[211]
	RBL 12, MO	(Ibn Sa'd)[212]

Now let us test the dates with the calendar.

11 H SFR	1	632 Apr 27 (MO)	-	28 (TU)
	19 (WE)	May 15 (FR)	-	16 (SA)
	26 (MO)	22 (FR)	-	23 (SA)
	30 (WE)	26 (TU)	-	**27 (WE)**
RBL	1	27 (WE)	-	28 (TH)
	2 (MO)	28 (TH)	-	29 (FR)
	10 (SA)	Jun 5 (FR)	-	**6 (SA)**
	12 (MO)	7 (SU)	-	**8 (MO)**

Only three of the dates can withstand the test. The Prophet ﷺ fell sick on Wednesday, May 27th (30th Safar), spoke on the appointment of Usamah on Saturday, June 6th (10th Rabi' al-Awwal), and breathed his last on Monday, June 8th, 632 (12th Rabi' al-Awwal).[213]

Burial

Regarding the burial of the Prophet ﷺ, opinions vary amongst the authorities – some say it was on Tuesday while others maintain that it was on a Wednesday as canbe seen from the following reports.

'Ali:	Tuesday[214]
Al-Waqidi:	Tuesday, after sunset[215]
Ibn Sa'd:	Wednesday[216]
'Ayishah:	Wednesday night[217]

The apparent conflicts were reconciled by a report of 'Ikrimah which read as follows: "The Prophet ﷺ died on Monday. His body was kept for the remaining part of the day, the night and the next day and was buried by night."[218] From this it is clear that the mortal remains of the Prophet ﷺ were buried on the evening of Tuesday, June 9th, 632 which was a Wednesday in the Muslim reckoning.

Notes

1. Ibn Sa'd: *at-Tabaqat*, Vol 1, p 110
2. Burhan, Apr 1965, p 229
3. Ibn Sa'd: *at-Tabaqat*, Vol 1, p 110
4. Ibn Sa'd: *at-Tabaqat*, Vol 1, p 109
5. Ibn Hisham: *as-Sirah*, Vol 1, p 182
6. Burhan, Apr 1965, p 232
7. Ibn Sa'd: *at-Tabaqat*, Vol 1, p 109
8. Burhan, Apr 1965, p 230
9. Sachau: *Chronology*, p 39
10. Ibn Sa'd: *at-Tabaqat*, Vol 2, p 384
11. Ibn Sa'd: *at-Tabaqat*, Vol 1, p 219
12. Ibn Sa'd: *at-Tabaqat*, Vol 1, p 224; Mirkhond: *Rawzatus Safa*, Pt II, p 140
13. At-Tabari: *at-Tarikh*, Vol 1, p 70
14. Bukhari, Vol 1, pp 432, 433
15. Bukhari, Vol 3, p 130
16. Bukhari, Vol 3, p 133
17. Bukhari, Vol 3, p 136
18. Abu Dawud, Vol 1, p 362
19. Bukhari, Vol 3, p 133
20. Muslim, Vol 2, p 573
21. *Tafsir Ibn Kathir*, Vol 3, p 33
22. Klein: *Religion*, p 9
23. Ibn Sa'd: *at-Tabaqat*, Vol 1, p 247
24. Ibn Sa'd: *at-Tabaqat*, Vol 1, p 246
25. Burhan, Oct 1964, p 204; Dec 1964, p 370
26. Ibn Sa'd: *at-Tabaqat*, Vol 1, p 270
27. At-Tabari: *at-Tarikh*, Vol 1, p 135
28. Ibn Hisham: *as-Sirah*, Vol 1, p 544
29. Ibn Hisham: *as-Sirah*, Vol 1, p 691; Ibn Sa'd: *at-Tabaqat*, Vol 2, p 5
30. At-Tabari: *at-Tarikh*, Vol 1, p 150; Burhan, Sep 1964, p 140
31. Burhan, Sep 1964, p 140
32. Burhan, May 1964, p 271
33. Ibn Hisham: *as-Sirah*, Vol 1, pp 693, 694
34. At-Tabari: *at-Tarikh*, Vol 1, p 153
35. Burhan, Sep 1964, p 137
36. Burhan, May 1964, p 283; Oct 1964, p 209
37. Burhan, May 1964, p 268
38. Ibn Sa'd: *at-Tabaqat*, Vol 1, pp 283, 284
39. Burhan, Oct 1964, p 209
40. Ibn Sa'd: *at-Tabaqat*, Vol 1, p 284
41. At-Tabari: *at-Tarikh*, Vol 1, p 158
42. Ibn Sa'd: *at-Tabaqat*, Vol 1, p 290
43. Ibn Sa'd: *at-Tabaqat*, Vol 2, p 10
44. Burhan, May 1964, p 269
45. At-Tabari: *at-Tarikh*, Vol 1, pp 70, 159
46. Ibn Sa'd: *at-Tabaqat*, Vol 2, p 21
47. At-Tabari: *at-Tarikh*, Vol 1, p 159
48. At-Tabari: *at-Tarikh*, Vol 1, p 208
49. Ibn Sa'd: *at-Tabaqat*, Vol 2, p 21
50. Asad: *Message*, p 239
51. Muir: *Life*, p 173
52. Ibn Hisham: *as-Sirah*, Vol 1, p 740
53. Ibn Sa'd: *at-Tabaqat*, Vol 2, p 28
54. At-Tabari: *at-Tarikh*, Vol 1, pp 208, 209; Burhan, Aug 1964, p 94
55. *Ibn Sa'd: at-Tabaqat, Vol 2, p 34; At-Tabari: at-Tarikh, Vol 1, p 208*
56. At-Tabari: *at-Tarikh*, Vol 1, p 208
57. Ibn Hisham: *as-Sirah*, Vol 2, p 21; At-Tabari: *at-Tarikh*, Vol 1, p 208
58. Burhan, Aug 1964, p 95
59. At-Tabari: *at-Tarikh*, Vol 1, p 209
60. At-Tabari: *at-Tarikh*, Vol 1, p 206
61. Burhan, May 1964, p 269
62. Ibn Sa'd: *at-Tabaqat*, Vol 2, p 32
63. Burhan, Aug 1964, p 94; Oct 1964, p 210
64. At-Tabari: *at-Tarikh*, Vol 1, p 208
65. Ibn Sa'd: *at-Tabaqat*, Vol 2, p 32
66. Ibn Sa'd: *at-Tabaqat*, Vol 2, p 32
67. Burhan, May 1964, p 270
68. Burhan, Sep 1964, p 139
69. At-Tabari: *at-Tarikh*, Vol 1, p 209
70. Ibn Sa'd: *at-Tabaqat*, Vol 2, p 33
71. Ibn Hisham: *as-Sirah*, Vol 2, p 23

[72] At-Tabari: *at-Tarikh*, Vol 1, pp 212, 215
[73] Burhan, May 1964, p 285; Aug 1964, p 80
[74] Ibn Sa'd: *at-Tabaqat*, Vol 2, p 40
[75] Ibn Sa'd: *at-Tabaqat*, Vol 2, p 40
[76] Ibn Sa'd: *at-Tabaqat*, Vol 2, p 42; At-Tabari: *at-Tarikh*, Vol 1, p 222; Burhan, Nov 1964, p 268
[77] Burhan, Nov 1964, p 267
[78] Ibn Hisham: *as-Sirah*, Vol 2, p 84; At-Tabari: *at-Tarikh*, Vol 1, pp 224, 249
[79] Sachau: *Chronology*, p 332
[80] At-Tabari: *at-Tarikh*, Vol 1, pp 224, 229
[81] Ibn Sa'd: *at-Tabaqat*, Vol 2, p 43
[82] Ibn Hisham: *as-Sirah*, Vol 2, p 44
[83] Ibn Sa'd: *at-Tabaqat*, Vol 2, p 51
[84] Ibn Sa'd: *at-Tabaqat*, Vol 2, p 54
[85] Ibn Sa'd: *at-Tabaqat*, Vol 2, p 57
[86] At-Tabari: *at-Tarikh*, Vol 1, p 249
[87] Burhan, May 1964, p 272
[88] Ibn Sa'd: *at-Tabaqat*, Vol 2, p 60
[89] Ibn Sa'd: *at-Tabaqat*, Vol 2, p 61
[90] Burhan, Sep 1964, p 137
[91] Ibn Sa'd: *at-Tabaqat*, Vol 2, p 68
[92] Ibn Hisham: *as-Sirah*, Vol 2, p 216
[93] Ibn Hisham: *as-Sirah*, Vol 2, p 235; At-Tabari: *at-Tarikh*, Vol 1, p 268
[94] At-Tabari: *at-Tarikh*, Vol 1, p 268
[95] At-Tabari: *at-Tarikh*, Vol 1, pp 483, 484
[96] Muslim, Vol 4, p 1335
[97] Bukhari, Vol 5, p 310
[98] Bukhari, Vol 5, pp 311, 312; Muslim, Vol 3, p 1006
[99] Muslim, Vol 3, p 1005 f
[100] Muslim, Vol 3, p 1006
[101] Ibn Hisham: *as-Sirah*, Vol 2, p 235
[102] Ibn Sa'd: *at-Tabaqat*, Vol 2, p 74; At-Tabari: *at-Tarikh*, Vol 1, p 268
[103] Burhan, Nov 1964, p 275
[104] Ibn Sa'd: *at-Tabaqat*, Vol 2, p 74
[105] Ibn Sa'd: *at-Tabaqat*, Vol 2, p 75
[106] At-Tabari: *at-Tarikh*, Vol 1, p 269
[107] Ibn Hisham: *as-Sirah*, Vol 2, p 242; At-Tabari: *at-Tarikh*, Vol 1, p 271
[108] Burhan, Aug 1964, p 81
[109] Burhan, Nov 1964, p 271
[110] Ibn Sa'd: *at-Tabaqat*, Vol 2, pp 71, 72
[111] Burhan, Nov 1964, p 273
[112] Burhan, Sep 1964, p 141
[113] Ibn Sa'd: *at-Tabaqat*, Vol 2, pp 81, 82, 86; Burhan, Sep 1964, pp 141, 142
[114] Bukhari, Vol 5, p 295
[115] At-Tabari: *at-Tarikh*, Vol 1, p 290
[116] Ibn Hisham: *as-Sirah*, Vol 2, p 332; At-Tabari: *at-Tarikh*, Vol 1, p 303
[117] Ibn Sa'd: *at-Tabaqat*, Vol 2, pp 92, 93
[118] Ibn Hisham: *as-Sirah*, Vol 2, p 271
[119] Ibn Sa'd: *at-Tabaqat*, Vol 2, pp 92, 94
[120] Ibn Hisham: *as-Sirah*, Vol 2, p 272
[121] At-Tabari: *at-Tarikh*, Vol 1, p 294
[122] Ibn Hisham: *as-Sirah*, Vol 2, p 282
[123] Mirkhond: *Rawzatus Safa*, Pt II, p 777
[124] Ibn Sa'd: *at-Tabaqat*, Vol 1, p 307; Burhan, Nov 1964, p 281
[125] At-Tabari: *at-Tarikh*, Vol 1, p 355
[126] Burhan, Nov 1964, p 283
[127] Burhan, Nov 1964, p 283; Margoliouth: *Rise*, p 367
[128] Ibn Hisham: *as-Sirah*, Vol 1, p 99
[129] At-Tabari: *at-Tarikh*, Vol 1, p 354
[130] Hamidullah: *Foreign Relations*, pp 13, 33
[131] Ibn Sa'd: *at-Tabaqat*, Vol 2, p 77; Margoliouth: *Rise*, p 339
[132] Ibn Hisham: *as-Sirah*, Vol 2, p 345; At-Tabari: *at-Tarikh*, Vol 1, p 311
[133] Bukhari, Vol 5, p 319
[134] Bukhari, Vol 5, pp 321, 327
[135] Bukhari, Vol 5, p 323
[136] Mirkhond: *Rawzatus Safa*, Pt II, pp 773, 774
[137] Burhan, Nov 1964, p 273
[138] Burhan, Nov 1964, p 273
[139] Ibn Sa'd: *at-Tabaqat*, Vol 2, pp 77, 80
[140] Bukhari, Vol 5, p 321
[141] Bukhari, Vol 5, pp 324, 325

[142] Bukhari, Vol 5, p 326
[143] Mirkhond: *Rawzatus Safa*, Pt II, pp 433, 442
[144] Ibn Sa'd: *at-Tabaqat*, Vol 2, p 117
[145] Burhan, Nov 1964, p 280
[146] Islamic Review, Feb 1969, p 7
[147] Ibn Sa'd: *at-Tabaqat*, Vol 2, p 130
[148] Ibn Sa'd: *at-Tabaqat*, Vol 2, p 122
[149] Ibn Sa'd: *at-Tabaqat*, Vol 2, pp 130, 131
[150] Ibn Sa'd: *at-Tabaqat*, Vol 2, p 121
[151] Muir says that ordinary time for travel from Makkah to Madinah was 11 days. - Muir: *Life*, p 168
[152] Ibn Sa'd: *at-Tabaqat*, Vol 1, p 304; At-Tabari: *at-Tarikh*, Vol 1, p 306
[153] Burhan, Nov 1964, p 283; Margoliouth: *Rise*, p 367
[154] Burhan, Nov 1964, p 280
[155] Ibn Hisham: *as-Sirah*, Vol 2, p 433; Ibn Sa'd: *at-Tabaqat*, Vol 2, p 150
[156] Burhan, Dec 1964, p 343
[157] Ibn Hisham: *as-Sirah*, Vol 2, pp 435, 436; Ibn Sa'd: *at-Tabaqat*, Vol 2, p 152
[158] Ibn Sa'd: *at-Tabaqat*, Vol 2, p 172
[159] Ibn Sa'd: *at-Tabaqat*, Vol 2, p 171
[160] Ibn Sa'd: *at-Tabaqat*, Vol 2, p 177
[161] Ibn Hisham: *as-Sirah*, Vol 2, p 473; At-Tabari: *at-Tarikh*, Vol 1, p 391
[162] Ibn Hisham: *as-Sirah*, Vol 2, p 522
[163] Burhan, Aug 1964, p 92
[164] Ibn Sa'd: *at-Tabaqat*, Vol 2, p 167
[165] Ibn Sa'd: *at-Tabaqat*, Vol 2, p 170
[166] Bashiruddin: *Holy Qur'an*, p clxxiii
[167] Ibn Sa'd: *at-Tabaqat*, Vol 2, p 165
[168] Ibn Hisham: *as-Sirah*, Vol 2, p 473; Ibn Sa'd: *at-Tabaqat*, Vol 2, p 167
[169] Ibn Sa'd: *at-Tabaqat*, Vol 2, p 185
[170] Bukhari, Vol 5, p 412
[171] Ibn Sa'd: *at-Tabaqat*, Vol 2, p 212
[172] Ibn Sa'd: *at-Tabaqat*, Vol 2, p 211
[173] Ibn Sa'd: *at-Tabaqat*, Vol 2, p 213
[174] Ibn Sa'd: *at-Tabaqat*, Vol 2, p 212
[175] Ibn Sa'd: *at-Tabaqat*, Vol 2, p 191
[176] Mirkhond: *Rawzatus Safa*, Pt II, p 639
[177] Ibn Sa'd: *at-Tabaqat*, Vol 2, p 191
[178] Ibn Sa'd: *at-Tabaqat*, Vol 2, p 191
[179] Ibn Hisham: *as-Sirah*, Vol 2, p 604
[180] Mirkhond: *Rawzatus Safa*, Pt II, p 640
[181] Burhan, Dec 1964, p 358
[182] Ibn Sa'd: *at-Tabaqat*, Vol 2, p 207; Bukhari, Vol 4, p 126
[183] Burhan, Dec 1964, p 357
[184] Ibn Sa'd: *at-Tabaqat*, Vol 2, p 208
[185] Ibn Hisham: *as-Sirah*, Vol 2, p 633
[186] Ibn Sa'd: *at-Tabaqat*, Vol 2, p 204; At-Tabari: *at-Tarikh*, Vol 1, p 435
[187] At-Tabari: *at-Tarikh*, Vol 1, p 436
[188] Bukhari, Vol 5, p 495
[189] Islamic Culture, Apr 1947, p 143
[190] Dinet: *The Prophet*, p 238
[191] Ibn Sa'd: *at-Tabaqat*, Vol 2, p 206; At-Tabari: *at-Tarikh*, Vol 1, p 445
[192] Mirkhond: *Rawzatus Safa*, Pt II, p 781
[193] Bukhari, Vol 2, p 196
[194] Ibn Sa'd: *at-Tabaqat*, Vol 1, p 161; Bukhari, Vol 2, p 84
[195] Ibn Sa'd: *at-Tabaqat*, Vol 1, p 163
[196] Ibn Sa'd: *at-Tabaqat*, Vol 1, p 152
[197] Ibn Sa'd: *at-Tabaqat*, Vol 1, p 162
[198] At-Tabari: *at-Tarikh*, Vol 1, p 430
[199] Yusuf Ali: *Holy Qur'an*, p 1078
[200] Burhan, May 1964, p 282; Margoliouth: *Rise*, p xvi
[201] At-Tabari: *at-Tarikh*, Vol 1, p 479
[202] Ibn Sa'd: *at-Tabaqat*, Vol 2, pp 214, 215, 218
[203] Bukhari, Vol 1, p 38; Muslim, Vol 4, p 1551
[204] Muslim, Vol 4, p 1551
[205] Ibn Sa'd: *at-Tabaqat*, Vol 2, p 233
[206] Muslim, Vol 4, p 1551
[207] Ibn Sa'd: *at-Tabaqat*, Vol 2, p 340
[208] Ibn Sa'd: *at-Tabaqat*, Vol 2, p 340
[209] Ibn Sa'd: *at-Tabaqat*, Vol 2, p 235
[210] Ibn Sa'd: *at-Tabaqat*, Vol 2, p 236
[211] Ibn Sa'd: *at-Tabaqat*, Vol 2, p 340

[212] Ibn Sa'd: *at-Tabaqat*, Vol 2, p 340

[213] A mnemonic aid to remember the dates of his birth and death is 22632 — the number of days he lived. The last three figures denote the year of his death. The middle one stands for June in which he was born and died. The first two indicate that after 22 days of the commencement of the month he was born and 22 days before its end he died.

[214] Ibn Sa'd: *at-Tabaqat*, Vol 2, p 341

[215] At-Tabari: *at-Tarikh*, Vol 1, p 526

[216] Ibn Sa'd: *at-Tabaqat*, Vol 2, p 341

[217] At-Tabari: *at-Tarikh*, Vol 1, p 541

[218] Ibn Sa'd: *at-Tabaqat*, Vol 2, p 341

7. The Pagan Calendar

The examples with which we have worked in the preceding chapter show that the 31.36N102 calendar agrees with the biographical reports in 32 cases – perfectly in 29 cases and with one day's difference in three. Biographical dates of one were found to have been recorded in terms of the Hijrah calendar and those of three were discovered to be wrong while, however, the calendar was able to show the true dates thereof. These results clearly indicate that this was the very calendar operative during the lifetime of the Prophet ﷺ.

With this discovery the exact point when the Arabs adopted intercalation will now become clear. Al-Biruni, Maqrizi and Muhammad Jarkasi maintained that they adopted it about two hundred years before the mission of the Prophet[1] ﷺ while Dr. Hamidullah was of the opinion that it could be much earlier than this. Now the identity of the calendar discloses that they did it 102 or 474 years (one cycle of repetition plus 102) before April 631 when they abandoned it for ever. Of the two possible points, the former is too near to agree with the hints provided by the earlier researches and must therefore be rejected.

Now we summarise the features of the pagan calendar as follows:

(1) the pagan Arabs had adopted the 31 year system of intercalation from October 23rd, 157 – 474 years before its abandonment in 631, that is, 452 years before Islam, in complete agreement with Dr. Hamidullah's view;

(2) in the first year of the intercalary epoch, the pagan pilgrimage fell on the autumnal equinox (September 21st, 158), exactly on the date at which they aimed;

(3) in the process they intercalated an additional month (also called Dhu'l-Hijjah) at the end of the following year numbers;

1st cycle	–	3,	6,	9,	...	27,	30,	31,
2nd cycle	–	34,	37,	40,	...	58,	61,	62,
3rd cycle	–	65,	68,	71,	...	89,	92,	93,
...			...		...		...	
15th cycle	–	437,	440,	443,	...	461,	464,	465,
16th cycle	–	468,	471,	474.				

The Pagan Calendar

(4) amidst 5688 ordinary lunar months the system incorporated 168 *nasi's* (– 146 before the commencement of *'Am al-Fil* – the Year of the Elephant, 19 in the Makkan period of the Prophet ﷺ and 3 in the Madinan) with the first *nasi'* turning up against September 20th – October 19th, 160 and the last against March 10th – April 9th, 631;

(5) in the *'Am al-Fil* era, which started from April 23rd, 570, they intercalated the following years --- 2 AF, 5 AF, 8 AF, 11 AF, 14 AF, 17 AF, 20 AF, 21 AF, 24 AF, 27 AF, 30 AF, 33 AF, 36 AF, 39 AF, 42 AF, 45 AF, 48 AF, 51 AF, 52 AF, 55 AF, 58 AF and 61 AF; and

(6) the very imperfection of the system dragged their pilgrimage backwards by 197 days in the Julian calendar from 21st September in 158 to 8th March in 632 when the Prophet ﷺ did his last pilgrimage as shown below:

Epoch	Cycle No.	Year No.	Date of pilgrimage (the day of 'Arafat)
Intercalary	1	1	21 Sep 158
	2	32	9 Sep 189
	3	63	27 Aug 220
	4	94	15 Aug 251
	5	125	3 Aug 282
	6	156	21 Jul 313
	7	187	8 Jul 344
	8	218	26 Jun 375
	9	249	13 Jun 406
	10	280	1 Jun 437
	11	311	19 May 468
	12	342	7 May 499
	13	373	24 Apr 530
	14	404	11 Apr 561
	15	435	30 Mar 592
	16	466	18 Mar 623
		467	6 Mar 624
		468	24 Feb 625
		469	14 Mar 626
		470	4 Mar 627
		471	21 Feb 628
		472	11 Mar 629
		473	28 Feb 630
		474	18 Feb 631
Non-intercalary		475	8 Mar 632

With this we have solved the fourteen centuries old puzzle of the pagan Arab calendar and have landed ourselves in a better position to handle the calendrical conflicts in the biographical works of the Prophet ﷺ.

The Hijrah Era and the Madinan Decade

Elsewhere we have discussed how the Hijrah calendar had been reconstructed at a later stage and how the epochal day had been wrongly fixed at July 15th, 622, the termination point of the backward reconstruction. Here we shall briefly deliberate where its epochal day really should be.

Our sources inform us that from the lifetime of the Prophet ﷺ himself the people had started referring to the Madinan years[2] by individual names derived from the major event of the year. So there was no immediate need of numbering them as they could be identified by such names. Nevertheless the years in their reckoning were with the usual thirteenth month wherever necessary. To the first Muslims the first ten years in Madinah consisted of 123 months (including the three *nasi's* intercalated against Shawwal, Dhu'l-Qa'dah and Dhu'l-Hijjah). Only at some later stage, oblivious of this important feature, did people backwardly reconstruct the Hijrah calendar of the first decade with twelve months a year uniformly. But the Prophet ﷺ spent his entire life, except the last fifteen months, under the old order. Any realistic attempt to locate the events of his life must therefore be necessarily linked to the old system. Moreover when the Companions decided to commence the new era from Muharram of the year of Hijrah, the reference could not be to any other Muharram but to that of the pagan calendar as the presently adopted Hijrah calendar was then non-existent. Abu Ja'far gives a clear picture in this regard by saying that the Hijrah epoch was counted from the beginning of the year, that is, 2 months and 12 days prior to the emigration of the Prophet[3] ﷺ. As the emigration took place on June 28th, 622, in the true reckoning the epoch should be considered from Sunday, April 18th, 622 the starting point of the pagan Muharram — three months prior to the presently adopted date.

The Hijrah calendar, with its erroneous epochal day, started immediately after the month of emigration, as the following Pagan-Hijrah concordance will show:

The Pagan Calendar

				Pagan	Hijrah
622	Apr 18	–	May 18	MHR	
	May 18	–	Jun 16	SFR	
	Jun 16	–	Jul 15	RBL	(Emigration)
	Jul 15	–	Aug 14	RBR	MHR

The first ten Madinan years worked out as follows in the two calendars – the pagan and the Hijrah. The table will help the reader to understand the lag between the two.

Year	Pagan (H)	Hijrah (AH)[4]
1	622 Apr 18 – 623 Apr 7	622 Jul 15 – 623 Jul 5
2	623 Apr 7 – 624 Mar 27	623 Jul 5 – 624 Jun 23
3	**624 Mar 27 – 625 Mar 15**	624 Jun 23 – 625 Jun 13
4	625 Mar 15 – 626 Apr 4	625 Jun 13 – 626 Jun 2
5	626 Apr 4 – 627 Mar 25	626 Jun 2 – 627 May 22
6	**627 Mar 25 – 628 Apr 11**	627 May 22 – 628 May 11
7	628 Apr 11 – 629 Mar 31	628 May 11 – 629 Apr 30
8	629 Mar 31 – 630 Mar 21	629 Apr 30 – 630 Apr 19
9	**630 Mar 21 – 631 Apr 9**	630 Apr 19 – 631 Apr 9
10	631 Apr 9 – 632 Mar 29	631 Apr 9 – 632 Mar 29

(Years in bold character consisted of 13 months in the pagan calendar).

Notes

[1] Sachau: *Chronology*, p 73; Islamic Culture, Apr 1947, pp 137, 146

[2] These were respectively known as the year of Permission, the year of the Command to Fight, the year of Trial, the year of Congratulation on the occasion of Marriage, the year of the Earthquake, the year of Inquiring, the year of the Opening [of Makkah to Islam], the year of Equality, the year of Exemption and the year of Farewell. – Sachau: *Chronology*, p 35

[3] At-Tabari: *at-Tarikh*, Vol 1, p 142

[4] It must be reiterated for the clear information of the reader that no calendar of this fashion ever existed at the time of the Prophet ﷺ. What the Muslims used was the pagan calendar. The Orientalists invented this design at a later date erroneously believing that the early Muslims disregarded intercalation in their chronology, which was not a fact.

8. Other Events

In respect of the other remaining events, the biographers recorded only the dates or the months without mentioning the weekdays. With the help of the calendar these may now be located in the Julian calendar and the corresponding weekdays ascertained wherever the dates were given.

In the course of this work we have seen that after the institution of the Hijrah calendar reporters sometimes narrated dates in relation to it without however specifying so. In respect of the following events, unless we have reasons to the contrary, the reported months are all cMi'rajered to be pagan, which presumption may not however be correct in all the cases. But there is no way out. Until further information is available we are to be content with such an assumption.

Pre-Prophethood Events

1. Abu Bakr's birth

Tabrizi recorded that Abu Bakr as-Siddiq was born 2 years 4 months and a few days after Abrahah's attack upon the Ka'bah.[1] As the attack was on 18th Muharram 1 AF, Abu Bakr must have been born in Jumada al-Ula 3 AF (August 26th – September 24th, 572).

2. Aminah's death

The Prophet's ﷺ mother 'Aminah died when he was only six years of age.[2] The sixth year of the his life extended from June 575 to May 576.

3. 'Abd al-Muttalib's death

When the Prophet ﷺ attained the age of eight years his grand-father 'Abd al-Muttalib left this world.[3] The eighth year of his lMaw'idrresponded to the period from June 577 – May 578.

4. First trip Muraysi'

Abu Talib took the Prophet ﷺ on a trip to Syria when the latter was 12.[4] The Prophet ﷺ entered his twelfth year in June 581.

5. Battles of Fijar

Abu 'Amr ibn Ula reports that the battles of Fijar was fought during the sacred months when the Prophet ﷺ was 14 to 15 years old.[5]

Other reports say that the battle, probably the last one, was fought in Shawwal[6] when the Prophet ﷺ was twenty.[7] This corresponded to December 14th, 589 – January 13th, 590.

6. Hilf al-Fudul

Shortly after the restoration of peace after the battles of Fijar, a confederacy was formed at Makkah for suppression of violence and injustice. Ma'shars known as Hilf al-Fudul.

Ibn Sa'd sayJa'far this was formed in Dhu'l-Qa'dah when the Prophet ﷺ was 20 years of age.[8] This coJa'farnds to January 13th – February 12th, 590.

7. Marriage to Khadijah

When he was 25 years old, the Prophet ﷺ married Khadijah.[9] The twenty-fifth year of his life commenced in June 594.

8. Zaynab's birth

The Prophet's ﷺ first daughter Zaynab was born 30 years after the incident of the Elephant.[10] The thirtieth year of the *'Am al-Fil* era ended in April 600.

9. 'Ali's birth

Al-Biruni recorded that 'Ali ibn Abi Talib was born on 15th Rabi' al-Akhir,[11] while at-Tabari stated on the authority of Mujahid that he was 10 years old when accepting Islam one year after Prophethood.[12]

The Prophet ﷺ received his call in 40 AF. To be 10 years old in 41 AF, 'Ali must have been born in 31 AF. It appears that he was born on Tuesday, August 2nd, 600 (15th Rabi' al-Akhir 31 AF).

10. Ruqayyah's birth

Ruqayyah, the second daughter of the Prophet ﷺ was stated to have been born in the thirty-third year of the *'Am al-Fil*.[13] The year corresponded to March 602 – March 603.

11. Fatimah's birth

Although al-Biruni stated that Fatimah, the youngest daughter of the Prophet ﷺ was born on the 4th of Jumada al-Akhirah,[14] there is A difference of opinionMuraysi'he year. Some say that it was 5 years before ProMas'udod while others maintain that it was in the 41st year of *'Am al-Fil* or 5 years after the Prophet ﷺ received his call.[15]

Surat ash-Shu'ara' (26) was one of the early Makkan surahs. Now when one of its ayat, **"Warn your near relatives..."** (26: 213) was revealed, the Prophet ﷺ summoned his kindred and addressed them as follows:

"Quraysh! Buy yourselves (from the Fire). I cannot save you from Allah. Bani 'Abd Manaf! I cannot save you from Allah. 'Abbas, son of 'Abd al-Muttalib! I cannot save you from Allah. Safiyyah! I cannot save you from Allah. Fatimah, daughter of Muhammad! Ask what you wish from my properties, but I cannot save you from Allah (if you disobey Him)."[16]

The Prophet's ﷺ inclusion of Fatimah in the address clearly indicates that she was by then old enough to understand and must have been born before the Prophet ﷺ was commissioned. Such inference is supported by Tabrizi who recorded that Fatimah expired six months after the Prophet ﷺ at an age of 28 years.[17] This places the birth of Fatimah in 35 AF, five years before the call.

4th Jumada al-Akhirah 35 AF Ka'bs out to Saturday, September 5th, 604.

12. Rebuilding the Ka'bah

Ibn Ishaq and at-Tabari agree in saying that the Ka'bah was re-built when the Prophet ﷺ attained the age of 35.[18] The thirty-fifth year of his life started in June 604.

13. A'ishah's birth

A'ishah started sharing the bed with the Prophet ﷺ in Shawwal 2 H eighteen months after the Emigration.[19] Bukhari recorded on the authority of 'Urwah that she was 9 years old then.[20]

If we accept 'Urwah's report, A'ishah must have been born in 46 AF. Contrary to this, Khatib al-Baghdadi wrote in *Akmal fi Asma ar-Rijal* that A'ishah was at least 18/19 years old when she started living with the Prophet ﷺ – thereby placing her birth sometime around 36 – 37 AF. It calls us to examine which of these two views is more acceptable.

A'ishah herself reports that she was already a playful girl when Surat al-Qamar (54) descended.[21] This was an early Makkan surah revealed sometime around the end of the early Makkan or the beginning of the middle Makkan period. If we follow 'Urwah she was then not yet born.

When Khawlah bint Hakim suggested that the Prophet ﷺ remarry (52 AF), she mentioned two women – A'ishah as a virgin and Sawdah as a widow.[22] It is evident that Khawlah could not have suggested the name of A'ishah if she was not of marriageable age by then, inasmuch as the immediate need of the Prophet's ﷺ household was for a woman who could fill the vacuum created by the loss of Khadijah.

There is also a report that when the Prophet ﷺ asked for the hand of A'ishah (52 AF) she was already engaged to the son of one Mu'tim ibn 'Adi. Abu Bakr broke this engagement and married her to the Prophet ﷺ.[23] If A'ishah had not reached puberty by then, there could not have been an engagement. The fact that she had already attained puberty in her Makkan days is also evident from the following report of A'ishah herself:

> I had seen my parents following Islam since I attained the age of puberty. Not a single day passed but that the Prophet ﷺ visited us, both in the morning and evening. My father Abu Bakr thought of building a mosque in the courtyard of his house and he did so. He used to pray and recite the Qur'an in it. The pagan women and their children used to stand by him and look at him with surprise. Abu Bakr was a soft-hearted person and could not help weeping while reciting the Qur'an. The chiefs of the Quraysh pagans became afraid of that.[24]

In the battle of Uhud which was fought in Shawwal 3 H, A'ishah was seen running in the battlefield carrying heavy water-skins on her back and emptying them into the mouths of the wounded and dying Muslim soldiers[25] which was definitely not possible for the girl of 10 years that A'ishah would have been according to 'Urwah.

On the other hand we are informed, in complete dismissal of 'Urwah's view, that all four children of Abu Bakr – 'Abdallah and Asma' from his first wife Qutaylah, and 'Abd ar-Rahman and A'ishah from his second wife Umm Ruman, had been born in the days of Ignorance.[26]

Tabrizi recorded that Asma', who was 10 years older than A'ishah, died in 73 AH at the age of 100 years[27] – thereby placing the birth of Asma' in 26 AF and that of A'ishah in 36 AF. If this is so, A'ishah would have been 8 around the end of the early Makkan period when Surat al-Qamar was revealed, 17 at the time of her betrothal, 19 at the time of cohabitation with the Prophet ﷺ and 20 when joining the battle of Uhud.

It appears that she was born in 36 AF (March 27th, 605 – April 15th, 606).

Pre-Hijrah events

14. Emigration of the Companions to Abyssinia

When the atrocities of the Makkans perpetrated against the adherents of the new faith increased beyond the limits of toleration, the Prophet ﷺ advised his Companions to seek asylum in Abyssinia; and a party of sixteen persons including four women left for the said country in Rajab of the fifth year of his mission[28] (44 AF). Shortly after, in Ramadan the Prophet ﷺ made a public recital of Surat an-Najm (53). The sublimity of the verses sent the Qurayshites into prostration, and so the news spread that they had accepted Islam and were no longer hostile to the faith. The little band of the emigrants picked up the heartening news and without further loss of time reappeared at Makkah in Shawwal of the same year.[29]

The corresponding Julian months were as follows – leaving in emigration: September 21st – October 22nd (Rajab); incident of mass prostration: November 20th – December 19th (Ramadan) and return of the emigrants: December 19th, 613 – January 18th, 614 (Shawwal 44 AF).

After the departure of his faithful Companions to Abyssinia, the Prophet ﷺ was almost alone. One day he sought the assembly of the Quraysh near the Ka'bah and there he recited: **"By the star when it descends."** When he reached **"Have you really considered al-Lat and al-'Uzza and Manat, the third, the other one?"** (53: 19-20), Shaytan inserted the words, "these idols are high and their intercession is expected." The Prophet ﷺ continued and completed the whole surah and fell in prostration. The people in the assembly also fell in prostration being pleased with what they had heard about their deities. They said, "We know that Allah gives life and causes death. He creates and gives us provision, but our deities will intercede with Him."

When it was evening Jibril came and pointed out the error. The Prophet ﷺ was upset that Shaytan had cast something into the recitation which Allah did not reveal to him. Thereupon the ayah descended:[30]

> They were very near to enticing you away from some of what We have revealed to you, hoping that you would invent something against Us. Then they would have taken you as their intimate. If We had not made you firm, you would have leaned towards them a little. Then We would have let you taste a double punishment in life and a double punishment in death. You would not have found any helper against Us. (17: 73-75)

This places the revelation of these ayat in Ramadan 44 AF (November-December 613).

15. The Isra'

Quoting the authority of Ibn 'Abbas, Ibn Sa'd says that the Prophet's ﷺ night journey to Jerusalem took place on 17th Rabi' al-Awwal one year before his exile to the glen of Abu Talib.[31] But al-Biruni maintains, without mentioning the year, tMas'ud was on 27th Rajab.[32] He did not make any distinction between the Isra and Mi'raj.

The Prophet ﷺ was exiled in the seventh year of his mission (46 AF) and therefore Ibn Sa'd's date corresponded to Sunday, June 2nd, 614 (17th Rabi' al-Awwal 45 AF).

Julian date corresponding to al-Biruni's report cannot be worked out for want of the year.

16. 'Umar's Islam

It is reported that 'Umar, later the second Caliph of Islam, accepted the deen in Dhu'l-Hijjah of the 6th year of the Prophet's ﷺ mission[33] (45 AF) which corresponded to February 5th – March 7th, 615.

17. Blockade in the Shi'b

Ibn Sa'd reports that the Prophet ﷺ took refuge in the glen (*Shi'b*) of

Abu Talib from the first of Muharram in the 7th year of Mission ('Uthman ibn Abi Sulayman).[34] This corresponded to Monday, April 7th, 615 (1st Muharram 46 AF).

The blockade extended for two years according to some authorities but three according to others.[35]

18. Khadijah's death

There is a confusion about who died first – Khadijah or Abu Talib. Al-Biruni places the death of Khadijah on 10th Ramadan[36] about one month before that of Abu Talib while Ibn Sa'd says on the authority of Muhammad ibn 'Umar al-Aslami that it was one month and five days after.[37]

There is exactly one month and five days' gap between al-Biruni's date of Khadijah's death and Ibn Sa'd's date of Abu Talib's death. Did Ibn 'Umar say one month and five days before or did Ibn Sa'd make an inadvertent mistake in taking down the report? – we cannot make out.

Al-Biruni's date corresponded to Tuesday, December 5th, 618 (10th Ramadan 49 AF).

19. Abu Talib's death

Ibn Sa'd stated the date of Abu Talib's death as in the middle of Shawwal in the 10th year of Mission[38] (49 AF) while al-Biruni gave it as 19th Shawwal.[39] These dates respectively correspond to Tuesday, January 9th (15th Shawwal) and Saturday, January 13th, 619 (19th Shawwal 49 AF).

Concern for the salvation of his uncle Abu Talib was so heavy in the mind of the Prophet ﷺ that even in the dying moments of the former he continued to insist upon his utterance of the Shahadah and assured him that if he did so he would be a witness before Allah of his being a Muslim. Dying, Abu Talib replied that had it not been for fear that Quraysh would say despondency had overwhelmed him, he would have surely done it and cooled the eyes of the Prophet ﷺ.

For several days after his death, the Prophet ﷺ did not come out of his house and remained praying for the forgiveness of Abu Talib. In emulation, his companions began to pray for the forgiveness of their dead relatives who died in idolatry. Then descended the ayah:[40]

It is not right for the Prophet and those who have iman to ask

forgiveness for the mushrikun – even if they are close relatives – after it has become clear to them that they are the Companions of the Blazing Fire. (9: 113)

It is also said that the following ayah was revealed in relation to Prophet's ﷺ labours to convert his uncle Abu Talib.[41]

You cannot guide those you would like to but Allah guides those He wills. He has best knowledge of the guided. (28: 56)

20. Visit to Ta'if

When the Prophet ﷺ met severe opposition from all sides he became disappointed of talking to the Makkans and looked for greener pasture and hit upon Ta'if, which was his childhood cradle, hoping that its people might give a sympathetic ear to his words. It is stated to have been around the end of Shawwal in the tenth year of his mission after the passing away of his beloved wife Khadijah and of his protecting uncle Abu Talib.[42] The period corresponded to December 24th, 618 – January 23rd, 619.

According to Ibn Sa'd he stayed at Ta'if for 10 days and on his return halted at Nakhlah a few days, where he recited Surat al-Jinn (72) in the night prayer which occasioned the revelation of ayah 46: 29.[43]

21. Meeting the chiefs of Khazraj

Ibn Hisham recorded that in Rajab of the 11th year of his mission (50 AF) six chiefs of the tribe of Khazraj of Madinah met the Prophet ﷺ at 'Aqabah.[44] It corresponded to September 16th – October 15th, 619.

22. The First Pledge of 'Aqabah

Twelve Madinans gave the pledge of acceptance of Islam at the hands of the Prophet ﷺ in Dhu'l-Hijjah of the 12th year of Mission[45] (51 AF) at 'Aqabah. This corresponded to January 30th – March 1st, 621.

23. Engagement to A'ishah

Talking about marriage in Shawwal, which was considered by the Arabs an ominous month, A'ishah used to say: "Allah's Messenger contracted marriage with me in Shawwal and took me to his house as a bride during Shawwal. And who amongst the wives of Allah's Messenger was dearer to him than I?"[46]

About the marriage we have the information that it was three years after Khadijah's death.[47] If Khadijah had expired in Ramadan 49 AF, the marriage was in Shawwal 52 AF. The period therefore corresponded to December 21st, 621 – January 20th, 622.

24. The Second Pledge of 'Aqabah

Seventy persons including two women gave the second pledge at 'Aqabah on the 11th and 12th Dhu'l-Hijjah in the 12th year of the mission according to Mirkhond.[48]

Quoting Abu Ja'far's authority, at-Tabari narrated that the Madinans came to the Prophet ﷺ in Dhu'l-Hijjah. After they left, the Prophet ﷺ spent the remaining days of Dhu'l-Hijjah, Muharram and Safar in Makkah. He came to Madinah in Rabi' al-Awwal.[49] This report provides a gap of only three months' between the second pledge and the migration. Since the Prophet ﷺ left Makkah in the 14th year of the mission (53 AF), the second pledge must necessarily have been in the 13th year and not in the 12th.

Perhaps the people gave the pledge in the nights of Sunday, February 28th (11th Dhu'l-Hijjah) and Monday, March 1st, 622 (12th Dhu'l-Hijjah 52 AF).

Events of 1 H
25. Increase in the length of the prayer

Ibn Ishaq and at-Tabari say that the length of the obligatory prayers was increased from the initial two rak'ahs[50] to four from 12th Rabi' al-Akhir 1 H.[51] This corresponded to Tuesday, July 27th, 622.

26. Sariyyah Hamzah ibn 'Abd al-Muttalib to Sif al-Bahr

Al-Waqidi contended that this expedition took place in Ramadan 2 H.[52] But this cannot be accepted. Because the sources tell us that Hamzah took part in the battle of Badr (2 H)[53] for which the people set out on the 3rd and returned on 22nd of Ramadan leaving no time for another expedition by Hamzah. Ibn Sa'd corrected this error and located the event in Ramadan 1 H.[54] This corresponded to December 10th, 622 – January 9th, 623.

27. Sariyyah 'Ubaydah ibn al-Harith towards Batn Rabigh

At-Tabari dated this event in Shawwal 2 H[55] while Ibn Sa'd assigned it to Shawwal 1 H.[56] Ibn Hisham informs us that the sariyyah of Hamzah and the sariyyah of 'Ubaydah were almost contemporaneous.[57] The more correct date could be Shawwal 1 H (January 9th – February 7th, 623).

28. Sariyyah Sa'd ibn Abi Waqqas towards al-Kharrar

This expedition is recorded to have been sent out in Dhu'l-Qa'dah 1 H[58] after Hamzah's sariyyah.[59] This corresponded to February 7th – March 9th, 623.

Events of 2 H
29. Ghazwah Dhu'l-'Ushayrah

According to Ibn Habib, the Prophet ﷺ set out on this expedition on the 1st Jumada al-Ula 2 H and returned when eight nights of Jumada al-Akhirah were still left.[60]

The date of setting out corresponded to Thursday, August 4th, 623.

We have already seen that the Prophet ﷺ set out for the Ghazwah Badr al-Ula on 12th Jumada al-Ula 2 H, indicating thereby that he had already returned from Dhu'l-'Ushayrah before the 12th Jumada al-Ula. Hence Ibn Habib's report of the Prophet's ﷺ return on 21st/22nd Jumada al-Akhirah cannot be correct.

It was the third ghazwah according to Ibn Ishaq.[61]

30. Ghazwah al-Abwa

Bukhari reported on the authority of Zayd ibn Arqam that Ghazwah Dhu'l-'Ushayrah was the first expedition[62] of the Prophet ﷺ while Ibn Ishaq, Ibn Hisham and Ibn Sa'd maintained that Ghazwah al-Abwa was the first.[63] Such a contradiction apparently stems from the fact that in the second year, Jumada al-Ula of the pagan calendar corresponded to Safar of the Hijrah calendar.

The narration reaching Ibn Ishaq, Ibn Hisham and Ibn Sa'd probably narrated the month of occurrence (Safar 2 AH) of Ghazwah al-Abwa in terms of the Hijrah calendar. This they confused for the pagan and maintained that Ghazwah al-Abwa was the first ghazwah.

Because of their proximity and their mistaking of the Hijrah month for that of the pagan, the *inter se* sequence was confused. Ghazwah al-Abwa appears to be a continuation of Ghazwah Dhu'l-'Ushayrah. The concordance was as follows:

	Pagan	Hijrah	Julian
Ghazwah Dhu'l-'Ushayrah	JML 2 H	(SFR 2 AH)	623 Aug 3 – Sep 2
Ghazwah al-Abwa	(JML 2 H)	SFR 2 AH	623 Aug 3 – Sep 2

It was recorded that Jihad was ordered on this occasion.[64]

31. Sariyyah 'Abdallah ibn Jahsh al-Asadi at Nakhlah

Ibn Sa'd says that the Nakhlah incident occurred in Rajab 2 H.[65] According to Ibn Hisham it was the last day of Rajab[66] while at-Tabari maintains that the day could have been either the last day of Jumada al-Akhirah or the first or the last day of Rajab.[67] Mirkhond says it was the first day of Rajab.[68]

It was as a consequence of this occasion that the following Quranic ayah was revealed:[69]

> They will ask you about the Sacred Month and fighting in it. Say, 'Fighting in it is a serious matter; but barring access to the Way of Allah and rejecting Him and barring access to the Masjid al-Haram and expelling its people from it are far more serious in the sight of Allah. Fitna is worse than killing.' … They are the Companions of the Fire, remaining in it timelessly, for ever. (2: 217)

In the pagan days, Rajab was considered a sacred month and fighting therein was not resorted to. When 'Abdallah killed one of the Quraysh at Nakhlah and took others captive in this expedition, the Makkans charged that Muhammad had violated the sanctity of the sacred month. On his return to Madinah 'Abdallah faced serious displeasure from the Prophet ﷺ. "I did not permit you to shed blood in the sacred month" reprimanded the Prophet ﷺ.[70] Also the Prophet ﷺ is reported to have refused the booty brought by 'Abdallah. Moreover the Qur'anic revelation clearly indicates that it was a fight that occurred in the sacred month. If it was in Jumada al-Akhirah, there was no room for the Prophet's ﷺ displeasure. All these suggest that it was in Rajab.

Regarding the date, the arguments are in favour of the last day of Rajab. As was narrated by Ibn Hisham, when Quraysh clamoured that during the sacred month the Companions of Muhammad had shed blood, looted property and captured people, the Muslims in Makkah tried to put up a defense by saying that they did these things in Sha'ban. Unless the event was in the close proximity to Sha'ban they could not have made such a reply.

It appears that the incident took place on Monday, 30th Rajab 2 H (October 31st, 623).

32. Command for the fast of Ramadan

Ibn Sa'd and at-Tabari stated that the command for the fast of Ramadan descended at the beginning of Sha'ban 2 H.[71] This corresponded to (October 31st – November 30th, 623).

33. Execution of Asma' bint Marwan

Asma', the daughter of Marwan of the tribe Aws, belonged to a family which had not yet thrown off their ancestral faith. She made no secret of her dislike for Islam. After the battle of Badr, she composed couplets on the folly of receiving and trusting a stranger and incited the people of Madinah to a murderous attack on the Prophet ﷺ.

According to Ibn Sa'd, 'Umayr ibn 'Adi volunteered to finish the poetess in Ramadan 2 H when still five nights of the month remained.[72] The date corresponded to Saturday, December 24th, 623 (24th Ramadan 2 H).

Margoliouth stated that her execution would not have been an inexcusably ruthless measure judged by any standard for it must not be forgotten that satire was a far more effective weapon in Arabia than elsewhere and during the Caliphate it was at times penalised.[73]

34. Celebrartion of the first 'Id al-Fitr

At-Tabari recorded that the first ever 'Id al-Fitr in the life of the new community was celebrated in Shawwal 2 H.[74] Since 'Id al-Fitr is always celebrated on the first day of Shawwal, the date of the first 'Id was Friday, December 30th, 623.

35. Elimination of Abu 'Afak

Abu 'Afak, a member of the tribe of 'Amir ibn 'Awf, failing to see that the Prophet's ﷺ arrival had united the people of Madinah, taunted them for being divided by the stranger whose notions of right and wrong were quite different from theirs. He proposed that if they believed in force and tyranny, they would have been better to have obeyed the old kings of Yemen. Although over a hundred years of age, he was active in his opposition to the new faith and like Asma' composed stinging verses satirising the Prophet ﷺ.

In the week immediately following Badr, Salim ibn 'Umayr undertook a sariyyah to finish this opponent. Al-Waqidi and Ibn Sa'd provide the date as Shawwal 2 H[75] which corresponded to (December 29th, 623 – January 28th, 624). It could have been in the beginning of Shawwal.

Ibn Sa'd stated that it was a hot night and the Jew was sleeping in the open courtyard[76] when he met his assassin. Our finding does not agree with the reported weather.

36. Cohabiting with A'ishah

About A'ishah's coming to stay together with the Prophet ﷺ, at-Tabari says that according to many reports it was either in Shawwal or in Dhu'l-Qa'dah, seventeen or eighteen months after the emigration to Madinah[77] while A'ishah herself states that it was in Shawwal.[78] Other authorities such as Imam an-Nawawi, Ibn Kathir and Qastalani also maintain that it was in Shawwal after the return from Badr.[79]

Of the consummation, Abu Ja'far remarked that it was on one of the Wednesdays.[80]

In Shawwal 2 H, the Prophet ﷺ was engaged in Ghazwah Qararat al-Kudr from the first to the tenth and in Ghazwah Bani Qaynuqa' from the sixteenth up to the end of the month. He was available in Madinah only from the eleventh up to the fifteenth during which period the only Wednesday available was the 13th (January 10th – 11th, 624).

Therefore the Prophet ﷺ consummated his marriage with A'ishah on the night of Tuesday, January 10th, 624 which was Wednesday in the Muslim reckoning.

37. Fatimah's marriage

Fatimah was married to 'Ali after Badr[81] on the first day of Dhu'l-Hijjah[82] in the twenty-second month of migration (Abu Ja'far).[83]

Counting twenty-two months from Rabi' al-Awwal 1 H we arrive at Dhu'l-Hijjah 2 H. Therefore the marriage took place on Monday, February 27th, 624 (1st Dhu'l-Hijjah 2 H).

As against this, at-Tabari maintains that the marriage was in Safar 2 H.[84] In view of Abu Ja'far's clear testimony, this report cannot be accepted as it is before both the 22 months and Badr. The other reports of Rabi' al-Awwal and Rajab 2 H as quoted by Mirkhond[85] must also be rejected on the same ground.

38. Celebration of the first 'Id al-Adha

According to Jabir ibn 'Abdallah, the first ever 'Id al-Adha was celebrated on 10th Dhu'l-Hijjah 2 H.[86] This corresponded to Wednesday, March 7th, 624.

Events of 3 H
39. Ghazwah Buhran against Bani Sulaym

Ibn Sa'd furnishes the date of this ghazwah as 6th Jumada al-Ula 3 H with the information that the Prophet ﷺ was absent from Madinah for ten nights in this expedition.[87] The date corresponds to Saturday, July 28th, 624.

Ibn Ishaq adds that in this expedition the Prophet ﷺ halted at Buhran some days of Rabi' al-Akhir and Jumada al-Ula.[88] Therefore the Prophet ﷺ apparently set out in the last days of Rabi' al-Akhir.

40. Sariyyah of Zayd ibn Harithah towards Kindah

About this expedition Ibn Sa'd furnishes the date as the 1st Jumada al-Akhirah 3 H[89] while Ibn Ishaq maintains that it was in Rabi' al-Awwal.[90]

In the third year, pagan Jumada al-Akhirah corresponded to Hijrah Rabi' al-Awwal showing that Ibn Ishaq reported his date with reference to the Hijrah calendar.

The date corresponds to Wednesday, August 22nd, 624.

As against this, Ibn Kathir, attributing to al-Waqidi, gives the date as 1st Jumada al-Ula.[91] Perhaps this was an error of al-Waqidi which Ibn Sa'd corrected.

41. The elimination of Ka'b ibn al-Ashraf

According to al-Waqidi and Ibn Sa'd, Ka'b ibn al-Ashraf, a poet and son of a Jewess of Bani Nadir, who stirred up the Quraysh in Makkah to avenge their heroes buried in the pit of Badr by elegies lamenting their fate and disquieted the Muslims in Madinah by amatory sonnets on their women, was finished by Muhammad ibn Maslamah (of the tribe Aws)[92] and his party on 14 Rabi' al-Awwal 3 H.[93] The party, who were seen off by the Prophet ﷺ up to Baqi' al-Gharqad (Ibn 'Abbas),[94] reported back to him the same night after the task.[95]

Earlier we have seen that the Prophet ﷺ had gone out from the 12th to 24th Rabi' al-Awwal for Ghazwah Dhu Amarr. Therefore he could not have been present in Madinah on 14th Rabi' al-Awwal, which indicates that the biographers' reference could not be to the pagan calendar but to the Hijrah.

14th Rabi' al-Awwal 3 AH corresponds to Tuesday, September 4, 624.

The sources stated that it was during a spring night that Ka'b and his would be assailants walked together under the brilliant moonlight for quite some time before the latter fell upon him. In September we normally get brilliant moonlight.

42. Umm Kulthum's marriage

Al-Waqidi reported that Prophet's ﷺ daughter Umm Kulthum married in Rabi' al-Awwal 3 H and consummation took place in Jumada al-Akhirah of the same year.[96]

Perhaps al-Waqidi got information from two sources – one saying that the marriage took place in Jumada al-Akhirah and the other saying that it was in Rabi' al-Awwal. As the cohabitation of the spouses may take place on a later date, as was in the case of A'ishah, he apparently believed that the marriage had taken place in Rabi' al-Awwal followed by cohabitation and consummation in Jumada al-Akhirah and reported accordingly. But it is not always necessary that the two occasions should be separated unless there was specific reason to do so. It may occur on the same day.

Our calendar tells us that in the third year the pagan Jumada al-Akhirah corresponded to Hijrah Rabi' al-Awwal. It appears that Umm

Kulthum married in Jumada al-Akhirah 3 H which corresponded to (August 21st – September 20th, 624).

43. Marriage to Hafsah

The Prophet ﷺ added Hafsah bint 'Umar to his espousal circle in Sha'ban 3 H.[97] This corresponded to (October 20th – November 18th, 624).

44. The birth of Hasan

As reported by at-Tabari, Hasan, the first issue of 'Ali and Fatimah, was born in the middle of Ramadan 3 H.[98] The date (15th Ramadan) corresponded to Sunday, December 2nd, 624.

This information reveals that exactly 280 days after the marriage (1st Dhu'l-Hijjah 2 H: February 27th, 624) Fatimah delivered her first baby which is perfectly in accord with medical science. This indirectly attests the authenticity of the two dates.

45. Marriage to Zaynab bint Khuzaymah

At-Tabari stated that the Prophet ﷺ married Zaynab bint Khuzaymah, the divorcee of Tufayl ibn al-Harith, in Ramadan 3 H[99] (November 18th – December 18th, 624).

Events of 4 H

46. Sariyyah of Abu Salamah ibn 'Abd al-Asad al-Makhzumi against Qatan

Ibn Sa'd gives the date of this expedition as 1st Muharram 4 H[100] which corresponded to Monday, April 15th, 625.

47. Betrayal at ar-Raji'

That was the tragic incident when some people of 'Adal and al-Qara came to the Prophet ﷺ and pleaded that he send some competent teachers to teach Islam to their tribe who were willing to accept the new faith. The Prophet ﷺ had sent six to ten of his Companions led by Marthad ibn Abi Marthad (or 'Asim ibn Thabit according to another narration).

On the way 'Adal and al-Qara acted treacherously. With the help of Bani Lihyan they killed the Companions near a spring called ar-Raji' except Khubayb ibn 'Adi and Zayd ibn ad-Dathinah whom they had taken to Makkah and sold to the Quraysh. They were kept there till the sacred months were over and then killed at Tan'im beyond the sacred precincts of the Ka'bah. Before his execution on the gallows Khubayb prayed: "O Allah! I have conveyed the message of Your Prophet ﷺ. Do You then convey to Your Prophet ﷺ before the morning itself what has been meted out to me."[101]

Ibn Habib dated this event around the end of Shawwal 3 H.[102] But al-Waqidi and Ibn Sa'd stated that it was an event of Safar 4 H, the 36th month after the Emigration.[103]

It appears that the people of 'Adal and al-Qara came around the end of Shawwal (December 18th, 624 – January 16th, 625) and the Prophet ﷺ sent off his Companions in Dhu'l-Qa'dah (January 16th – February 15th, 625). Khubayb was arrested and sold to the Makkans the same month but was executed in Safar 4 H (May 14th – June 13th, 625) after the sacred months (Dhu'l-Qa'dah to Muharram) were over.

48. The massacre of Bi'r Ma'unah

Full four months after Uhud, Abu Bara 'Amir Mula'ib al-Asinnah ibn Malik came to the Prophet ﷺ in Safar 4 H and suggested he send a delegation of his Companions to his people to teach them Islam. The Prophet ﷺ expressed his apprehension that the people of Najd would maltreat them, whereupon Abu Bara took the responsibility of their safety.

The Prophet ﷺ sent a delegation of 50 to 70 of his Companions with al-Mundhir ibn 'Amr as its leader. On the way at the spring of Bi'r Ma'unah, 'Amir ibn Tufayl with the help of the people of Usayyah, Ri'l and Dhakwan attacked and killed all of them except Ka'b ibn Zayd. He was left for dead and was later picked up from amongst the dead.

'Amr ibn Umayyah ad-Damri, who happened to be in that locality, witnessed the massacre. He was arrested too, but later 'Amir ibn Tufayl, the mastermind of the plot released him, after cutting off his forelocks, in fulfilment of his mother's wish to release a slave.[104] 'Amr returned to the Prophet ﷺ after walking for four days on foot. Ibn Sa'd says that the same night the Prophet ﷺ also received the news of the fate of Khubayb.[105]

Then the Prophet ﷺ sent 'Amr ibn Umayyah to Makkah on a mission as a spy. 'Amr found Khubayb's body still hanging on the gallows.

Approaching stealthily he lowered the corpse to the ground. But he was espied and was chased by the Makkans.[106]

All classical biographers without exception agree that this tragedy occurred in Safar 4 H. This corresponded to May 14th – June 13th, 625.

49. The death of Zaynab bint Khuzaymah

Only after six months of becoming the wife of the Prophet ﷺ, Zaynab is reported to have expired in Rabi' al-Awwal/Rabi' al-Akhir 4 H[107] (June 13th – July 12th, 625 /July 12th – August 11th, 625).

50. The death of Abu Salamah

Abu Salamah is recorded to have died on 8th Jumada al-Akhirah 4 H.[108] This works out to have been Tuesday, September 17th, 625.

51. The lunar eclipse

Diyarbakri recorded that there was a lunar eclipse in Jumada al-Akhirah 5 H[109] and the Jews of Madinah started beating dishes thinking that some one had cast a spell on the moon.

This appears to be an event of 4 H which Diyarbakri erroneously thought to be of 5 H. The reference must have been to the Hijrah calendar for in Jumada al-Akhirah 4 AH there was a lunar eclipse on November 19th – 20th, 625.[110]

The corresponding pagan date was 13th Sha'ban 4 H.

52. The birth of Hussein

At-Tabari did not specify the date of birth of Hussein (the second child of Fatimah), but said that it was in the beginning of Shawwal 4 H[111] while Tabrizi pinpointed it as 5th Sha'ban.[112]

In the fourth year after emigration, the pagan Shawwal corresponded to the Hijrah Sha'ban indicating that at-Tabari reported it according to the pagan calendar while Tabrizi did so according to the Hijrah.

5th Shawwal 4 H works out to be Friday, January 10th, 626.

Al-Biruni maintained that Hussein was born on 6th Ramadan.[113]

53. Marriage to Umm Salamah

The Prophet ﷺ married Umm Salamah bint Abi Umayyah, widow of Abu Salamah, in Shawwal 4 H[114] (January 6th – February 4th, 626).

Events of 5 H

54. Ghazwah Dumat al-Jandal

According to Ibn Sa'd the Prophet ﷺ set out on this expedition on 25th Rabi' al-Awwal 5 H and returned when 10 nights of Rabi' al-Akhir were still left.[115] Mirkhond says that the start was on a Monday.[116] The dates corresponded to Friday, June 27th and Monday, July 21st, 626.

The pagan calendar does not corroborate Mirkhond's weekday.

55. The deputation of Muzaynah

Ibn Sa'd narrates that the first deputation that ever called on the Prophet ﷺ was that of Mudar. Four hundred persons of Muzaynah visited him in Rajab 5 H.[117]

This corresponded to September 28th – October 28th, 626.

56. Marriage to Zaynab bint Jahsh

In Dhu'l-Qa'dah 5 H,[118] the Prophet ﷺ married Zaynab bint Jahsh after her divorce from Zayd ibn Harithah. This corresponded to January 24th – February 23rd, 627.

Anas ibn Malik reported that the ayah on the veil (Qur'an 33:59) was revealed on the day of Zaynab's marriage.[119]

57. Deputation of Ashja'

It is said that a deputation consisting of a hundred persons of Ashja' led by Mas'ud ibn Rukhaylah visited the Prophet ﷺ in 5 H after the execution of Bani Quraydah.[120]

This places it sometime in Dhu'l-Qa'dah or Dhu'l-Hijjah 5 H (January-February or February-March 627).

Events of 6 H

58. Sariyyah of Muhammad ibn Maslamah against al-Qurata

Ibn Sa'd says that this expedition set out on 10th Muharram 6 H and returned when still one day of the month was remaining.[121] The dates corresponded to Friday, April 3rd and Wednesday, April 22nd, 627.

59. The ghazwah of Bani Lihyan

There are contradictory reports about this ghazwah. Ibn Ishaq in his work (translated into Persian) says that it took place in Jumada al-Ula 6 H.[122] At-Tabari also mentions the same month.[123] As against this Ibn Sa'd maintains that it was on 1st Rabi' al-Awwal 6 H with the added information that in this occasion the Prophet ﷺ was absent from Madinah for 14 nights.[124]

If we accept Ibn Ishaq's report as correct, the Prophet's ﷺ start and return work out to have been 1st Jumada al-Ula and 15th Jumada al-Ula respectively. In that case the day (13th Jumada al-Ula) on which the Prophet ﷺ predicted the murder of the Persian Emperor Chosroe falls during this period whereas the prediction was made in Madinah.[125] The report about Jumada al-Ula cannot therefore be accepted.

It appears that Ibn Ishaq got the information that this ghazwah occurred in Rabi' al-Awwal, which he considered to be a reference to the Hijrah calendar and then converted to the corresponding pagan month. (In the sixth year, pagan Jumada al-Ula corresponded to Hijrah Rabi' al-Awwal.)

Accepting Ibn Sa'd's date, the dates of setting out and returning work out to have been Sunday, May 24th (1st Rabi' al-Awwal) and Sunday, June 7th, 627 (15th Rabi' al-Awwal).

Diyarbakri says that in another report Ibn Ishaq dated this expedition in Sha'ban 6 H.[126] It could not have been so, because for almost the whole of Sha'ban (1st to 22nd) the Prophet ﷺ was engaged in Ghazwah al-Muraysi'.

60. Ghazwah al-Ghabah (Ghazwah Dhu Qarad)

A few nights after the Prophet's ﷺ return from Bani Lihyan, 'Uyaynah ibn Hisn came down upon the plain of Ghabah in the northern side of Madinah, fell upon the milch camels of the Prophet ﷺ grazing there, drove off the whole herd, and having killed the keeper carried off his wife. On receiving the news of that the Prophet ﷺ immediately despatched Sa'd ibn Zayd and his party in pursuit of the marauders.[127] He too soon followed and reached as far as the hills of Dhu Qarad.[128]

Ibn Sa'd stated that it was in Rabi' al-Awwal 6 H and the camels were driven off on the night of Wednesday and the Prophet ﷺ returned to Madinah five days later on the Monday.[129]

If the Prophet ﷺ returned from Ghazwah Bani Lihyan on Sunday, 15th Rabi' al-Awwal, the camels had been driven off on Wednesday, June 10th (18th Rabi' al-Awwal) and he returned to Madinah on Monday, June 15th, 627 (23rd Rabi' al-Awwal).

But at-Tabari says that, according to a story narrated by Salamah ibn al-Akwa', who was the first person who noticed the movement of the offenders, it was when the Prophet ﷺ was returning from Hudaybiyyah to Madinah.[130] Apparently inferring from this narration, Bukhari says that it occurred three days before Khaybar.[131]

61. The sariyyah of 'Ukkashah ibn Mihsan al-Asadi towards al-Ghamr

Ibn Sa'd dated this sariyyah in Rabi' al-Awwal[132] while al-Waqidi put it in Rabi' al-Akhir 6 H.[133]

It appears that the expedition extended over a few days of Rabi' al-Awwal and a few days of Rabi' al-Akhir 6 H (May 22nd – July 20th, 627).

62. The sariyyah of Muhammad ibn Maslamah towards Dhu'l-Qassah

The Prophet ﷺ sent Muhammad ibn Maslamah, as is narrated by Muir, to ascertain the whereabouts of the suspected gathering of the Ghatafan tribes at Dhu'l-Qassah with the motive of driving away the herds of camels grazing there. Ibn Maslamah and his party of ten were overpowered and all his party were slain; and Ibn Maslamah himself survived having been left on the field for dead.[134]

Both al-Waqidi and Ibn Sa'd furnish the date of this sariyyah as Rabi' al-Akhir 6 H.[135] This corresponded to June 21st – July 20th, 627.

63. The sariyyah of Abu 'Ubaydah ibn al-Jarrah towards Dhu'l-Qassah

In pursuit of the marauders and to retaliate for the murder of Maslamah's party, the Prophet ﷺ sent out Abu 'Ubaydah towards Dhu'l-Qassah at the head of forty well-mounted soldiers.

Al-Waqidi and Ibn Sa'd placed the event in Rabi' al-Akhir 6 H.[136] Therefore it corresponds to the same period as that of Sariyyah Muhammad ibn Maslamah i.e. June 21st – July 20th, 627.

64. The sariyyah of Zayd ibn Harithah against Bani Sulaym at al-Jamum

Ibn Sa'd says that this expedition took place in Rabi' al-Akhir 6 H[137] which corresponded to (June 21st – July 20th, 627).

65. The sariyyah of Zayd ibn Harithah against al-'Is

Ibn Sa'd and at-Tabari agree in placing this event in Jumada al-Ula 6 H[138] which corresponded to July 20th – August 19th, 627.

66. The sariyyahs of Zayd ibn Harithah to at-Taraf and al-Hisma

In Jumada al-Akhirah 6 H[139] (August 19th – September 17th, 627), Zayd ibn Harithah undertook two expeditions – one against Bani Tha'labah at at-Taraf and the other against Bani Judham at al-Hisma.

In relation to the second, Ibn Sa'd narrates that Dihyah ibn Khalifah al-Kalbi was plundered by the people of Judham at al-Hisma when he was returning from Caesar. This occasioned the Prophet ﷺ to send Zayd with five hundred fighters for a punitive action against them.[140]

67. The sariyyah of Zayd ibn Harithah against Wadi al-Qura

Zayd ibn Harithah undertook another expedition against Wadi al-Qura in Rajab 6 H[141] (September 17th – October 17th, 627).

68. The sariyyah of 'Abd ar-Rahman ibn 'Awf to Dumat al-Jandal

In Sha'ban 6 H (October 17th – November 16th, 627) 'Abd ar-Rahman ibn 'Awf undertook an expedition towards Dumat al-Jandal.[142] This and the following expedition must have been in the later part of the month after the Prophet's ﷺ return from Ghazwah al-Muraysi'.

69. The sariyyah of 'Ali ibn Abi Talib against Bani Sa'd ibn Bakr

Ibn Sa'd and at-Tabari recorded that in Sha'ban 6 H[143] (October 17th – November 16th, 627) 'Ali ibn Abi Talib led an expedition towards Fadak against Bani Sa'd ibn Bakr.

70. The elmination of Abu Rafi'

There was a rivalry between the two tribes of Madinah, Aws and Khazraj, regarding their sincerity in the deen. Aws had eliminated Ka'b ibn al-Ashraf, who was a great enemy of the new deen, in Rabi' al-Awwal 3 AH (Jumada al-Akhirah 3 H). Khazraj sought out another enemy of the deen in the person of Abu Rafi' and eliminated him.

But causing a confusion to us, the biographers furnish different dates for this – Jumada al-Akhirah 3 H (at-Tabari),[144] Dhu'l-Hijjah 4 H (al-Waqidi)[145] and Ramadan 6 H (Ibn Sa'd).[146] At-Tabari adds that it was on the 15th of the month. However Ibn Ishaq recorded that Abu Rafi' was one of the chiefs who took a leading role in collecting the confederate forces against the Prophet ﷺ in the battle of the Trench[147] making it clear that at least up to the time of the battle of al-Khandaq Abu Rafi' was alive.

It appears that Abu Rafi' was executed in Ramadan 6 H (November 16th – December 15th, 627), more precisely on Tuesday, December 1st, 627 if at-Tabari's date is to be accepted.

71. Marriage to Juwayriyyah

In Ramadan 6 H (November 16th – December 15th, 627), the Prophet ﷺ added Juwayriyah bint al-Harith to his wives.[148] She was made captive in the Ghazwah al-Muraysi' and was the widow of Dhu'sh-Shafar ibn Musafi who was killed in the encounter.

72. The sariyyah of Zayd ibn Harithah against Umm Qirfah

Zayd set out on a mercantile expedition to Syria. But he was waylaid near Wadi al-Qura, maltreated and plundered by the Bani Fazarah. This occasioned much exasperation in Madinah. When recovered sufficiently from his injuries, Zayd was sent out with a strong force to execute retaliation upon them. Approaching stealthily, he surprised and captured the marauders' stronghold. Umm Qirfah, aunt of 'Uyaynah ibn Hisn, a lady who had gained celebrity as the mistress of this nest of robbers, was taken captive along with her daughter (Muir).

Ibn Sa'd and at-Tabari placed this expedition in Ramadan 6 H[149] which corresponded to (November 16th – December 15th, 627).

73. The sariyyah of 'Abdallah ibn Rawahah against Usayr ibn Razim

This expedition was undertaken in Shawwal 6 H[150] which corresponded to December 15th, 627 – January 14th, 628.

74. The sariyyah of Kurz ibn Jabir al-Fihri towards 'Uraniyin

Some people of the 'Uraynah tribe visited Madinah and accepted Islam. The damp climate of Madinah affected their spleens and for a cure the Prophet ﷺ bade them to join his herd of milch camels grazing in the plain south of Quba and to drink of their milk and urine. Following his advice they soon recovered; but with the returning health also the lust of plunder revived. They drove off the herd and attempted to escape. The herdsman who pursued them was seized and barbarously handled; his hands and legs were cut off, and thorny spikes thrust into his tongue and eyes till he died. In pursuit of these offenders Kurz ibn Jabir al-Fihri set out with twenty horsemen.

But the biographers furnished different dates for this expedition – Jumada al-Ula by Ibn Ishaq,[151] Jumada al-Akhirah by al-Qastalani,[152] Shawwal 6 H by al-Waqidi, Ibn Sa'd and at-Tabari.[153]

Ibn Sa'd says that by the time the offenders were brought to book, the Prophet ﷺ was at al-Ghabah.[154] Perhaps the story reaching him became mixed up with that of another such incident wherein 'Uyaynah ibn Hisn made an attempt to escape with the milch camels of the Prophet ﷺ grazing in the plain of al-Ghabah.

In view of the conflicting reports, it is difficult to decide the true date of this sariyyah.

As punishment, the offenders' hands and feet were amputated, eyes extracted and then they were crucified. Then descended the ayah:

The reprisal against those who wage war on Allah and His Messenger, and go about the earth corrupting it, is that they should be killed or crucified, or have their alternate hands and feet cut off, or be banished from the land. That will be their degradation in the dunya and in the akhira they will have a terrible punishment, except for those who make tawba before you gain power over them. Know that Allah is Ever-Forgiving, Most Merciful. (5: 33-34)

After that the Prophet ﷺ did not extract anyone's eyes.[155]

75. A solar eclipse

Alvi says that there are reports from many biographers that there was a solar eclipse in the year of Hudaybiyyah, apparently after the treaty. He also says that Cunningham had located one eclipse on April 10th, 628.[156] This date corresponds to 29th Dhu'l-Hijjah (*Nasi*) 6 H.

Events of 7 H

76. Letters to rulers

By the close of the sixth year, the Prophet ﷺ thought of inviting neighbouring rulers to Islam and sent out a number of emissaries carrying letters addressed to them.

At-Tabari reports that it was in Dhu'l-Hijjah 6 H that he wrote to Heraclius, the Byzantine Emperor; al-Harith, the Prince of Bani Ghassan; Chosroe, the Persian Emperor; al-Muqawqis, the Byzantine Governor of Egypt; Negus, the King of Abyssinia; and Hawdhah, the Chief of Bani Hanifah in Yamamah.[157] But Ibn Sa'd gives the date as Muharram 7 H.[158]

Now in the pagan-Hijrah concordance, Muharram 7 H corresponded to Dhu'l-Hijjah 6 AH (April 11th – May 11th, 628). It appears that Ibn Sa'd reported the event in the pagan calendar and at-Tabari in the Hijrah.

77. The return of Zaynab

Al-Waqidi stated that in fulfilment of the conditions agreed in the treaty of Hudaybiyyah, in Muharram 7 H[159] (April 11th – May 11th, 628) the Prophet ﷺ returned his daughter Zaynab to her husband Abu'l-'As who was still a pagan.

78. Ghazwah Khaybar

Ibn Ishaq and at-Tabari dated this expedition as Muharram 7 H.[160] According to Ibn Sa'd it was in Jumada al-Ula 7 H.[161] We shall have to look deeper to resolve this contradiction.

In the narration we find an indication of the season of the expedition. Anas stated that when the Muslims raided Khaybar in the morning, the Jews had already come out from their houses for the day's work with their shovels, date-baskets and asses.[162] This indicates that it was in the season of collecting ripe dates. Elsewhere we have discussed that in Arabia dates are plucked in August. Now we are to see which one of the reports come closer to it. Muharram corresponded to April-May while Jumada al-Ula corresponded to August-September falling exactly in the season. The expedition was undertaken in Jumada al-Ula 7 H (August 7th – September 5th, 628).

It was on this occasion that the Prophet ﷺ married Safiyyah, widow of Kinanah[163] and that a woman of Khaybar named Zaynab offered poisoned meat to the Prophet[164] ﷺ from the after-effects of which he later suffered a lot.

Ibn Hisham says that the first missed prayer (*qada*) was offered while returning from this expedition.[165]

79. The deputation of Ash'aris

Ibn Sa'd stated that the Ash'aris came to the Prophet ﷺ in a group of fifty persons including Abu Musa and two members of the 'Akk tribe when the Prophet ﷺ was on his way to Khaybar.[166]

As the expedition to Khaybar was undertaken in Jumada al-Ula 7 H, the party's arrival must have been in the same month. It corresponded with August-September 628.

80. The sariyyahs of 'Umar ibn al-Khattab, Abu Bakr as-Siddiq and Bashir ibn Sa'd al-Ansari

In Sha'ban 7 H (November 3rd – December 4th, 628) three expeditions set out – one led by 'Umar against Turabah, the second by Abu Bakr against Bani Kilab at Najd[167] and the third by Bashir Ibn Sa'd towards Fadak.[168]

81. The sariyyah of Ghalib ibn 'Abdallah al-Laythi towards Mayfa'ah

In Ramadan 7 H (December 4th, 628 – January 2nd, 629) Ghalib ibn 'Abdallah al-Laythi led a sariyyah to Mayfa'ah.[169]

82. The sariyyah of Bashir ibn Sa'd al-Ansari

Bashir ibn Sa'd al-Ansari undertook an expedition towards al-Yaman and Jamar in Shawwal 7 H[170] (January 2nd – February 1st, 629).

83. The sariyyah of Ibn Abi'l-Awja as-Sulami

According to al-Waqidi, Ibn Abi al-Awja as-Sulami undertook a sariyyah against Bani Sulaym in Dhu'l-Qa'dah 7 H.[171] But Ibn Sa'd says that this was in Dhu'l-Hijjah 7 H and the return was on 1st Safar 8 H.[172] Now in the seventh year, pagan Dhu'l-Hijjah corresponded to Hijrah Dhu'l-Qa'dah. Perhaps al-Waqidi reported with reference to the Hijrah calendar.

The return was on Sunday, April 30th, 629 (1st Safar 8 H).

EVENTS OF 8 H

84. Sariyyah of Ghalib ibn 'Abdallah al-Laythi

In Safar 8 H (April 30th – May 30th, 629) Ghalib ibn 'Abdallah al-Laythi undertook two expeditions – one against Bani al-Mulawwih at al-Kadid[173] and the other against Bani Murrah towards Fadak.[174]

85. Sariyyahs of Shuja ibn Wahb al-Asadi and Ka'b ibn 'Umayr al-Ghifari

In Rabi' al-Awwal 8 H (May 30th – June 29th, 629) two expeditions set out – one led by Shuja ibn Wahb al-Asadi against Bani 'Amir at as-Siyyi[175] and the other by Ka'b ibn 'Umayr al-Ghifari towards Dhat Atlah beyond Wadi al-Qura.[176]

86. The sariyyah of Zayd ibn Harithah to Mu'tah

The expedition to Mu'tah was led by Zayd ibn Harithah in Jumada al-Ula 8 H[177] (July 29th – August 27th, 629).

87. The sariyyah of 'Amr ibn al-'As towards Dhat as-Salasil

Ibn Sa'd and at-Tabari reported that in Jumada al-Akhirah 8 H (August 27th – September 25th, 629) 'Amr ibn al-'As led an expedition towards Dhat as-Salasil beyond Wadi al-Qura.[178] It is also said that it was in an extremely cold weather.[179] But the pagan calendar does not disclose cold weather against this month.

There are contradictory reports about 'Amr's coming to the Prophet ﷺ. According to at-Tabari he came in the beginning of Safar 8 H.[180] In contradiction, Ibn Hisham maintains, quoting 'Amr's own narration, that he came to the Prophet ﷺ a few days before the capture of Makka[181] indicating that his coming might have been in Sha'ban. If this was correct, 'Amr could not have undertaken the expedition in Jumada al-Akhirah as he had not yet joined the Prophet ﷺ then. If we are to believe the report about the weather it looks like to have been undertaken in Sha'ban (October – November 629).

88. The sariyyah Sif al-Bahr

According to al-Waqidi and Ibn Sa'd, Abu 'Ubaydah ibn al-Jarrah undertook an expedition at al-Khabt in Rajab 8 H[182] (September 25th – October 24th, 629). It was recorded to be the occasion of eating of a dead whale when the party ran short of provisions.[183]

Another story says that al-Khabt was not the name of a place but was the leaves of a thorny desert plant known as Salam and for some days the party lived on these leaves.

89. The sariyyah of Abu Qatadah ibn Rib'i al-Ansari towards Khudrah in the territory of Muharib

Ibn Sa'd and at-Tabari dated this expedition in Sha'ban 8 H[184] (October 24th – November 23rd, 629). Ibn Sa'd added that in this expedition Abu Qatadah was absent from Madinah for 15 nights.

90. The sariyyahs of 'Amr ibn al-'As, Hisham ibn al-'As, Khalid ibn Sa'id, Abu Qatadah, Sa'd ibn Zayd al-Ashhali and Khalid ibn al-Walid

'Amr ibn al-'As, Hisham ibn al-'As and Khalid ibn Sa'id undertook one sariyyah each in Ramadan 8 H (November 23rd – December 23rd, 629). 'Amr's expedition was against Suwa' while Hisham and Khalid respectively headed for the destinations of Yalamlam and 'Uranah.[185]

In addition the following three expeditions had been undertaken in the same month.

| Sariyyah Abu Qatadah ibn Rib'i al-Ansari towards Batn Idam | **1 RMD**[186] (Friday, November 24, 629) |

It was on this occasion that the following Qur'anic ayah descended: **You who have iman! when you go out to fight in the Way of Allah verify things carefully. Do not say, 'You are not a mumin', to some-**

one who greets you as a Muslim, simply out of desire for the goods of this world. With Allah there is booty in abundance. ... Allah is aware of what you do. (4:94)

| Sariyyah Sa'd ibn Zayd al-Ashhali against Manat | Start | 18 RMD[188] | (Monday, December 11, 629) |
| Sariyyah Sa'd ibn Zayd al-Ashhali against Manat | Return | 24 RMD[189] | (Sunday, December 17, 629) |

Sariyyah Khalid ibn al-Walid against al-'Uzza at Nakhlah   25 RMD[190] (Monday, December 18, 629)

91. The sariyyahs of Khalid ibn al-Walid and Tufayl ibn 'Amr ad-Dawsi

In Shawwal 8 H (December 23rd, 629 – January 21st, 630) Khalid ibn al-Walid and Tufayl ibn 'Amr ad-Dawsi undertook expeditions respectively against Bani Jadhimah[191] and Dhu'l-Kaffayn.[192]

The date on which Khalid set out for this expedition is stated to be the Day of Procyon (the brightest star in the constellation *Canis Minor*).[193]

92. The ghazwah of Ta'if

Bukhari says on the authority of Musa ibn 'Uqbah that this ghazwah occurred in Shawwal 8 H.[194] Ibn Sa'd also gives the same period and says that the siege continued for 18 days.[195]

Since this ghazwah was a sequel to Ghazwah Hunayn which took place in Shawwal, it must have been an event of the latter part of Shawwal (December 23rd, 629 – January 21st, 630).

93. Marriage to Fatimah bint ad-Dahhak

Abu Dukhbarat as-Sa'di narrates that the Prophet ﷺ married Fatimah bint ad-Dahhak ibn Sufyan al-Kilabi in the month of Dhu'l-Qa'dah 8 H[196] (January 21st – February 20th, 630).

94. The letter to Jayfar

Ibn Sa'd recorded that in Dhu'l-Qa'dah 8 H[197] (January 21st – February 20th, 630) the Prophet ﷺ wrote a letter to Jayfar, the ruler of Uman inviting him to Islam.

95. The sariyyah of Qays ibn Sa'd

Ibn Sa'd narrates that when the Prophet ﷺ returned from al-Ji'ranah in

8 H he sent Qays Ibn Sa'd ibn 'Ubadah to al-Yaman to devastate Suda.[198]

With four hundred warriors Qays encamped in the suburbs of Qanat when a resident of Suda named Ziyad ibn al-Harith happened to meet them. On learning the motive of the army he hastened to the Prophet ﷺ and entreated withdrawal of the force. The Prophet ﷺ ordered its withdrawal. Shortly thereafter a deputation of fifteen persons of Suda visited the Prophet ﷺ and embraced Islam.

As the Prophet ﷺ returned from Ji'ranah around the end of Dhu'l-Qa'dah this must have been an expedition of Dhu'l-Hijjah 8 H (February-March 630).

Events of 9 H

96. The first zakat collections

Ibn Sa'd stated that the Prophet ﷺ sent out the first zakat collectors on 1st Muharram 9 H.[199] He mentioned eight collectors in all. The date corresponded to Thursday, March 22nd, 630.

The Prophet ﷺ sent al-Walid ibn 'Uqbah to Bani al-Mustaliq who had already embraced Islam and built mosques. On hearing of al-Walid's arrival, twenty of their men came out to welcome him. Al-Walid misunderstood their motive and forthwith returned to Madinah and told the Prophet ﷺ that they confronted him with arms. No sooner had the Prophet ﷺ taken a decision to send a force against them than the party who encountered al-Walid arrived and apprised the Prophet ﷺ of the true position. Thereupon descended the ayah:[200]

> You who have iman! if a deviator brings you a report, scrutinize it carefully in case you attack people in ignorance and so come to greatly regret what you have done. (49:6)

97. The sariyyah 'Uyaynah ibn Badr al-Fazari

To Bani Ka'b the Prophet ﷺ sent Bishr ibn Sufyan. The people were ready to pay the zakat. But Bani Tamim obstructed the collection. Bishr returned and reported the matter to the Prophet ﷺ. The Prophet ﷺ sent 'Uyaynah with fifty horsemen[201] in Muharram 9 H.[202]

Some people of Banim Tamim were grazing their cattle at as-Suqya.

On seeing 'Uyaynah's party they fled leaving their women and children. 'Uyaynah captured 11 men, 11 women and 30 children, brought them to Madinah and kept them imprisoned in a house. Then several of their chiefs arrived at Madinah to seek their release. On seeing them the women and children began to weep. The chiefs hurried to the door of the Prophet ﷺ and called loudly for him to come out.

It was with reference to these people that the following ayah descended:[203]

> As for those who call out to you from outside your private quarters, most of them do not use their intellect. If they had only been patient until you came out to them, it would have been better for them. But Allah is Ever-Forgiving, Most Merciful. (49:4,5)

The period corresponded to (March 21st – April 20th, 630).

98. The sariyyah of Qutbah ibn 'Amir

Against Khath'am, Qutbah ibn 'Amir ibn Hadidah undertook an expedition in Safar 9 H[204] (April 20th – May 20th, 630).

99. The sariyyahs of 'Ali ibn Abi Talib and ad-Dahhak ibn Sufyan al-Kilabi

In Rabi' al-Awwal 9 H (May 20th – June 18th, 630) 'Ali ibn Abi Talib led an expedition at Tayy[205] and ad-Dahhak ibn Sufyan al-Kilabi against Bani Kilab.[206]

100. The deputation of Bani Kilab

Ibn Sa'd says that thirteen persons of Bani Kilab called on the Prophet ﷺ in 9 H. They informed him that ad-Dahhak ibn Sufyan had invited them to Islam with the Book of Allah and the Sunnah of the Prophet ﷺ.[207]

As ad-Dahhak undertook the expedition to Bani Kilab in Rabi' al-Awwal 9 H (May-June 630), the visit of the delegation must have been after that.

101. The sariyyahs of 'Alqamah ibn Mujazziz, 'Ali ibn Abi Talib and 'Ukkashah ibn Mihsan

In Rabi' al-Akhir 9 H (June 18th – July 17th, 630) three expeditions were undertaken – one by 'Alqamah ibn Mujazziz al-Mudliji against al-Habashah,[208] the second by 'Ali ibn Abi Talib against the idol of al-Fuls[209] and the third by 'Ukkashah ibn Mihsan al-Asadi against al-Jinab.[210]

102. The death of the Negus and the sariyyah of Khalid ibn al-Walid

In Rajab 9 H[211] (September 14th – October 14th, 630) the Negus (Ashamah ibn Bahr),[212] the Abyssinian ruler, expired and while still at Tabuk the Prophet ﷺ sent out Khalid ibn al-Walid for an expedition against Ukaydir ibn 'Abd al-Malik at Dumat al-Jandal.[213]

103. The death of Umm Kulthum

The Prophet's ﷺ daughter Umm Kulthum passed away in Sha'ban 9 H[214] (October 14th – November 13th, 630).

104. The death of 'Abdallah ibn Ubayy

In Dhu'l-Qa'dah 9 H[215] (January 11th – February 13th, 631) the hypocrite 'Abdallah ibn Ubayy died and the Prophet ﷺ said his funeral prayers whereupon descended the ayah:[216]

> Never pray over any of them who die or stand at their graves. They rejected Allah and His Messenger and died as deviators. (9:84)

105. Abu Bakr's Hajj

In Dhu'l-Hijjah 9 H (February 9th – March 11th, 631) Abu Bakr led the Hajj.[217] It was on this occasion that the ayat of Immunity (9:1-6) were announced on Yawm an-Nahr, the day of sacrifice, which corresponded to 10th Dhu'l-Hijjah 9 H (Tuesday, February 19th, 631). The command allowed the polytheists four months in which to leave Makkah from the day of its declaration up to 10th Rabi' al-Awwal 10 H[218] (June 17th, 631).

106. The deputation of Bani Asad

Ibn Sa'd narrates that a delegation consisting of ten persons of Bani Asad visited the Prophet ﷺ in 9 H. One of the delegates (Hadrami ibn 'Amir) said to the Prophet ﷺ: "We came to you travelling in dark nights in a year of drought although you never sent a force against us." Thereupon descended the ayah:[219]

"They think they have done you a favour by becoming Muslims! Say: 'Do not consider your Islam a favour to me. No indeed! It is Allah who has favoured you by guiding you to iman if you are telling the truth.'" (49:17)

This places the revelation of this verse in 9 H (March 630 - March 631)

Events of 10 H

107. The sariyyah of Khalid ibn al-Walid against Bani al-Harith

In the early part of 10 H, the Prophet ﷺ sent Khalid ibn al-Walid in an expedition against Bani 'Abd al-Madan – in Rabi' al-Awwal according to Ibn Sa'd.[220] But it was in Rabi' al-Awwal, Rabi' al-Akhir or Jumada al-Ula according to at-Tabari.[221] These corresponded to June-July, July-August or August-September 631.

The people readily accepted Islam, and Khalid informed the Prophet ﷺ about this. The Prophet ﷺ wrote to Khalid to come with a deputation of their people. After staying some time in Madinah, the delegates returned to their people before the end of Shawwal (January 631).

108. The sariyyah of of 'Ali ibn Abi Talib against al-Yaman

'Ali undertook this expedition in Ramadan 10 H[222] (December 1 - 30, 631).

Initially the people refused to join the fold of Islam and fought with the raiders. After losing twenty of their men in the fight they decided to accept the deen. Bringing the sadaqat due from them, 'Ali joined the Prophet ﷺ at Makkah in the Farewell Hajj.

109. Visit of the Christian delegation of Najran

Ibn Sa'd narrates that in response to the Prophet's ﷺ letter to the people of Najran, a deputation of 14 Christian nobles called on the Prophet ﷺ. He invited them to accept Islam. There was a difference of opinion about the nature of 'Isa and there ensued a long argument. Quoting ayat from the Qur'an, the Prophet ﷺ endeavoured to convince them that 'Isa was not God, but a man and a prophet. Finding them sticking tenaciously to their false concept, he finally invited them to a contest in accordance with the divine ayah:

> If anyone argues with you about him after the knowledge that has come to you, say, 'Come then! Let us summon our sons and your sons, our women and your women, ourselves and yourselves. Then let us make earnest supplication and call down the curse of Allah upon the liars.' (3:61)

On receiving the challenge they retired. The next morning they turned up and said: We do not think it proper to curse each other.[223]

Al-Biruni stated that the argumentation took place on 4th Shawwal 10 H.[224] This fixes the date of the event and revelation of this ayah. It corresponded to Friday, January 3rd, 632.

110. The sariyyah of of Jarir ibn 'Abdallah

Ibn Sa'd narrates that Jarir ibn 'Abdallah came to the Prophet ﷺ in 10 H with one hundred and fifty of his people and embraced Islam. The Prophet ﷺ enquired of him about Dhu'l-Khalasah. He replied that it was still there. Then the Prophet ﷺ sent him to destroy it. Not long after, Jarir returned after destroying it.[225]

Jarir narrated that Dhu al-Khalasah was a house in Yemen called al-Ka'bah al-Yamaniyah where people used to worship idols.[226]

Although it occurred in 10 H (April 631 - March 632), the month was not stated.

Events of 11 H

111. The deputation of an-Nakha'

Ibn Sa'd narrates that the last deputation that called on the Prophet ﷺ was that of an-Nakha'. They came from al-Yaman in the middle of Muharram 11 H and were two hundred in number.[227]

This corresponded to April 632.

Notes

1. *Mishkat*, Vol 3, p 306
2. Ibn Hisham: *as-Sirah*, Vol 1, p 189
3. Ibn Hisham: *as-Sirah*, Vol 1, p 190; Ibn Sa'd: *at-Tabaqat*, Vol 1, p 132; at-Tabari: *at-Tarikh*, Vol 1, p 58
4. Ibn Sa'd: *at-Tabaqat*, Vol 1, pp 134, 174
5. Ibn Hisham: *as-Sirah*, Vol 1, p 208
6. Ibn Sa'd: *at-Tabaqat*, Vol 1, p 144
7. Ibn Hisham: *as-Sirah*, Vol 1, p 210; Ibn Sa'd: *at-Tabaqat*, Vol 1, p 143
8. Ibn Sa'd: *at-Tabaqat*, Vol 1, p 144
9. Ibn Hisham: *as-Sirah*, Vol 1, p 211
10. Mirkhond: *Rawzatus Safa*, Pt II, p 779
11. Sachau: *Chronology*, pp 329, 330
12. at-Tabari: *at-Tarikh*, Vol 1, pp 83, 85
13. Mirkhond: *Rawzatus Safa*, Pt II, p 780
14. Sachau: *Chronology*, p 329
15. Mirkhond: *Rawzatus Safa*, Pt II, p 782
16. Bukhari, Vol 6, p 277
17. Mishkat, Vol 3, p 407
18. Ibn Hisham: *as-Sirah*, Vol 1, p 216; at-Tabari: *at-Tarikh*, Vol 1, p 63
19. *Mishkat*, Vol 3, p 390
20. Bukhari, Vol 7, p 65
21. Bukhari, Vol 6, p 370
22. at-Tabari: *at-Tarikh*, Vol 1, p 492
23. at-Tabari: *at-Tarikh*, Vol 1, p 492
24. Bukhari, Vol 1, p 276
25. Bukhari, Vol 5, p 98
26. at-Tabari: *at-Tarikh*, Vol 2, p 250
27. *Mishkat*, Vol 3, pp 300, 301
28. Ibn Sa'd: *at-Tabaqat*, Vol 1, p 236
29. Ibn Sa'd: *at-Tabaqat*, Vol 1, p 239
30. Ibn Sa'd: *at-Tabaqat*, Vol 1, pp 237, 238
31. Ibn Sa'd: *at-Tabaqat*, Vol 1, p 247
32. Sachau: *Chronology*, p 329
33. Margoliouth: *Rise*, p 162; Maududi: *Sarware Alam*, Vol 2, p 612
34. Ibn Sa'd: *at-Tabaqat*, Vol 1, p 241
35. Ibn Sa'd: *at-Tabaqat*, Vol 1, p 243
36. Sachau: *Chronology*, p 330
37. Ibn Sa'd: *at-Tabaqat*, Vol 1, pp 139, 243
38. Ibn Sa'd: *at-Tabaqat*, Vol 1, p 139
39. Sachau: *Chronology*, p 332
40. Ibn Sa'd: *at-Tabaqat*, Vol 1, p 138
41. Ibn Sa'd: *at-Tabaqat*, Vol 1, p 137
42. Ibn Sa'd: *at-Tabaqat*, Vol 1, p 244; Muslim, Vol 3, p 988 f
43. Ibn Sa'd: *at-Tabaqat*, Vol 1, p 245
44. Mirkhond: *Rawzatus Safa*, Pt II, pp 219, 220
45. Mirkhond: *Rawzatus Safa*, Pt II, p 222
46. Muslim, Vol 2, pp 716, 717
47. Bukhari, Vol 8, p 22
48. Mirkhond: *Rawzatus Safa*, Pt II, p 226
49. at-Tabari: *at-Tarikh*, Vol 1, p 123
50. Ibn Hisham: *as-Sirah*, Vol 1, p 269
51. at-Tabari: *at-Tarikh*, Vol 1, p 147
52. at-Tabari: *at-Tarikh*, Vol 1, p 148
53. Ibn Hisham: *as-Sirah*, Vol 1, p 789
54. Ibn Sa'd: *at-Tabaqat*, Vol 2, p 2
55. at-Tabari: *at-Tarikh*, Vol 1, p 148
56. Ibn Sa'd: *at-Tabaqat*, Vol 2, p 3
57. Ibn Hisham: *as-Sirah*, Vol 1, p 686
58. Ibn Sa'd: *at-Tabaqat*, Vol 2, p 4; at-Tabari: *at-Tarikh*, Vol 1, p 149
59. Ibn Hisham: *as-Sirah*, Vol 1, p 693
60. Burhan, Sep 1964, p 137
61. Bukhari, Vol 5, p 195
62. Bukhari, Vol 5, p 195

63. Ibn Hisham: *as-Sirah*, Vol 1, p 681; Ibn Sa'd: *at-Tabaqat*, Vol 2, p 5; Bukhari, Vol 5, p 195; Burhan, May 1964, p 287
64. Burhan, Oct 1964, pp 212, 213
65. Ibn Sa'd: *at-Tabaqat*, Vol 2, p 7
66. Ibn Hisham: *as-Sirah*, Vol 1, p 695
67. at-Tabari: *at-Tarikh*, Vol 1, pp 154, 157
68. Mirkhond: *Rawzatus Safa*, Pt II, p 279
69. Ibn Hisham: *as-Sirah*, Vol 1, p 696
70. Ibn Hisham: *as-Sirah*, Vol 1, p 696
71. Ibn Sa'd: *at-Tabaqat*, Vol 1, p 284; at-Tabari: *at-Tarikh*, Vol 1, p 158
72. Ibn Sa'd: *at-Tabaqat*, Vol 2, p 30
73. Margoliouth: Rise, pp 278, 279
74. at-Tabari: *at-Tarikh*, Vol 1, p 159
75. Ibn Sa'd: *at-Tabaqat*, Vol 2, p 31; Burhan, May 1964, p 274
76. Ibn Sa'd: *at-Tabaqat*, Vol 2, p 31
77. at-Tabari: *at-Tarikh*, Vol 1, p 146
78. at-Tabari: *at-Tarikh*, Vol 1, p 147
79. Maududi: *Sarware Alam*, Vol 2, p 629
80. at-Tabari: *at-Tarikh*, Vol 1, p 147
81. Bukhari, Vol 5, p 226
82. Sachau: *Chronology*, p 332
83. at-Tabari: *at-Tarikh*, Vol 1, p 211
84. at-Tabari: *at-Tarikh*, Vol 1, p 153
85. Mirkhond: *Rawzatus Safa*, Pt II, p 273
86. at-Tabari: *at-Tarikh*, Vol 1, p 208
87. Ibn Sa'd: *at-Tabaqat*, Vol 2, p 41
88. Ibn Hisham: *as-Sirah*, Vol 2, p 23
89. Ibn Sa'd: *at-Tabaqat*, Vol 2, p 41
90. Burhan, Nov 1964, p 262
91. Burhan, Sep 1964, p 137
92. Ibn Hisham: *as-Sirah*, Vol 2, p 327
93. Ibn Sa'd: *at-Tabaqat*, Vol 2, p 35; Burhan, Sep 1964, p 138
94. Ibn Hisham: *as-Sirah*, Vol 2, p 35
95. Ibn Hisham: *as-Sirah*, Vol 2, p 36; Bukhari, Vol 5, p 250
96. at-Tabari: *at-Tarikh*, Vol 1, p 215
97. at-Tabari: *at-Tarikh*, Vol 1, p 222
98. at-Tabari: *at-Tarikh*, Vol 1, p 252
99. at-Tabari: *at-Tarikh*, Vol 1, pp 259, 260
100. Ibn Sa'd: *at-Tabaqat*, Vol 2, p 59
101. Ibn Hisham: *as-Sirah*, Vol 2, p 194
102. Burhan, Aug 1964, p 81
103. Ibn Sa'd: *at-Tabaqat*, Vol 2, p 66; Burhan, Aug 1964, p 85
104. Ibn Hisham: *as-Sirah*, Vol 2, p 210; Ibn Sa'd: *at-Tabaqat*, Vol 2, p 62; at-Tabari: *at-Tarikh*, Vol 1, p 261
105. Ibn Sa'd: *at-Tabaqat*, Vol 2, p 62
106. at-Tabari: *at-Tarikh*, Vol 1, p 256
107. Naeem Siddiqi: *The Benefactor*, p 269; Zakaria: *Sahabah*, p 191
108. Zakaria: *Sahabah*, p 182
109. Burhan, May 1964, p 282
110. Margoliouth: *Rise*, p xvi
111. at-Tabari: *at-Tarikh*, Vol 1, p 268
112. Mishkat, Vol 3, p 320
113. Sachau: *Chronology*, p 330
114. at-Tabari: *at-Tarikh*, Vol 1, p 273
115. Ibn Sa'd: *at-Tabaqat*, Vol 2, p 76
116. Mirkhond: *Rawzatus Safa*, Pt II, p 426
117. Ibn Sa'd: *at-Tabaqat*, Vol 1, p 345
118. Mirkhond: *Rawzatus Safa*, Pt II, p 773
119. Bukhari, Vol 7, p 71
120. Ibn Sa'd: *at-Tabaqat*, Vol 1, p 362
121. Ibn Sa'd: *at-Tabaqat*, Vol 2, pp 96, 97
122. Burhan, Sep 1964, p 142
123. at-Tabari: *at-Tarikh*, Vol 1, p 305
124. Ibn Sa'd: *at-Tabaqat*, Vol 2, pp 97, 98
125. at-Tabari: *at-Tarikh*, Vol 1, p 355
126. Burhan, Sep 1964, p 142
127. Ibn Hisham: *as-Sirah*, Vol 2, p 336; at-Tabari: *at-Tarikh*, Vol 1, pp 305, 309
128. Ibn Hisham: *as-Sirah*, Vol 2, p 338; at-Tabari: *at-Tarikh*, Vol 1, p 311
129. Ibn Sa'd: *at-Tabaqat*, Vol 2, pp 99, 101
130. at-Tabari: *at-Tarikh*, Vol 1, p 306
131. Bukhari, Vol 5, p 355
132. Ibn Sa'd: *at-Tabaqat*, Vol 2, p 104
133. at-Tabari: *at-Tarikh*, Vol 1, p 341
134. Muir: *Life*, p 343

135 Ibn Sa'd: *at-Tabaqat*, Vol 2, p 105; Burhan, Sep 1964, p 136
136 Ibn Sa'd: *at-Tabaqat*, Vol 2, p 106; at-Tabari: *at-Tarikh*, Vol 1, p 341
137 Ibn Sa'd: *at-Tabaqat*, Vol 2, p 106
138 Ibn Sa'd: *at-Tabaqat*, Vol 2, p 107; at-Tabari: *at-Tarikh*, Vol 1, p 341
139 Ibn Sa'd: *at-Tabaqat*, Vol 2, p 108; at-Tabari: *at-Tarikh*, Vol 1, pp 341, 342
140 Ibn Sa'd: *at-Tabaqat*, Vol 2, p 108
141 Ibn Sa'd: *at-Tabaqat*, Vol 2, p 109; at-Tabari: *at-Tarikh*, Vol 1, p 342
142 Ibn Sa'd: *at-Tabaqat*, Vol 2, p 110; at-Tabari: *at-Tarikh*, Vol 1, p 342
143 Ibn Sa'd: *at-Tabaqat*, Vol 2, p 111; at-Tabari: *at-Tarikh*, Vol 1, p 342
144 at-Tabari: *at-Tarikh*, Vol 1, p 217
145 at-Tabari: *at-Tarikh*, Vol 1, p 218
146 Ibn Sa'd: *at-Tabaqat*, Vol 2, p 112
147 Ibn Hisham: *as-Sirah*, Vol 2, p 327
148 Mirkhond: *Rawzatus Safa*, Pt II, p 774
149 Ibn Sa'd: *at-Tabaqat*, Vol 2, p 111; at-Tabari: *at-Tarikh*, Vol 1, p 342
150 Ibn Sa'd: *at-Tabaqat*, Vol 2, p 113
151 Burhan, Aug 1964, p 82
152 Burhan, May 1964, p 287
153 Ibn Sa'd: *at-Tabaqat*, Vol 2, p 115; at-Tabari: *at-Tarikh*, Vol 1, p 344; Burhan, May 1964, pp 286, 287; Aug 1964, p 82
154 Muir: *Life*, p 350
155 Ibn Sa'd: *at-Tabaqat*, Vol 2, p 115
156 Burhan, Nov 1964, p 285
157 at-Tabari: *at-Tarikh*, Vol 1, p 345
158 Ibn Sa'd: *at-Tabaqat*, Vol 1, p 305
159 at-Tabari: *at-Tarikh*, Vol 1, p 367
160 Ibn Hisham: *as-Sirah*, Vol 2, p 392; at-Tabari: *at-Tarikh*, Vol 1, p 357
161 Ibn Sa'd: *at-Tabaqat*, Vol 2, p 131
162 Ibn Sa'd: *at-Tabaqat*, Vol 2, p 136
163 Ibn Hisham: *as-Sirah*, Vol 2, p 402
164 Ibn Hisham: *as-Sirah*, Vol 2, p 404
165 Ibn Hisham: *as-Sirah*, Vol 2, p 406
166 Ibn Sa'd: *at-Tabaqat*, Vol 1, p 409
167 Ibn Sa'd: *at-Tabaqat*, Vol 2, p 146; at-Tabari: *at-Tarikh*, Vol 1, p 368
168 Ibn Sa'd: *at-Tabaqat*, Vol 2, p 147; at-Tabari: *at-Tarikh*, Vol 1, p 368
169 Ibn Sa'd: *at-Tabaqat*, Vol 2, p 148; at-Tabari: *at-Tarikh*, Vol 1, p 368
170 Ibn Sa'd: *at-Tabaqat*, Vol 2, p 149; at-Tabari: *at-Tarikh*, Vol 1, p 368
171 at-Tabari: *at-Tarikh*, Vol 1, p 371
172 Ibn Sa'd: *at-Tabaqat*, Vol 2, p 153
173 Ibn Sa'd: *at-Tabaqat*, Vol 2, p 154; at-Tabari: *at-Tarikh*, Vol 1, p 372
174 Ibn Sa'd: *at-Tabaqat*, Vol 2, p 156
175 Ibn Sa'd: *at-Tabaqat*, Vol 2, p 157; at-Tabari: *at-Tarikh*, Vol 1, p 374
176 Ibn Sa'd: *at-Tabaqat*, Vol 2, p 158
177 Ibn Hisham: *as-Sirah*, Vol 2, p 437; Ibn Sa'd: *at-Tabaqat*, Vol 2, p 158; at-Tabari: *at-Tarikh*, Vol 1, p 380
178 Ibn Sa'd: *at-Tabaqat*, Vol 2, p 162; at-Tabari: *at-Tarikh*, Vol 1, p 376
179 Burhan, May 1964, p 275
180 at-Tabari: *at-Tarikh*, Vol 1, p 374
181 Ibn Hisham: *as-Sirah*, Vol 2, p 331
182 Ibn Sa'd: *at-Tabaqat*, Vol 2, p 163; at-Tabari: *at-Tarikh*, Vol 1, p 377
183 Ibn Sa'd: *at-Tabaqat*, Vol 2, p 163; Bukhari, Vol 7, pp 293, 294
184 Ibn Sa'd: *at-Tabaqat*, Vol 2, p 164; at-Tabari: *at-Tarikh*, Vol 1, p 378
185 Ibn Sa'd: *at-Tabaqat*, Vol 2, p 180; Watt: *Muhammad at Madinah*, p 342
186 Ibn Sa'd: *at-Tabaqat*, Vol 2, p 164
187 Ibn Sa'd: *at-Tabaqat*, Vol 2, p 165
188 Ibn Sa'd: *at-Tabaqat*, Vol 2, p 181
189 Ibn Sa'd: *at-Tabaqat*, Vol 2, p 182
190 Ibn Sa'd: *at-Tabaqat*, Vol 2, p 180; at-Tabari: *at-Tarikh*, Vol 1, p 404
191 Ibn Sa'd: *at-Tabaqat*, Vol 2, p 182
192 Ibn Sa'd: *at-Tabaqat*, Vol 2, p 194
193 Ibn Sa'd: *at-Tabaqat*, Vol 2, p 182
194 Bukhari, Vol 5, p 428
195 Ibn Sa'd: *at-Tabaqat*, Vol 2, pp 195, 196
196 at-Tabari: *at-Tarikh*, Vol 1, p 430

[197] Ibn Sa'd: *at-Tabaqat*, Vol 1, p 309
[198] Ibn Sa'd: *at-Tabaqat*, Vol 1, pp 384, 385
[199] Ibn Sa'd: *at-Tabaqat*, Vol 2, p 198
[200] Ibn Sa'd: *at-Tabaqat*, Vol 2, p 200
[201] Ibn Sa'd: *at-Tabaqat*, Vol 1, p 348
[202] Ibn Sa'd: *at-Tabaqat*, Vol 2, p 198
[203] Ibn Sa'd: *at-Tabaqat*, Vol 2, p 199
[204] Ibn Sa'd: *at-Tabaqat*, Vol 2, p 200
[205] at-Tabari: *at-Tarikh*, Vol 1, p 445
[206] Ibn Sa'd: *at-Tabaqat*, Vol 2, p 201
[207] Ibn Sa'd: *at-Tabaqat*, Vol 1, p 355
[208] Ibn Sa'd: *at-Tabaqat*, Vol 2, p 201
[209] Ibn Sa'd: *at-Tabaqat*, Vol 2, p 202
[210] Ibn Sa'd: *at-Tabaqat*, Vol 2, p 203
[211] at-Tabari: *at-Tarikh*, Vol 1, p 456
[212] Ibn Sa'd: *at-Tabaqat*, Vol 1, p 541 f
[213] Ibn Sa'd: *at-Tabaqat*, Vol 2, p 205
[214] at-Tabari: *at-Tarikh*, Vol 1, p 457
[215] at-Tabari: *at-Tarikh*, Vol 1, p 454
[216] Bukhari, Vol 6, p 154
[217] Ibn Hisham: *as-Sirah*, Vol 2, p 655; Ibn Sa'd: *at-Tabaqat*, Vol 2, p 208
[218] at-Tabari: *at-Tarikh*, Vol 1, p 457
[219] Ibn Sa'd: *at-Tabaqat*, Vol 1, p 347
[220] Ibn Sa'd: *at-Tabaqat*, Vol 1, p 399; Vol 2, p 209
[221] at-Tabari: *at-Tarikh*, Vol 1, p 460
[222] Ibn Sa'd: *at-Tabaqat*, Vol 2, p 210
[223] Ibn Sa'd: *at-Tabaqat*, Vol 1, p 419
[224] Sachau: *Chronology*, p 332
[225] Ibn Sa'd: *at-Tabaqat*, Vol 1, pp 407, 408
[226] Bukhari, Vol 5, pp 450, 452
[227] Ibn Sa'd: *at-Tabaqat*, Vol 1, p 407

Postscript

In the beginning of this work we have talked about various imperfect models of the calendar. Now we shall discuss their disastrous effects on modern biographical works and a comparative historical study. As the Christian calendar has become a universal frame of reference for all comparative studies, all modern writers and researchers want to put all dates within this frame. For a representative survey we shall consider the Julian dates of eight landmark events of the early days of Islam as put forward by various writers working in this field. This will show the reader vividly the calendrical corruption wrought into modern works and the need to rewrite them.

1. Birth of the Prophet ﷺ (Monday, 2nd Rabi' al-Awwal 1st AF / June 23rd, 570)

Arabian society was steeped in idolatry, polytheism and all sorts of vicious customs immediately before Muhammad ﷺ. Slaves were doomed to lifelong bondage, the properties of orphans were misappropriated and female infants were buried alive. Prostitution flourished and adultery was rampant. Wine and usury soaked the society. Robbery was part of their culture and homicide was the order of the day. Amidst such people so deeply immersed in evil and at such a time when they were on the brink of irreparable ruin, Destiny decreed that the Prophet ﷺ should be born to call them back to the Benevolent God, to a life of piety and to a future of unending reward.

We have been able to show in complete agreement with classical reports that it was on June 23rd, 570 that the Prophet ﷺ was born. But working with imperfect models of the calendar, people suggested various other dates. Let us examine these with reference to the actual pagan calendar and ascertain the extent of their departure from the real date. The table below will indicate this.

	Julian date	**Corresponding pagan date**
Dr. Hamidullah	Jun 17, 569[1]	Monday 15 SFR 1 BF
Habibur Rahman Khan	Dec 9, 569[2]	Monday 13 SHB 1 BF
Zafrullah Khan	Apr 20, 570[3]	Sunday 26 DLH 1 BF
Jamal N. Hussein	May 2, 570[4]	Friday 9 MHR 1 AF
Caussin de Perceval	Aug 20, 570[5]	Wednesday 1 JML 1 AF
Syed Ameer Ali	Aug 29, 570[6]	Friday 10 JML 1 AF
Sulaiman & Salman Mansur	Apr 15, 571[7]	Wednesday 3 MHR 2 AF
Mahmud Pasha Falaki	Apr 20, 571[8]	Monday 8 MHR 2 AF
Abdul Hamid Siddiqi	Apr 22, 571[9]	Wednesday 10 MHR 2 AF
Muhammad Akbar Khan	Apr 23, 571[10]	Thursday 11 MHR 2 AF
Abdur Rahman Shad	Apr 29, 571[11]	Wednesday 17 MHR 2 AF

Perceval believed that the Arabs regularly intercalated one month every three years and there arrived at the end of the tenth year of Hijrah against month number 5869 (March 29th – April 27th, 632) one *nasi'* operation of which was discontinued as per orders of the Prophet ﷺ. If one intercalation was due against this month, month number 5107 (August 18th – September 17th, 570) will work out to a Rabi' al-Awwal (— place in Appendix 2 one *nasi'* against 5869, another against 5832, the next against 5795, and so on every thirty-six months). Then he contended that the Prophet ﷺ was born on August 20th, 570.

Mahmud Pasha Falaki wrote a book on the birth of the Prophet ﷺ. Inasmuch as his date occurs on the undisputed weekday of Monday and because of his being an astronomer, many lent credence to his result and started adopting his date which became very popular in many recent works. But he believed that there was no such thing as *nasi'* in the pagan calendar and that the Arab year was purely a lunar one, as already discussed in the beginning of this work. This erroneous idea led him to reconstruct the pagan calendar purely on a twelve monthly basis without inter-stitching any *nasi'*. If we extend the Hijrah calendar backward beyond the epochal day, presently believed to be July 15th, 622, in 571 we get a Rabi' al-Awwal commencing from April 12th and the 8th of that month works out to a Monday on April 20th. This was the date which Falaki believed the Prophet ﷺ was born.

2. First revelation of the Qur'an (Monday, 18th Ramadan 40 AF / December 22nd, 609)

It is narrated that actual revelation to the Prophet ﷺ was preceded by strange events and true dreams. In the valleys and mountains of Makkah he did not pass a stone or a tree but it greeted him. He turned around and looked to his right and to his left but did not notice any one. This period was followed by true visions. These used to come to him like the breaking of the dawn. Thereafter solitude became dear to him and he would retire to a cave on Mt. Hira for a certain number of nights. There he used to apply himself to ardent devotions consisting of long vigils and prayers. Then he would return to his family for provisions for a similar stay. Thus passed some years.

Then one night in one of such sojourn the Angel of Revelation unexpectedly appeared to him and said, "Read". The Prophet ﷺ at first thought that he was called upon to read actual script. Being unlettered he answered "I cannot read" – whereupon the Angel seized him and pressed him to himself until all strength went out of him; then he released him and said, "Read". Again the Prophet ﷺ answered "I cannot read". Then the Angel seized him and pressed him to himself until all strength went out of him; then he released him and said, "Read". The Prophet ﷺ again answered "I cannot read". For a third time the Angel seized him and pressed him to himself until all strength went out of him; then he released him and said: **"Recite: In the Name of your Lord who created, created man from clots of blood. Recite: And your Lord is the Most Generous, He who taught by the pen, taught man what he did not know."** (Surah 96: 1-5) Then in sudden illumination the Prophet ﷺ understood that he was called upon to recite the divine commands to mankind. Thus did he receive the first revelation. This occurred in the night of the 18th Ramadan when he was forty years old.

Various Julian dates were regarded as corresponding with this this night:

	Julian date	**Corresponding pagan date**
Dr. Hamidullah	Dec 22, 609[12]	Monday 18 RMD 40 AF
Hashim Amir Ali	Jun 17, 610	Wednesday 18 RBL 41 AF
Safiur Rahman	Aug 10, 610[13]	Monday 13 JML 41 AF
Caussin de Perceval	Jan 10, 611	Sunday 18 SHW 41 AF

Opposing the winter theory, Amir Ali argued that a sagacious man such as Muhammad ﷺ could not have chosen to meditate on a hillside during a winter night. Instead it should have been during June, when the Arab summer was at its height and resorting to the hillside was a pleasant escape from the suffocating valley surrounded by hills, and thus it was then that the Prophet ﷺ experienced the glories of the night of enlightenment.[14]

Safiur Rahman held that it was in the Ramadan of the backwardly extended Hijrah system (as worked out by Falaki) that the Prophet ﷺ received the mantle of Prophethood. However as the lunar date 18th turned out to be a Saturday, he moved away to the 13th to get a Monday.

Hamidullah found out the real date.

3. Emigration to Madinah (Monday, 12th Rabi' al-Awwal 1 H / June 28th, 622)

When the number of Muslims gradually grew and Islam became the topic of common talk, the non-believing Quraysh imprisoned the Muslims, tortured and tried to reconvert them. The Prophet ﷺ advised his followers: "Be scattered in the earth." They migrated to Abyssinia. But when they returned to Makkah on the false information that the Quraysh had accepted Islam, their relatives meted out to them harsh and cruel treatment. The Prophet ﷺ had to send them off to Abyssinia for a second time.

With the passage of time, the relationship became even more estranged and the Makkans launched a boycott against Bani Hashim in whose house the Prophet ﷺ was born. They cut off all matrimonial alliances, commercial transactions and social intercourse with them. In addition, they decided to assassinate the Prophet ﷺ at the first available opportunity. For three years he had to take refuge in a mountain pass. After that, the boycott was called off due to divine intervention and the Prophet ﷺ and Bani Hashim returned to Makkah. But, the Prophet's protecting uncle Abu Talib breathed his last, leaving him with no human protector.

Nevertheless the Prophet ﷺ did not shrink; he re-directed his call to people in the annual pilgrimage. People from Madinah responded and offered shelter to his followers in Madinah. Secretly, batch by batch, the Prophet ﷺ started sending his men to Madinah. The Quraysh soon discovered this and became more enraged, and intensified their tyranny over the Muslims. They showered intolerable abuses on them and made their lives miserable. Moreover, they assembled at Dar an-Nadwah and took the decision jointly to butcher the Prophet ﷺ with a group of men among whom all the clans of the Quraysh were represented.

Continuing for even a single moment longer in Makkah became precarious for him. He had to leave his native land. This opened a new chapter in the history of Islam. Adieu to the years of untold suffering, tribulation and torture in Makkah and welcome to the life of mutual understanding, love and loyalty in Madinah!

Various Julian dates suggested for the day of his arrival in Quba (in the outskirts of Madinah) were as follows:

	Julian date		Corresponding pagan date			
Dr. Hamidullah	May 31,	622[15]	Monday	13	SFR	1 H
Caussin de Perceval	Jun 28,	622[16]	Monday	12	RBL	1 H
Abdul Hamid Siddiqi	Sep 20,	622[17]	Monday	8	JMR	1 H
Naeem Siddiqi	Sep 23,	622[18]	Thursday	11	JMR	1 H
Edward Mahler	Sep 24,	622[19]	Friday	12	JMR	1 H
Ishaqun Nabi Alvi	Nov 22,	622[20]	Monday	12	SHB	1 H

Those who contended that the emigration took place in September do so according to the mistaken belief that the reported month of Rabi' al-Awwal was that of the Hijrah calendar. Al-Biruni was one of those who so believed. In the Hijrah calendar, Rabi' al-Awwal started on the sunset of Sunday, September 12th, 622 and the 12th turned out to be a Friday as against the popular tradition that the Prophet ﷺ arrived at Quba on a Monday. Therefore he argued that to be a Monday the arrival could not have been on the 12th but on the 8th. Abdul Hamid Siddiqi appears to have relied on him.

While assigning the event to November, Alvi tries to justify such a placing by arguing that Ali's sleeping in the bed of the Prophet ﷺ covered by the latter's blanket was indicative of winter. But this cannot be a conclusive proof. 'Ali could have used the Prophet's ﷺ blanket to mislead the enemies into believing that it was the Prophet ﷺ himself who was sleeping on the bed.

Speaking about the Madinan people's waiting for the Prophet's ﷺ arrival in their city, at-Tabari recorded that it was during a very hot season that the people went out for several days in the morning to the outskirts to watch for his arrival and they waited till the heat of the day increased and no shadows were left, when they returned to their houses only to resume the watch in the afternoon. This rather indicates summer.

Only Perceval accidentally arrived at the true date.

4. The battle of Badr (Friday, 16th Ramadan 2 H / December 16th, 623)

The Prophet ﷺ wanted to intercept the Makkan trade caravan returning from Syria and so set out with 313 of his followers, seventy camels and two horses. While in Syria, the polytheists had somehow learnt that the Prophet ﷺ was watching for their return and therefore they had sent messages in advance to Makkah for help. Putting Badr to his left, Abu Sufyan, the leader of the caravan, took the coastal route, moved fast, travelling day and night and eluded the Muslims. After that he sent messages to the defence forces to return to Makkah. But Abu Jahl refused to return without showing his strength. Thus a force 950 strong with one hundred horses arrived at Badr.

It proved to be one of the most historic battles ever fought. Only 313 ardent believers had to fight an army three times as strong. The handful fought tooth and nail, killed seventy, captured an equal number and routed the rest.

While truly the battle was fought on December 16th, 623 the various erroneous dates given in modern biographical works were:

	Julian date		Corresponding pagan date			
Dr. Hamidullah	Nov 18,	623[21]	Friday	18	SHB	2 H
Caussin de Perceval	Jan 15,	624	Sunday	17	SHW	2 H
Montgomery Watt	Mar 15,	624[22]	Thursday	18	DLH	2 H
Hashim Amir Ali	May 11,	624	Friday	17	SFR	2 H
Ishaqun Nabi Alvi	Jun 11,	624	Monday	17	RBL	3 H

5. The battle of Uhud (Saturday, 11th Shawwal 3 H / December 29th, 624)

The Quraysh were terribly exasperated at their utter defeat at Badr, which had come about despite the fact that they heavily outnumbered the Muslims. On their return from Badr, they confided with Abu Sufyan.

He agreed to finance raising an army strong enough to hook Muhammad ﷺ and for that purpose offered all the profits of his Syrian trade journey. Then in Shawwal 3 H, with an army three thousand strong the Quraysh arrived at Uhud.

The Prophet ﷺ desired to fight the battle at Madinah itself, if the enemy would dare to come there. But younger people opted for a battle outside Madinah. In his strategy, the Prophet ﷺ stationed a contingent of archers in the rear with instructions to guard against enemy attack from the rear. He advised them never to leave their position even if all the Muslims in the field were slain.

In a battle tactic, the enemy retreated and the Muslims chased them. The archers could not resist the temptation of joining the fight and disregarding the orders of the Prophet ﷺ they left their position. The enemy cavalry came around the hill and launched an attack from the rear and the Muslim army were caught in the middle. The Muslims suffered a humiliating defeat and a number of them were killed.

The traditions say that the battle took place on Saturday, 11th Shawwal 3 H and we have successfully proved that it was on December 29th, 624. Various other erroneous dates suggested for this battle were as follows:

	Julian date		Corresponding pagan date		
Caussin de Perceval	Jan 26,	625[23]	Saturday	9	DLQ 3 H
Montgomery Watt	Mar 23,	625[24]	Saturday	7	DLH (N) 3 H
Margoliouth	Mar 24,	625[25]	Sunday	8	DLH (N) 3 H
Ishaqun Nabi Alvi	Jun 24,	625	Monday	11	RBL 4 H

In his calendar, Perceval could not get a Saturday against the reported date of the battle; instead he got a Monday. Therefore he moved to January 26th, 625 – a nearby date to get a Saturday and presumed that to be the real date of the battle. But as per his own calendar this date actually corresponded to the 9th Shawwal which was none of the reported dates.

6. The battle of al-Khandaq (Saturday, 1st Dhu'l-Qa'dah 5 H / January 24th, 627)

The Jews and the Quraysh could not find peace while thinking that Muhammad with a handful of followers was day by day getting supremacy over Arabian affairs. In less than five years from the time of his expulsion, he had twice waged full-scale battles with the Quraysh, had ambushed Makkan trade caravans, expelled the Jews of Qaynuqa' and Nadir from Madinah. Muhammad's ﷺ rise to power was a signal of a crushing death of pagan religion and an ultimate threat to the Makkan oligarchy. Unless the spark were doused in time, it might soon burst into flames and spread all over Arabia and consume everything they cherished. Mustering all their strength and the forces unfriendly to Muhammad ﷺ, the Quraysh and their allies raised an army ten thousand strong. Bani Nadir, Ghatafan, Sulaym, Asad, Fazarah, Ashja', and Murrah – all joined. It was the greatest force of Arabs that could ever rise together against the Prophet ﷺ. If they could not finish him this time, never would they do so in future.

The confederate force besieged Madinah for nearly one month until a fierce gale came, uprooted their tents, upset the kettles, buried the camel's saddles and broke the tent-pegs. They fled in panic and the battle ended in victory for the Messenger of Allah ﷺ.

The biographers dated the end of the siege as Saturday, 1st Dhu'l-Qa'dah 5 H; and it really corresponded to January 24th, 627. Dates furnished by others were as follows:

	Julian date	Corresponding pagan date
Dr. Hamidullah	Jan 24, 627[26]	Saturday 29 SHW 5 H
Caussin de Perceval	Feb 24, 627	Tuesday 1 DLH 5 H
Ishaqun Nabi Alvi	Mar 25, 627	Wednesday 29 DLH 5 H

Montgomery Watt believed that the siege began on March 31st, 627 (which actually corresponded to 6th Muharram 6 H in the pagan calendar) and lasted about a fortnight.[27]

Dr. Hamidullah successfully found the correct Julian date.

7. The treaty of al-Hudaybiyyah (Thursday, 1st Dhu'l-Qa'dah 6 H / January 14th, 628)

Towards the end of the sixth year of emigration, with about 1,500 of his followers, the Prophet ﷺ made a march to Makkah to perform an 'Umrah, a 'lesser pilgrimage'. Now, it was a serious blow to the pride of the pagan Quraysh that their eternal enemy should be allowed to set foot in Makkah, with all the animosity between them intact. Yet they could not violate the sanctity of the sacred month by taking up arms against him. Circumstances compelled them to enter into negotiations with him. They put forth the condition that he should postpone his pilgrimage by one year. By this they could boast to the Arab world that they had refused the Muslims and Muhammad ﷺ entry to the sacred land.

Among other things, the truce contained other conditions which, though initially insignificant, had far-reaching consequences for the rise of Islam. It stipulated that hostilities should cease for ten years between the two parties. For the first time in six years of almost permanent warfare, the possibility was established of peaceful contact between the Muslim community in Madinah and the pagan oligarchy of Makkah and a way was opened for the penetration of Islamic truth into the citadel of Arabian paganism. The Makkans who had occasion to visit the Muslim camp at Hudaybiyyah returned deeply impressed by the spirit and unity of the Prophet's ﷺ followers, and many of them began to waver in their hostility to the new deen. As soon as warfare came to an end and people of both sides could meet freely and discuss the issues intimately, the truth dawned and new converts rallied around the Prophet ﷺ – so much so that when the Quraysh broke the truce two years later, the Prophet ﷺ could lay his hands on Makkah almost without resistance. Thus the truce proved to be of utmost value to the Muslims. This is what the divine ayah, appropriately revealed just after the treaty, foretold: **"Truly We have granted you a clear victory."** (48:1)

Our sources placed the date of this march to Makkah on Thursday, 1st Dhu'l-Qa'dah 6 H and we have successfully found that it corresponded to January 14th, 628. Other erroneous dates suggested by other writers were:

	Julian dates		**Corresponding pagan date**		
Caussin de Perceval	Feb 13,	628	Saturday	1	DLH 6 H
William Muir	Mar 13,	628[28]	Sunday	1	DLH (N) 6 H

8. The Opening of Makkah [to Islam] (Monday, 18th Ramadan 8 H / December 11th, 629)

About the Ka'bah, the Qur'an says, "We contracted with Ibrahim and Isma'il: 'Purify My House for those who circle it, and those who stay

there, and those who bow and who prostrate.'" (2:124) – which command meant that it should remain an inviolable place of pure and unadulterated worship. With the passage of time the forces of evil misled its children from taqwa, usurped their rights and turned it into a citadel of idolatry. Three hundred and sixty idols were worshipped in this house of Allah. The Prophet's ﷺ cleansing of the Ka'bah by devastating the idols was truly a coronation of tawhid and must be hailed as a landmark in the annals of the eternal struggle of truth against falsehood.

Traditional works give the date of this historic day as Monday, 18th Ramadan 8 H. This corresponded to December 11th, 629. But some people place it in January and others in June 630, as shown below:

	Julian date	Corresponding pagan date
Caussin de Perceval	Jan 10, 630	Wednesday 18 SHW 8 H
Montgomery Watt	Jan 11, 630[29]	Thursday 19 SHW 8 H
Ishaqun Nabi Alvi	Jun 6, 630	Wednesday 18 RBL 8 H

The foregoing examples enable the reader to form a fair idea as to how far from the real dates the modern writers put events and thus draw a faulty perspective of the early history of Islam. Every time they come to a Julian date, they invariably use one such erroneous date.

While truly most of these errors originate from the wrong models of the pagan calendar designed by them, the researchers try to put all the blame on the sources and their authors. They hold them either to be careless or manipulative. At the cost of repetition we may recall that failing to reconcile the apparent conflicts, within the sources, of weekdays and seasons with those of the calendars they devised, some orientalists were of the impression that all chronological details in the classical works were simply fabrications of the early Muslims. Some tried to explain and reconcile the discrepancies on the assumption that the dates had been recorded with reference to two parallel calendars. Some went so far as to allege that the Prophet ﷺ did the Farewell Hajj in Rajab but the early ruler had insidiously changed its name to Dhu'l-Hijjah in order to eliminate the existence of *nasi's* in the first decade. Yet some others, especially Orientalists, held that the early historians recorded the dates disregarding *nasi's* although the people might have actually been practising intercalation.

All these theories and arguments were however advanced in order to explain the apparent contradictions abounding in the classical records and to give some meaning and reliability to them. Unfortunately, not even once in the long history of the debate did it ever occur to the thinking of these scholars, perhaps with the sole exception of Dr. Hamidullah, that they might be comparing the records with a model of the calendar dissimilar to the actual calendar used in those days. On the other hand, relying too much on the Orientalists, the belief that the presently used Hijrah calendar was the very calendar used then has so firmly taken roots in the mind of some of our scholars that even now they are hesitant to accept the fact that the calendar of that time was different from it. It may take some time to dissuade them of such an erroneous view.[30]

Although ever since the dawn of the age of research, the classical historians had undeservedly been made the target of accusations, the results accruing from these studies leave us amazed at their sincerity and accuracy, and overwhelmingly bear out the fact that blaming them was unfair and wholly unfounded. Our own inability to dig out the lost calendar led us to the hasty conclusion that they were not accurate. With this study we have ultimately solved the mystery of the Arab calendar and have successfully come out of the seemingly inexplicable chronological mess in which we used to be caught time and again.

'Truth has come and falsehood has vanished. Falsehood is always bound to vanish.' (17:81)

NOTES

[1] Hamidullah: *Rasulullah*, p 1
[2] Burhan, Apr 1965, p 236
[3] Zafrullah: *Muhammad*, p 12
[4] Islamic Culture, Jan 1997, p 82
[5] Muir: Life, p 5
[6] Ameer Ali: *The Saracens*, p 7
[7] Sulaiman & Salman: *Mercy*, Vol 1, p 409
[8] Mirkhond: *Rawzatus Safa*, Pt II, p 88; Shibli: *as-Sirah*, Vol 1, p 171
[9] Siddiqi: *Life*, p 39
[10] Ghulam Mustafa: *Biswanabi*, p 370 f
[11] Shad: *Adam*, p 139
[12] Islamic Review, Feb 1969, p 10
[13] Rahman: *Sealed Nectar*, p 68
[14] Ali: *Upstream*, pp 15, 16
[15] Islamic Review, Feb 1969, p 10
[16] Muir: *Life*, p 168
[17] Siddiqi: *Life* 129
[18] Naeem Siddiqi: *the Benefactor*, p 265
[19] Ibn Saʻd: *at-Tabaqat*, Vol 2, p 2 f
[20] Burhan, Oct 1964, p 207
[21] Islamic Review, Feb 1969, p 9
[22] Watt: *Muhammad at Madinah*, p 339
[23] Ameer Ali: *Spirit*, p 70 f
[24] Watt: *Muhammad at Madinah*, p 21
[25] Margoliouth: *Rise*, p 294
[26] Islamic Review, Feb 1969, p 9
[27] Watt: *Muhammad at Madinah*, pp 35, 36
[28] Muir: *Life*, p 353
[29] Watt: *Muhammad at Madinah*, p 66
[30] Some time ago I sent an article on this issue to Islamic Culture for publication. They published it; but against my date of Badr they inserted a query mark as to whether it should not be in March 624 (as according to the Hijrah calendar) and they included this query in the print too.

Appendix 1
LOCATIONS OF INTERCALARY MONTHS

Calendar			Locations				
31.12N34		5090	5127	5164	5201	5238	5275	5312
	5349	5386	5423	5436	5473	5510	5547	5584
	5621	5658	5695	5732	5769	5806	5819	5856
31.24N68		5090	5127	5164	5201	5238	5275	5312
	5349	5386	5399	5436	5473	5510	5547	5584
	5621	5658	5695	5732	5769	5782	5819	5856
31.36N102		**5090**	**5127**	**5164**	**5201**	**5238**	**5275**	**5312**
	5349	**5362**	**5399**	**5436**	**5473**	**5510**	**5547**	**5584**
	5621	**5658**	**5695**	**5732**	**5745**	**5782**	**5819**	**5856**
31.48N136		5090	5127	5164	5201	5238	5275	5312
	5325	5362	5399	5436	5473	5510	5547	5584
	5621	5658	5695	5708	5745	5782	5819	5856
31.60N170		5090	5127	5164	5201	5238	5275	5288
	5325	5362	5399	5436	5473	5510	5547	5584
	5621	5658	5695	5708	5745	5782	5819	5856
31.72N204		5090	5127	5164	5201	5238	5251	5288
	5325	5362	5399	5436	5473	5510	5547	5584
	5621	5658	5671	5708	5745	5782	5819	5856
31.84N238		5090	5127	5164	5201	5214	5251	5288
	5325	5362	5399	5436	5473	5510	5547	5584
	5597	5634	5671	5708	5745	5782	5819	5856
31.96N272		5090	5127	5164	5177	5214	5251	5288
	5325	5362	5399	5436	5473	5510	5547	5560
	5597	5634	5671	5708	5745	5782	5819	5856
31.108N306		5090	5127	5140	5177	5214	5251	5288
	5325	5362	5399	5436	5473	5510	5523	5560
	5597	5634	5671	5708	5745	5782	5819	5856
31.120N340		5090	5103	5140	5177	5214	5251	5288
	5325	5362	5399	5436	5473	5486	5523	5560
	5597	5634	5671	5708	5745	5782	5819	5856
31.132N372		5103	5140	5177	5214	5251	5288
	5325	5362	5399	5436	5449	5486	5523	5560
	5597	5634	5671	5708	5745	5782	5819	5856

Note: From October 23rd, 157 whence the pagan Arabs started the intercalary epoch to April 9th, 631 (the last day of the epoch) there were altogether 5856 lunar months. The numbers in the above table indicate the serial numbers of these months as considered from the beginning of the epoch. Month numbers 5105 to 5872 covered the life span of the Prophet ﷺ.

Appendix 2
Pagan and Hijrah Calendars

Month serial	Pagan Calendar AF/H		Date of commencement	Hijrah Calendar BH/AH	Intercalary month serial
(1)	(2)		(3)	(4)	(5)
5091	1 BF	MHR	May 3	RBL 55 BH	
92		SFR	Jun 2	RBR	
93		RBL	Jul 2	JML	
94		RBR	Jul 31	JMR	
95		JML	Aug 29	RJB	
96		JMR	Sept 28	SHB	
97		RJB	Oct 28	RMD	
98		SHB	Nov 26	SHW	
99		RMD	Dec 25	DLQ	
5100		SHW	570 Jan 24	DLH	
01		DLQ	Feb 23	MHR 54 BH	
02		DLH	Mar 25	SFR	
03	1 AF	MHR	Apr 23	RBL	
04		SFR	May 22	RBR	
05		RBL	Jun 21	JML	
06		RBR	Jul 20	JMR	
07		JML	Aug 19	RJB	
08		JMR	Sept 17	SHB	
09		RJB	Oct 17	RMD	
5110		SHB	Nov 15	SHW	
11		RMD	Dec 15	DLQ	
12		SHW	571 Jan 13	DLH	
13		DLQ	Feb 12	MHR 53 BH	
14		DLH	Mar 14	SFR	
15	2 AF	MHR	Apr 12	RBL	
16		SFR	May 12	RBR	
17		RBL	Jun 10	JML	
18		RBR	Jul 10	JMR	
19		JML	Aug 8	RJB	
5120		JMR	Sept 6	SHB	
21		RJB	Oct 6	RMD	
22		SHB	Nov 4	SHW	
23		RMD	Dec 4	DLQ	
24		SHW	572 Jan 3	DLH	
25		DLQ	Feb 1	MHR 52 BH	

1. The lunar month commences from the sunset of the Julian dates shown in the table.
2. The serial of the months is as considered from the beginning of the intercalary epoch.
3. The last column indicates the serial of the intercalary month in the cycle of repetition as well as in the intercalary epoch.

Pagan and Hijrah Calendars

Month serial (1)	Pagan Calendar AF/H (2)	Date of commencement (3)	Hijrah Calendar BH/AH (4)	Intercalary month serial (5)
26	DLH	Mar 2	SFR	
27	**DLH**	Apr 1	RBL	15 N43; 147
28	3 AF MHR	Apr 30	RBR	
29	SFR	May 29	JML	
5130	RBL	Jun 28	JMR	
31	RBR	Jul 27	RJB	
32	JML	Aug 26	SHB	
33	JMR	Sept 24	RMD	
34	RJB	Oct 24	SHW	
35	SH	Nov 22	DLQ	
36	RMD	Dec 22	DLH	
37	SHW	573 Jan 21	MHR 51 BH	
38	DLQ	Feb 19	SFR	
39	DLH	Mar 21	RBL	
5140	4 AF MHR	Apr 19	RBR	
41	SFR	May 19	JML	
42	RBL	Jun 17	JMR	
43	RBR	Jul 17	RJB	
44	JML	Aug 15	SHB	
45	JMR	Sept 14	RMD	
46	RJB	Oct 13	SHW	
47	SHB	Nov 12	DLQ	
48	RMD	Dec 11	DLH	
49	SHW	574 Jan 10	MHR 50 BH	
5150	DLQ	Feb 8	SFR	
51	DLH	Mar 10	RBL	
52	5 AF MHR	Apr 9	RBR	
53	SFR	May 8	JML	
54	RBL	Jun 7	JMR	
55	RBR	Jul 6	RJB	
56	JML	Aug 4	SHB	
57	JMR	Sept 3	RMD	
58	RJB	Oct 3	SHW	
59	SHB	Nov 1	DLQ	
5160	RMD	Dec 1	DLH	

1. The lunar month commences from the sunset of the Julian dates shown in the table.
2. The serial of the months is as considered from the beginning of the intercalary epoch.
3. The last column indicates the serial of the intercalary month in the cycle of repetition as well as in the intercalary epoch.

Pagan and Hijrah Calendars

Month serial (1)	Pagan Calendar AF/H (2)	Date of commencement (3)	Hijrah Calendar BH/AH (4)	Intercalary month serial (5)
61		SHW		Dec 30	MHR 49 BH	
62		DLQ	575	Jan 29	SFR	
63		DLH		Feb 27	RBL	
64		**DLH**		Mar 29	RBR	**16N46; 148**
65	6 AF	MHR		Apr 28	JML	
66		SFR		May 27	JMR	
67		RBL		Jun 26	RJB	
68		RBR		Jul 25	SHB	
69		JML		Aug 23	RMD	
5170		JMR		Sept 22	SHW	
71		RJB		Oct 22	DLQ	
72		SHB		Nov 20	DLH	
73		RMD		Dec 20	MHR 48 BH	
74		SHW	576	Jan 18	SFR	
75		DLQ		Feb 17	RBL	
76		DLH		Mar 17	RBR	
77	7 AF	MHR		Apr 16	JML	
78		SFR		May 15	JMR	
79		RBL		Jun 14	RJB	
5180		RBR		Jul 13	SHB	
81		JML		Aug 12	RMD	
82		JMR		Sept 10	SHW	
83		RJB		Oct 10	DLQ	
84		SHB		Nov 8	DLH	
85		RMD		Dec 8	MHR 47 BH	
86		SHW	577	Jan 7	SFR	
87		DLQ		Feb 5	RBL	
88		DLH		Mar 7	RBR	
89	8 AF	MHR		Apr 5	JML	
5190		SFR		May 5	JMR	
91		RBL		Jun 3	RJB	
92		RBR		Jul 3	SHB	
93		JML		Aug 1	RMD	
94		JMR		Aug 31	SHW	
95		RJB		Sept 29	DLQ	

1. The lunar month commences from the sunset of the Julian dates shown in the table.
2. The serial of the months is as considered from the beginning of the intercalary epoch.
3. The last column indicates the serial of the intercalary month in the cycle of repetition as well as in the intercalary epoch.

Pagan and Hijrah Calendars

Month serial	Pagan Calendar AF/H		Date of commencement	Hijrah Calendar BH/AH		Intercalary month serial
(1)	(2)		(3)	(4)		(5)
96		SHB	Oct 29	DLH		
97		RMD	Nov 27	MHR	46 BH	
98		SHW	Dec 27	SFR		
99		DLQ	578 Jan 26	RBL		
5200		DLH	Feb 24	RBR		
01		**DLH**	Mar 26	JML		17N49; 149
02	9 AF	MHR	Apr 24	JMR		
03		SFR	May 24	RJB		
04		RBL	Jun 22	SHB		
05		RBR	Jul 22	RMD		
06		JML	Aug 20	SHW		
07		JMR	Sept 19	DLQ		
08		RJB	Oct 18	DLH		
09		SHB	Nov 17	MHR	45 BH	
5210		RMD	Dec 16	SFR		
11		SHW	579 Jan 15	RBL		
12		DLQ	Feb 13	RBR		
13		DLH	Mar 15	JML		
14	10 AF	MHR	Apr 14	JMR		
15		SFR	May 13	RJB		
16		RBL	Jun 12	SHB		
17		RBR	Jul 11	RMD		
18		JML	Aug 9	SHW		
19		JMR	Sept 8	DLQ		
5220		RJB	Oct 8	DLH		
21		SHB	Nov 6	MHR	44 BH	
22		RMD	Dec 6	SFR		
23		SHW	580 Jan 4	RBL		
24		DLQ	Feb 3	RBR		
25		DLH	Mar 3	JML		
26	11 AF	MHR	Apr 2	JMR		
27		SFR	May 1	RJB		
28		RBL	May 31	SHB		
29		RBR	Jun 30	RMD		
5230		JML	Jul 29	SHW		

1. The lunar month commences from the sunset of the Julian dates shown in the table.
2. The serial of the months is as considered from the beginning of the intercalary epoch.
3. The last column indicates the serial of the intercalary month in the cycle of repetition as well as in the intercalary epoch.

Pagan and Hijrah Calendars

Month serial	Pagan Calendar AF/H	Date of commencement	Hijrah Calendar BH/AH	Intercalary month serial
(1)	(2)	(3)	(4)	(5)
31	JMR	Aug 27	DLQ	
32	RJB	Sept 26	DLH	
33	SHB	Oct 25	MHR 43 BH	
34	RMD	Nov 24	SFR	
35	SHW	Dec 24	RBL	
36	DLQ	581 Jan 22	RBR	
37	DLH	Feb 21	JML	
38	**DLH**	Mar 22	JMR	18N52; 150
39	12 AF MHR	Apr 21	RJB	
5240	SFR	May 20	SHB	
41	RBL	Jun 19	RMD	
42	RBR	Jul 18	SHW	
43	JML	Aug 16	DLQ	
44	JMR	Sept 15	DLH	
45	RJB	Oct 15	MHR 42 BH	
46	SHB	Nov 13	SFR	
47	RMD	Dec 13	RBL	
48	SHW	582 Jan 11	RBR	
49	DLQ	Feb 10	JML	
5250	DLH	Mar 12	JMR	
51	13 AF MHR	Apr 10	RJB	
52	SFR	May 10	SHB	
53	RBL	Jun 8	RMD	
54	RBR	Jul 8	SHW	
55	JML	Aug 6	DLQ	
56	JMR	Sept 5	DLH	
57	RJB	Oct 4	MHR 41 BH	
58	SHB	Nov 3	SFR	
59	RMD	Dec 2	RBL	
5260	SHW	583 Jan 1	RBR	
61	DLQ	Jan 31	JML	
62	DLH	Mar 1	JMR	
63	14 AF MHR	Mar 31	RJB	
64	SFR	Apr 29	SHB	
65	RBL	May 28	RMD	

1. The lunar month commences from the sunset of the Julian dates shown in the table.
2. The serial of the months is as considered from the beginning of the intercalary epoch.
3. The last column indicates the serial of the intercalary month in the cycle of repetition as well as in the intercalary epoch.

Pagan and Hijrah Calendars

Month serial	Pagan Calendar AF/H	Date of commencement	Hijrah Calendar BH/AH	Intercalary month serial
(1)	(2)	(3)	(4)	(5)
66	RBR	Jun 27	SHW	
67	JML	Jul 26	DLQ	
68	JMR	Aug 25	DLH	
69	RJB	Sept 23	MHR 40 BH	
5270	SHB	Oct 23	SFR	
71	RMD	Nov 22	RBL	
72	SHW	Dec 21	RBR	
73	DLQ	584 Jan 20	JML	
74	DLH	Feb 18	JMR	
75	**DLH**	Mar 19	RJB	19N55; 151
76	15 AF MHR	Apr 17	SHB	
77	SFR	May 17	RMD	
78	RBL	Jun 15	SHW	
79	RBR	Jul 15	DLQ	
5280	JML	Aug 13	DLH	
81	JMR	Sept 12	MHR 39 BH	
82	RJB	Oct 11	SFR	
83	SHB	Nov 10	RBL	
84	RMD	Dec 10	RBR	
85	SHW	585 Jan 8	JML	
86	DLQ	Feb 7	JMR	
87	DLH	Mar 8	RJB	
88	16 AF MHR	Apr 7	SHB	
89	SFR	May 6	RMD	
5290	RBL	Jun 5	SHW	
91	RBR	Jul 4	DLQ	
92	JML	Aug 2	DLH	
93	JMR	Sept 1	MHR 38 BH	
94	RJB	Oct 1	SFR	
95	SHB	Oct 30	RBL	
96	RMD	Nov 29	RBR	
97	SHW	Dec 28	JML	
98	DLQ	586 Jan 27	JMR	
99	DLH	Feb 26	RJB	
5300	17 AF MHR	Mar 27	SHB	

1. The lunar month commences from the sunset of the Julian dates shown in the table.
2. The serial of the months is as considered from the beginning of the intercalary epoch.
3. The last column indicates the serial of the intercalary month in the cycle of repetition as well as in the intercalary epoch.

Pagan and Hijrah Calendars

Month serial	Pagan Calendar AF/H	Date of commencement	Hijrah Calendar BH/AH	Intercalary month serial
(1)	(2)	(3)	(4)	(5)
01	SFR	Apr 26	RMD	
02	RBL	May 25	SHW	
03	RBR	Jun 24	DLQ	
04	JML	Jul 23	DLH	
05	JMR	Aug 21	MHR 37 BH	
06	RJB	Sept 20	SFR	
07	SHB	Oct 20	RBL	
08	RMD	Nov 18	RBR	
09	SHW	Dec 18	JML	
5310	DLQ	587 Jan 16	JMR	
11	DLH	Feb 15	RJB	
12	**DLH**	Mar 17	SHB	20N58; 152
13	18 AF MHR	Apr 15	RMD	
14	SFR	May 14	SHW	
15	RBL	Jun 13	DLQ	
16	RBR	Jul 12	DLH	
17	JML	Aug 11	MHR 36 BH	
18	JMR	Sept 9	SFR	
19	RJB	Oct 9	RBL	
5320	SHB	Nov 8	RBR	
21	RMD	Dec 7	JML	
22	SHW	588 Jan 6	JMR	
23	DLQ	Feb 4	RJB	
24	DLH	Mar 5	SHB	
25	19 AF MHR	Apr 3	RMD	
26	SFR	May 3	SHW	
27	RBL	Jun 1	DLQ	
28	RBR	Jul 1	DLH	
29	JML	Jul 30	MHR 35 BH	
5330	JMR	Aug 29	SFR	
31	RJB	Sept 27	RBL	
32	SHB	Oct 27	RBR	
33	RMD	Nov 25	JML	
34	SHW	Dec 25	JMR	
35	DLQ	589 Jan 24	RJB	

1. The lunar month commences from the sunset of the Julian dates shown in the table.
2. The serial of the months is as considered from the beginning of the intercalary epoch.
3. The last column indicates the serial of the intercalary month in the cycle of repetition as well as in the intercalary epoch.

Pagan and Hijrah Calendars

Month serial (1)	Pagan Calendar AF/H (2)	Date of commencement (3)	Hijrah Calendar BH/AH (4)	Intercalary month serial (5)
36	DLH	Feb 22	SHB	
37	20 AF MHR	Mar 24	RMD	
38	SFR	Apr 22	SHW	
39	RBL	May 22	DLQ	
5340	RBR	Jun 20	DLH	
41	JML	Jul 20	MHR 34 BH	
42	JMR	Aug 18	SFR	
43	RJB	Sept 17	RBL	
44	SHB	Oct 16	RBR	
45	RMD	Nov 15	JML	
46	SHW	Dec 14	JMR	
47	DLQ	590 Jan 13	RJB	
48	DLH	Feb 12	SHB	
49	**DLH**	Mar 13	RMD	21N61; 153
5350	21 AF MHR	Apr 12	SHW	
51	SFR	May 11	DLQ	
52	RBL	Jun 10	DLH	
53	RBR	Jul 9	MHR 33 BH	
54	JML	Aug 7	SFR	
55	JMR	Sept 6	RBL	
56	RJB	Oct 6	RBR	
57	SHB	Nov 4	JML	
58	RMD	Dec 4	JMR	
59	SHW	591 Jan 2	RJB	
5360	DLQ	Feb 1	SHB	
61	DLH	Mar 3	RMD	
62	**DLH**	Apr 1	SHW	22N62; 154
63	22 AF MHR	May 1	DLQ	
64	SFR	May 30	DLH	
65	RBL	Jun 29	MHR 32 BH	
66	RBR	Jul 28	SFR	
67	JML	Aug 26	RBL	
68	JMR	Sept 25	RBR	
69	RJB	Oct 25	JML	
5370	SHB	Nov 23	JMR	

1. The lunar month commences from the sunset of the Julian dates shown in the table.
2. The serial of the months is as considered from the beginning of the intercalary epoch.
3. The last column indicates the serial of the intercalary month in the cycle of repetition as well as in the intercalary epoch.

Pagan and Hijrah Calendars

Month serial (1)	Pagan Calendar AF/H (2)	Date of commencement (3)	Hijrah Calendar BH/AH (4)	Intercalary month serial (5)
71	RMD	Dec 23	RJB	
72	SHW	592 Jan 21	SHB	
73	DLQ	Feb 20	RMD	
74	DLH	Mar 20	SHW	
75	23 AF MHR	Apr 18	DLQ	
76	SFR	May 18	DLH	
77	RBL	Jun 16	MHR 31 BH	
78	RBR	Jul 16	SFR	
79	JML	Aug 14	RBL	
5380	JMR	Sept 13	RBR	
81	RJB	Oct 12	JML	
82	SHB	Nov 11	JMR	
83	RMD	Dec 11	RJB	
84	SHW	593 Jan 9	SHB	
85	DLQ	Feb 8	RMD	
86	DLH	Mar 10	SHW	
87	24 AF MHR	Apr 8	DLQ	
88	SFR	May 8	DLH	
89	RBL	Jun 6	MHR 30 BH	
5390	RBR	Jul 6	SFR	
91	JML	Aug 4	RBL	
92	JMR	Sept 3	RBR	
93	RJB	Oct 2	JML	
94	SHB	Nov 1	JMR	
95	RMD	Nov 30	RJB	
96	SHW	Dec 30	SHB	
97	DLQ	594 Jan 29	RMD	
98	DLH	Feb 27	SHW	
99	**DLH**	Mar 29	DLQ	23N65; 155
5400	25 AF MHR	Apr 27	DLH	
01	SFR	May 27	MHR 29 BH	
02	RBL	Jun 25	SFR	
03	RBR	Jul 25	RBL	
04	JML	Aug 23	RBR	
05	JMR	Sept 22	JML	

1. The lunar month commences from the sunset of the Julian dates shown in the table.
2. The serial of the months is as considered from the beginning of the intercalary epoch.
3. The last column indicates the serial of the intercalary month in the cycle of repetition as well as in the intercalary epoch.

Pagan and Hijrah Calendars

Month serial (1)	Pagan Calendar AF/H (2)	Date of commencement (3)	Hijrah Calendar BH/AH (4)	Intercalary month serial (5)
06	RJB	Oct 21	JMR	
07	SHB	Nov 20	RJB	
08	RMD	Dec 19	SHB	
09	SHW	595 Jan 18	RMD	
5410	DLQ	Feb 16	SHW	
11	DLH	Mar 18	DLQ	
12	26 AF MHR	Apr 17	DLH	
13	SFR	May 16	MHR 28 BH	
14	RBL	Jun 15	SFR	
15	RBR	Jul 14	RBL	
16	JML	Aug 12	RBR	
17	JMR	Sept 11	JML	
18	RJB	Oct 11	JMR	
19	SHB	Nov 9	RJB	
5420	RMD	Dec 9	SHB	
21	SHW	596 Jan 7	RMD	
22	DLQ	Feb 6	SHW	
23	DLH	Mar 7	DLQ	
24	27 AF MHR	Apr 5	DLH	
25	SFR	May 5	MHR 27 BH	
26	RBL	Jun 3	SFR	
27	RBR	Jul 2	RBL	
28	JML	Aug 1	RBR	
29	JMR	Aug 30	JML	
5430	RJB	Sept 29	JMR	
31	SHB	Oct 28	RJB	
32	RMD	Nov 27	SHB	
33	SHW	Dec 27	RMD	
34	DLQ	597 Jan 25	SHW	
35	DLH	Feb 24	DLQ	
36	**DLH**	Mar 25	DLH	**24N68; 156**
37	28 AF MHR	Apr 24	MHR 26 BH	
38	SFR	May 23	SFR	
39	RBL	Jun 22	RBL	
5440	RBR	Jul 21	RBR	

1. The lunar month commences from the sunset of the Julian dates shown in the table.
2. The serial of the months is as considered from the beginning of the intercalary epoch.
3. The last column indicates the serial of the intercalary month in the cycle of repetition as well as in the intercalary epoch.

Pagan and Hijrah Calendars

Month serial	Pagan Calendar AF/H	Date of commencement	Hijrah Calendar BH/AH	Intercalary month serial
(1)	(2)	(3)	(4)	(5)
41	JML	Aug 20	JML	
42	JMR	Sept 18	JMR	
43	RJB	Oct 18	RJB	
44	SHB	Nov 16	SHB	
45	RMD	Dec 16	RMD	
46	SHW	598 Jan 15	SHW	
47	DLQ	Feb 13	DLQ	
48	DLH	Mar 15	DLH	
49	29 AF MHR	Apr 13	MHR 25 BH	
5450	SFR	May 13	SFR	
51	RBL	Jun 11	RBL	
52	RBR	Jul 11	RBR	
53	JML	Aug 9	JML	
54	JMR	Sept 8	JMR	
55	RJB	Oct 7	RJB	
56	SHB	Nov 6	SHB	
57	RMD	Dec 5	RMD	
58	SHW	599 Jan 4	SHW	
59	DLQ	Feb 2	DLQ	
5460	DLH	Mar 4	DLH	
61	30 AF MHR	Apr 3	MHR 24 BH	
62	SFR	May 2	SFR	
63	RBL	Jun 1	RBL	
64	RBR	Jun 30	RBR	
65	JML	Jul 30	JML	
66	JMR	Aug 28	JMR	
67	RJB	Sept 27	RJB	
68	SHB	Oct 26	SHB	
69	RMD	Nov 25	RMD	
5470	SHW	Dec 24	SHW	
71	DLQ	600 Jan 23	DLQ	
72	DLH	Feb 21	DLH	
73	**DLH**	Mar 22	MHR 23 BH	**25N71; 157**
74	31 AF MHR	Apr 20	SFR	
75	SFR	May 20	RBL	

1. The lunar month commences from the sunset of the Julian dates shown in the table.
2. The serial of the months is as considered from the beginning of the intercalary epoch.
3. The last column indicates the serial of the intercalary month in the cycle of repetition as well as in the intercalary epoch.

Pagan and Hijrah Calendars

Month serial	Pagan Calendar AF/H	Date of commencement	Hijrah Calendar BH/AH	Intercalary month serial
(1)	(2)	(3)	(4)	(5)
76	RBL	Jun 18	RBR	
77	RBR	Jul 18	JML	
78	JML	Aug 16	JMR	
79	JMR	Sept 15	RJB	
5480	RJB	Oct 14	SHB	
81	SHB	Nov 13	RMD	
82	RMD	Dec 13	SHW	
83	SHW	601 Jan 11	DLQ	
84	DLQ	Feb 10	DLH	
85	DLH	Mar 11	MHR 22 BH	
86	32 AF MHR	Apr 10	SFR	
87	SFR	May 9	RBL	
88	RBL	Jun 8	RBR	
89	RBR	Jul 7	JML	
5490	JML	Aug 5	JMR	
91	JMR	Sept 4	RJB	
92	RJB	Oct 4	SHB	
93	SHB	Nov 2	RMD	
94	RMD	Dec 2	SHW	
95	SHW	602 Jan 1	DLQ	
96	DLQ	Jan 30	DLH	
97	DLH	Mar 1	MHR 21 BH	
98	33 AF MHR	Mar 30	SFR	
99	SFR	Apr 29	RBL	
5500	RBL	May 28	RBR	
01	RBR	Jun 27	JML	
02	JML	Jul 26	JMR	
03	JMR	Aug 25	RJB	
04	RJB	Sept 23	SHB	
05	SHB	Oct 23	RMD	
06	RMD	Nov 21	SHW	
07	SHW	Dec 21	DLQ	
08	DLQ	603 Jan 20	DLH	
09	DLH	Feb 18	MHR 20 BH	
5510	**DLH**	Mar 20	SFR	26N74; 158

1. The lunar month commences from the sunset of the Julian dates shown in the table.
2. The serial of the months is as considered from the beginning of the intercalary epoch.
3. The last column indicates the serial of the intercalary month in the cycle of repetition as well as in the intercalary epoch.

Pagan and Hijrah Calendars

Month serial	Pagan Calendar AF/H	Date of commencement	Hijrah Calendar BH/AH	Intercalary month serial
(1)	(2)	(3)	(4)	(5)
11	34 AF MHR	Apr 18	RBL	
12	SFR	May 17	RBR	
13	RBL	Jun 16	JML	
14	RBR	Jul 15	JMR	
15	JML	Aug 14	RJB	
16	JMR	Sept 12	SHB	
17	RJB	Oct 12	RMD	
18	SHB	Nov 11	SHW	
19	RMD	Dec 10	DLQ	
5520	SHW	604 Jan 9	DLH	
21	DLQ	Feb 7	MHR	19 BH
22	DLH	Mar 8	SFR	
23	35 AF MHR	Apr 6	RBL	
24	SFR	May 6	RBR	
25	RBL	Jun 4	JML	
26	RBR	Jul 4	JMR	
27	JML	Aug 2	RJB	
28	JMR	Sept 1	SHB	
29	RJB	Sept 30	RMD	
5530	SHB	Oct 30	SHW	
31	RMD	Nov 28	DLQ	
32	SHW	Dec 28	DLH	
33	DLQ	605 Jan 27	MHR	18 BH
34	DLH	Feb 25	SFR	
35	36 AF MHR	Mar 27	RBL	
36	SFR	Apr 25	RBR	
37	RBL	May 25	JML	
38	RBR	Jun 23	JMR	
39	JML	Jul 23	RJB	
5540	JMR	Aug 21	SHB	
41	RJB	Sept 20	RMD	
42	SHB	Oct 19	SHW	
43	RMD	Nov 18	DLQ	
44	SHW	Dec 17	DLH	
45	DLQ	606 Jan 16	MHR	17 BH

1. The lunar month commences from the sunset of the Julian dates shown in the table.
2. The serial of the months is as considered from the beginning of the intercalary epoch.
3. The last column indicates the serial of the intercalary month in the cycle of repetition as well as in the intercalary epoch.

Pagan and Hijrah Calendars

Month serial	Pagan Calendar AF/H	Date of commencement	Hijrah Calendar BH/AH	Intercalary month serial
(1)	(2)	(3)	(4)	(5)
46	DLH	Feb 15	SFR	
47	**DLH**	Mar 16	RBL	27N77; 159
48	37 AF MHR	Apr 15	RBR	
49	SFR	May 14	JML	
5550	RBL	Jun 13	JMR	
51	RBR	Jul 12	RJB	
52	JML	Aug 10	SHB	
53	JMR	Sept 9	RMD	
54	RJB	Oct 9	SHW	
55	SHB	Nov 7	DLQ	
56	RMD	Dec 7	DLH	
57	SHW	607 Jan 5	MHR 16 BH	
58	DLQ	Feb 4	SFR	
59	DLH	Mar 6	RBL	
5560	38 AF MHR	Apr 4	RBR	
61	SFR	May 3	JML	
62	RBL	Jun 2	JMR	
63	RBR	Jul 1	RJB	
64	JML	Jul 31	SHB	
65	JMR	Aug 29	RMD	
66	RJB	Sept 28	SHW	
67	SHB	Oct 28	DLQ	
68	RMD	Nov 26	DLH	
69	SHW	Dec 26	MHR 15 BH	
5570	DLQ	608 Jan 24	SFR	
71	DLH	Feb 23	RBL	
72	39 AF MHR	Mar 24	RBR	
73	SFR	Apr 22	JML	
74	RBL	May 21	JMR	
75	RBR	Jun 20	RJB	
76	JML	Jul 19	SHB	
77	JMR	Aug 18	RMD	
78	RJB	Sept 16	SHW	
79	SHB	Oct 16	DLQ	
5580	RMD	Nov 14	DLH	

1. The lunar month commences from the sunset of the Julian dates shown in the table.
2. The serial of the months is as considered from the beginning of the intercalary epoch.
3. The last column indicates the serial of the intercalary month in the cycle of repetition as well as in the intercalary epoch.

Pagan and Hijrah Calendars

Month serial	Pagan Calendar AF/H	Date of commencement	Hijrah Calendar BH/AH	Intercalary month serial
(1)	(2)	(3)	(4)	(5)
81	SHW	Dec 14	MHR 14 BH	
82	DLQ	609 Jan 13	SFR	
83	DLH	Feb 11	RBL	
84	**DLH**	Mar 13	RBR	**28N80; 160**
85	40 AF MHR	Apr 11	JML	
86	SFR	May 11	JMR	
87	RBL	Jun 9	RJB	
88	RBR	Jul 9	SHB	
89	JML	Aug 7	RMD	
5590	JMR	Sept 6	SHW	
91	RJB	Oct 5	DLQ	
92	SHB	Nov 4	DLH	
93	RMD	Dec 4	MHR 13 BH	
94	SHW	610 Jan 2	SFR	
95	DLQ	Feb 1	RBL	
96	DLH	Mar 2	RBR	
97	41 AF MHR	Apr 1	JML	
98	SFR	Apr 30	JMR	
99	RBL	May 30	RJB	
5600	RBR	Jun 28	SHB	
01	JML	Jul 28	RMD	
02	JMR	Aug 26	SHW	
03	RJB	Sept 25	DLQ	
04	SHB	Oct 25	DLH	
05	RMD	Nov 23	MHR 12 BH	
06	SHW	Dec 23	SFR	
07	DLQ	611 Jan 21	RBL	
08	DLH	Feb 20	RBR	
09	42 AF MHR	Mar 21	JML	
5610	SFR	Apr 20	JMR	
11	RBL	May 19	RJB	
12	RBR	Jun 18	SHB	
13	JML	Jul 17	RMD	
14	JMR	Aug 15	SHW	
15	RJB	Sept 14	DLQ	

1. The lunar month commences from the sunset of the Julian dates shown in the table.
2. The serial of the months is as considered from the beginning of the intercalary epoch.
3. The last column indicates the serial of the intercalary month in the cycle of repetition as well as in the intercalary epoch.

Pagan and Hijrah Calendars

Month serial	Pagan Calendar AF/H	Date of commencement	Hijrah Calendar BH/AH	Intercalary month serial
(1)	(2)	(3)	(4)	(5)
16	SHB	Oct 14	DLH	
17	RMD	Nov 12	MHR 11 BH	
18	SHW	Dec 12	SFR	
19	DLQ	612 Jan 10	RBL	
5620	DLH	Feb 9	RBR	
21	**DLH**	Mar 10	JML	29N83; 161
22	43 AF MHR	Apr 8	JMR	
23	SFR	May 7	RJB	
24	RBL	Jun 6	SHB	
25	RBR	Jul 5	RMD	
26	JML	Aug 4	SHW	
27	JMR	Sept 2	DLQ	
28	RJB	Oct 2	DLH	
29	SHB	Nov 1	MHR 10 BH	
5630	RMD	Nov 30	SFR	
31	SHW	Dec 30	RBL	
32	DLQ	613 Jan 28	RBR	
33	DLH	Feb 27	JML	
34	44 AF MHR	Mar 28	JMR	
35	SFR	Apr 27	RJB	
36	RBL	May 26	SHB	
37	RBR	Jun 25	RMD	
38	JML	Jul 24	SHW	
39	JMR	Aug 23	DLQ	
5640	RJB	Sept 21	DLH	
41	SHB	Oct 21	MHR 9 BH	
42	RMD	Nov 19	SFR	
43	SHW	Dec 19	RBL	
44	DLQ	614 Jan 18	RBR	
45	DLH	Feb 16	JML	
46	45 AF MHR	Mar 18	JMR	
47	SFR	Apr 16	RJB	
48	RBL	May 16	SHB	
49	RBR	Jun 14	RMD	
5650	JML	Jul 14	SHW	

1. The lunar month commences from the sunset of the Julian dates shown in the table.
2. The serial of the months is as considered from the beginning of the intercalary epoch.
3. The last column indicates the serial of the intercalary month in the cycle of repetition as well as in the intercalary epoch.

Appendices

Pagan and Hijrah Calendars

Month serial	Pagan Calendar AF/H	Date of commencement	Hijrah Calendar BH/AH	Intercalary month serial
(1)	(2)	(3)	(4)	(5)
51	JMR	Aug 12	DLQ	
52	RJB	Sept 11	DLH	
53	SHB	Oct 10	MHR 8 BH	
54	RMD	Nov 9	SFR	
55	SHW	Dec 8	RBL	
56	DLQ	615 Jan 7	RBR	
57	DLH	Feb 5	JML	
58	**DLH**	Mar 7	JMR	30N86; 162
59	46 AF MHR	Apr 6	RJB	
5660	SFR	May 5	SHB	
61	RBL	Jun 4	RMD	
62	RBR	Jul 3	SHW	
63	JML	Aug 1	DLQ	
64	JMR	Aug 31	DLH	
65	RJB	Sept 30	MHR 7 BH	
66	SHB	Oct 29	SFR	
67	RMD	Nov 28	RBL	
68	SHW	Dec 27	RBR	
69	DLQ	616 Jan 26	JML	
5670	DLH	Feb 24	JMR	
71	47 AF MHR	Mar 25	RJB	
72	SFR	Apr 23	SHB	
73	RBL	May 23	RMD	
74	RBR	Jun 21	SHW	
75	JML	Jul 21	DLQ	
76	JMR	Aug 19	DLH	
77	RJB	Sept 18	MHR 6 BH	
78	SHB	Oct 17	SFR	
79	RMD	Nov 16	RBL	
5680	SHW	Dec 16	RBR	
81	DLQ	617 Jan 14	JML	
82	DLH	Feb 13	JMR	
83	48 AF MHR	Mar 14	RJB	
84	SFR	Apr 13	SHB	
85	RBL	May 12	RMD	

1. The lunar month commences from the sunset of the Julian dates shown in the table.
2. The serial of the months is as considered from the beginning of the intercalary epoch.
3. The last column indicates the serial of the intercalary month in the cycle of repetition as well as in the intercalary epoch.

Pagan and Hijrah Calendars

Month serial	Pagan Calendar AF/H	Date of commencement	Hijrah Calendar BH/AH	Intercalary month serial
(1)	(2)	(3)	(4)	(5)
86	RBR	Jun 11	SHW	
87	JML	Jul 10	DLQ	
88	JMR	Aug 9	DLH	
89	RJB	Sept 7	MHR 5 BH	
5690	SHB	Oct 7	SFR	
91	RMD	Nov 5	RBL	
92	SHW	Dec 5	RBR	
93	DLQ	618 Jan 4	JML	
94	DLH	Feb 2	JMR	
95	**DLH**	Mar 4	RJB	31N89; 163
96	49 AF MHR	Apr 2	SHB	
97	SFR	May 2	RMD	
98	RBL	May 31	SHW	
99	RBR	Jun 30	DLQ	
5700	JML	Jul 29	DLH	
01	JMR	Aug 28	MHR 4 BH	
02	RJB	Sept 26	SFR	
03	SHB	Oct 26	RBL	
04	RMD	Nov 25	RBR	
05	SHW	Dec 24	JML	
06	DLQ	619 Jan 23	JMR	
07	DLH	Feb 21	RJB	
08	50 AF MHR	Mar 23	SHB	
09	SFR	Apr 21	RMD	
5710	RBL	May 21	SHW	
11	RBR	Jun 19	DLQ	
12	JML	Jul 19	DLH	
13	JMR	Aug 17	MHR 3 BH	
14	RJB	Sept 16	SFR	
15	SHB	Oct 15	RBL	
16	RMD	Nov 14	RBR	
17	SHW	Dec 13	JML	
18	DLQ	620 Jan 12	JMR	
19	DLH	Feb 10	RJB	
5720	51 AF MHR	Mar 11	SHB	

1. The lunar month commences from the sunset of the Julian dates shown in the table.
2. The serial of the months is as considered from the beginning of the intercalary epoch.
3. The last column indicates the serial of the intercalary month in the cycle of repetition as well as in the intercalary epoch.

Pagan and Hijrah Calendars

Month serial	Pagan Calendar AF/H	Date of commencement	Hijrah Calendar BH/AH	Intercalary month serial
(1)	(2)	(3)	(4)	(5)
21	SFR	Apr 9	RMD	
22	RBL	May 9	SHW	
23	RBR	Jun 7	DLQ	
24	JML	Jul 7	DLH	
25	JMR	Aug 5	MHR 2 BH	
26	RJB	Sept 4	SFR	
27	SHB	Oct 4	RBL	
28	RMD	Nov 2	RBR	
29	SHW	Dec 2	JML	
5730	DLQ	Dec 31	JMR	
31	DLH	621 Jan 30	RJB	
32	**DLH**	Feb 28	SHB	**32N92; 164**
33	52 AF MHR	Mar 30	RMD	
34	SFR	Apr 28	SHW	
35	RBL	May 28	DLQ	
36	RBR	Jun 26	DLH	
37	JML	Jul 25	MHR 1 BH	
38	JMR	Aug 24	SFR	
39	RJB	Sept 23	RBL	
5740	SHB	Oct 22	RBR	
41	RMD	Nov 21	JML	
42	SHW	Dec 21	JMR	
43	DLQ	622 Jan 19	RJB	
44	DLH	Feb 18	SHB	
45	**DLH**	Mar 19	RMD	**33N93; 165**
46	1 H MHR	Apr 18	SHW	
47	SFR	May 18	DLQ	
48	RBL	Jun 16	DLH	
49	RBR	Jul 15	MHR 1 AH	
5750	JML	Aug 14	SFR	
51	JMR	Sept 12	RBL	
52	RJB	Oct 12	RBR	
53	SHB	Nov 10	JML	
54	RMD	Dec 10	JMR	
55	SHW	623 Jan 9	RJB	

1. The lunar month commences from the sunset of the Julian dates shown in the table.
2. The serial of the months is as considered from the beginning of the intercalary epoch.
3. The last column indicates the serial of the intercalary month in the cycle of repetition as well as in the intercalary epoch.

Pagan and Hijrah Calendars

Month serial	Pagan Calendar AF/H		Date of commencement		Hijrah Calendar BH/AH		Intercalary month serial
(1)	(2)		(3)		(4)		(5)
56		DLQ	Feb	7	SHB		
57		DLH	Mar	9	RMD		
58	2 H	MHR	Apr	7	SHW		
59		SFR	May	7	DLQ		
5760		RBL	Jun	6	DLH		
61		RBR	Jul	5	MHR	2 AH	
62		JML	Aug	3	SFR		
63		JMR	Sept	2	RBL		
64		RJB	Oct	1	RBR		
65		SHB	Oct	31	JML		
66		RMD	Nov	30	JMR		
67		SHW	Dec	29	RJB		
68		DLQ	624 Jan	28	SHB		
69		DLH	Feb	26	RMD		
5770	3 H	MHR	Mar	27	SHW		
71		SFR	Apr	25	DLQ		
72		RBL	May	25	DLH		
73		RBR	Jun	23	MHR	3 AH	
74		JML	Jul	23	SFR		
75		JMR	Aug	21	RBL		
76		RJB	Sept	19	RBR		
77		SHB	Oct	19	JML		
78		RMD	Nov	18	JMR		
79		SHW	Dec	18	RJB		
5780		DLQ	625 Jan	16	SHB		
81		DLH	Feb	15	RMD		
82		**DLH**	Mar	16	SHW		34N96; 166
83	4 H	MHR	Apr	15	DLQ		
84		SFR	May	14	DLH		
85		RBL	Jun	13	MHR	4 AH	
86		RBR	Jul	12	SFR		
87		JML	Aug	10	RBL		
88		JMR	Sept	9	RBR		
89		RJB	Oct	9	JML		
5790		SHB	Nov	7	JMR		

1. The lunar month commences from the sunset of the Julian dates shown in the table.
2. The serial of the months is as considered from the beginning of the intercalary epoch.
3. The last column indicates the serial of the intercalary month in the cycle of repetition as well as in the intercalary epoch.

Pagan and Hijrah Calendars

Month serial (1)	Pagan Calendar AF/H (2)		Date of commencement (3)		Hijrah Calendar BH/AH (4)		Intercalary month serial (5)
91		RMD	Dec	6	RJB		
92		SHW	626 Jan	5	SHB		
93		DLQ	Feb	4	RMD		
94		DLH	Mar	5	SHW		
95	5 H	MHR	Apr	4	DLQ		
96		SFR	May	3	DLH		
97		RBL	Jun	2	MHR	5 AH	
98		RBR	Jul	2	SFR		
99		JML	Jul	31	RBL		
5800		JMR	Aug	29	RBR		
01		RJB	Sept	28	JML		
02		SHB	Oct	28	JMR		
03		RMD	Nov	26	RJB		
04		SHW	Dec	26	SHB		
05		DLQ	627 Jan	24	RMD		
06		DLH	Feb	23	SHW		
07	6 H	MHR	Mar	25	DLQ		
08		SFR	Apr	23	DLH		
09		RBL	May	22	MHR	6 AH	
5810		RBR	Jun	21	SFR		
11		JML	Jul	20	RBL		
12		JMR	Aug	18	RBR		
13		RJB	Sept	17	JML		
14		SHB	Oct	17	JMR		
15		RMD	Nov	15	RJB		
16		SHW	Dec	15	SHB		
17		DLQ	628 Jan	14	RMD		
18		DLH	Feb	12	SHW		
19		**DLH**	Mar	13	DLQ		**35N99; 167**
5820	7 H	MHR	Apr	11	DLH		
21		SFR	May	11	MHR	7 AH	
22		RBL	Jun	9	SFR		
23		RBR	Jul	8	RBL		
24		JML	Aug	7	RBR		
25		JMR	Sept	5	JML		

1. The lunar month commences from the sunset of the Julian dates shown in the table.
2. The serial of the months is as considered from the beginning of the intercalary epoch.
3. The last column indicates the serial of the intercalary month in the cycle of repetition as well as in the intercalary epoch.

Pagan and Hijrah Calendars

Month serial	Pagan Calendar AF/H		Date of commencement		Hijrah Calendar BH/AH		Intercalary month serial
(1)	(2)		(3)		(4)		(5)
26		RJB	Oct	5	JMR		
27		SHB	Nov	3	RJB		
28		RMD	Dec	4	SHB		
29		SHW	629 Jan	2	RMD		
5830		DLQ	Feb	1	SHW		
31		DLH	Mar	2	DLQ		
32	8 H	MHR	Mar	31	DLH		
33		SFR	Apr	30	MHR	8 AH	
34		RBL	May	30	SFR		
35		RBR	Jun	28	RBL		
36		JML	Jul	27	RBR		
37		JMR	Aug	26	JML		
38		RJB	Sept	25	JMR		
39		SHB	Oct	24	RJB		
5840		RMD	Nov	23	SHB		
41		SHW	Dec	23	RMD		
42		DLQ	630 Jan	21	SHW		
43		DLH	Feb	19	DLQ		
44	9 H	MHR	Mar	21	DLH		
45		SFR	Apr	19	MHR	9 AH	
46		RBL	May	19	SFR		
47		RBR	Jun	17	RBL		
48		JML	Jul	17	RBR		
49		JMR	Aug	15	JML		
5850		RJB	Sept	14	JMR		
51		SHB	Oct	13	RJB		
52		RMD	Nov	12	SHB		
53		SHW	Dec	11	RMD		
54		DLQ	631 Jan	10	SHW		
55		DLH	Feb	9	DLQ		
56		**DLH**	Mar	10	DLH		36N102; 168
57	10 H	MHR	Apr	9	MHR	10 AH	
58		SFR	May	8	SFR		
59		RBL	Jun	7	RBL		
5860		RBR	Jul	6	RBR		

1. The lunar month commences from the sunset of the Julian dates shown in the table.
2. The serial of the months is as considered from the beginning of the intercalary epoch.
3. The last column indicates the serial of the intercalary month in the cycle of repetition as well as in the intercalary epoch.

Pagan and Hijrah Calendars

Month serial	Pagan Calendar AF/H	Date of commencement	Hijrah Calendar BH/AH	Intercalary month serial
(1)	(2)	(3)	(4)	(5)
61	JML	Aug 5	JML	
62	JMR	Sept 3	JMR	
63	RJB	Oct 3	RJB	
64	SHB	Nov 1	SHB	
65	RMD	Dec 1	RMD	
66	SHW	Dec 30	SHW	
67	DLQ	632 Jan 29	DLQ	
68	DLH	Feb 28	DLH	
69	11 H MHR	Mar 29	MHR 11 AH	
5870	SFR	Apr 27	SFR	
71	RBL	May 27	RBL	
72	RBR	Jun 25	RBR	
73	JML	Jul 25	JML	
74	JMR	Aug 24	JMR	
75	RJB	Sept 22	RJB	
76	SHB	Oct 22	SHB	
77	RMD	Nov 20	RMD	
78	SHW	Dec 20	SHW	
79	DLQ	633 Jan 18	DLQ	
5880	DLH	Feb 17	DLH	

1. The lunar month commences from the sunset of the Julian dates shown in the table.
2. The serial of the months is as considered from the beginning of the intercalary epoch.
3. The last column indicates the serial of the intercalary month in the cycle of repetition as well as in the intercalary epoch.

Appendix 3
Tsybulsky's Chart
FOR CALCULATION OF ASTRONOMICAL DATES OF NEW MOON

No.	Millennium	Century	Decade	Year		Month
(0)	0.0	0.0	0.0	0.0	Mar	24.2
(1)	13.9	4.3	9.3	18.6	Apr	22.6
(2)	27.7	8.7	18.6	7.8	May	22.0
(3)		13.0	27.9	26.4	Jun	20.6
(4)		17.4	7.6	15.5	Jul	20.0
(5)		21.7	16.9	4.6	Aug	18.0
(6)		26.0	26.2	23.3	Sept	17.0
(7)		0.8	6.0	12.4	Oct	16.6
(8)		5.2	15.3	1.5	Nov	15.1
(9)		9.5	24.6	20.2	Dec	14.8
					Jan	13.4
					Feb	11.9

How to use the chart:

To determine the date of new moon in a given year and month (accuracy, within 0.5 day in GMT),

(1) add the figures standing in the columns Millennium, Century, Decade, Year and Month against the given year and month,

(2) add correction 0.0, 0.2, 0.5 or 0.8 depending on whether the remainder after dividing the serial of the year by four is 0, 1, 2 or 3 respectively,

(The data for the months of January and February are calculated according to the preceding year. For example, the dates of new moon in January and February 1925 would be calculated for the year 1924),

(3) For the months after September, 1582 add 13.0 for change of the calendar from the Julian style to the Gregorian, and

(4) Subtract 29.5, 59.1 or 88.6 from the sum obtained, depending on which of these numbers is exceeded by the sum; the remainder will give the date of the first new moon in the given month (for there may be two of them).

Appendix 4
HOURS OF SUNSET
Makkah: 21° N; 40° E, Madinah: 25° N; 40° E

Date	January 20° N	January 24° N	February 20° N	February 24° N	March 20° N	March 24° N	April 20° N	April 24° N
1	1732	1724						
2			1752	1747	1805	1803		
3							1815	1817
4								
5	1735	1727						
6			1755	1750	1807	1805		
7							1816	1818
8								
9	1737	1730						
10			1757	1752	1808	1807		
11							1817	1820
12								
13	1740	1733						
14			1759	1755	1809	1809		
15							1818	1822
16								
17	1742	1735						
18			1801	1757	1810	1810		
19							1819	1823
20								
21	1745	1738						
22			1802	1759	1812	1812		
23							1821	1825
24								
25	1748	1741						
26			1804	1801	1813	1814		
27							1822	1827
28								
29	1750	1744						
30					1814	1815		
31								

Hours of Sunset

Makkah: 21° N; 40° E, Madinah: 25° N; 40° E

Date	May		June		July		August	
	20° N	24° N	20° N	24° N	20° N	24° N	20° N	24° N
1	1824	1829					1837	1843
2			1836	1844				
3								
4					1844	1852		
5	1825	1831					1835	1841
6			1838	1846				
7								
8					1844	1851		
9	1827	1833					1833	1838
10			1839	1847				
11								
12					1843	1851		
13	1828	1835					1830	1835
14			1840	1849				
15								
16					1843	1850		
17	1830	1836					1827	1832
18			1841	1850				
19								
20					1842	1849		
21	1831	1838					1824	1829
22			1842	1851				
23								
24					1840	1847		
25	1833	1840					1821	1825
26			1843	1851				
27								
28					1839	1845		
29	1835	1842					1818	1821
30			1843	1852				
31								

Hours of Sunset
Makkah: 21° N; 40° E, Madinah: 25° N; 40° E

Date	September 20° N	September 24° N	October 20° N	October 24° N	November 20° N	November 24° N	December 20° N	December 24° N
1					1726	1721		
2	1815	1817						
3							1720	1712
4			1746	1744				
5					1724	1719		
6	1811	1813						
7							1721	1713
8			1742	1741				
9					1722	1717		
10	1808	1809						
11							1722	1714
12			1739	1737				
13					1721	1715		
14	1804	1805						
15							1723	1715
16			1736	1733				
17					1720	1714		
18	1800	1801						
19							1725	1717
20			1733	1730				
21					1719	1713		
22	1757	1757						
23							1727	1719
24			1730	1727				
25					1719	1712		
26	1753	1753						
27							1729	1721
28			1728	1724				
29					1719	1712		
30	1749	1748						
31							1731	1723

(Data extracted from Dr. Muhammad Ilyas' *Islamic Calendar, Times and Qiblah*)

Appendix 5

Millennium Calendar (0001–2299)

		B. YEARS Last two digits of the year				
00	01	02	03		04	05
06	07		08	09	10	11
	12	13	14	15		16
17	18	19		20	21	22
23		24	25	26	27	
28	29	30	31		32	33
34	35		36	37	38	39
	40	41	42	43		44
45	46	47		48	49	50
51		52	53	54	55	
56	57	58	59		60	61
62	63		64	65	66	67
	68	69	70	71		72
73	74	75		76	77	78
79		80	81	82	83	
84	85	86	87		88	89
90	91		92	93	94	95
	96	97	98	99		

A. CENTURIES — First two digits of the year

Julian		Gregorian		D. KEY LETTERS							C. MONTHS	
	04	11	15	19	H	F	M	R	A	E	N	JAN OCT
	05	12	16	20	N	H	F	M	R	A	E	MAY
	06	13			E	N	H	F	M	R	A	*FEB* AUG
00	07	14	17	21	A	E	N	H	F	M	R	FEB MAR NOV
01	08	15			R	A	E	N	H	F	M	JUN
02	09		18	22	M	R	A	E	N	H	F	SEPT DEC
03	10				F	M	R	A	E	N	H	*JAN* APR JUL

E. DATES					F. DAYS					
01	08	15	22	29	MO	TU	WE	TH	FR	SA	SU
02	09	16	23	30	TU	WE	TH	FR	SA	SU	MO
03	10	17	24	31	WE	TH	FR	SA	SU	MO	TU
04	11	18	25		TH	FR	SA	SU	MO	TU	WE
05	12	19	26		FR	SA	SU	MO	TU	WE	TH
06	13	20	27		SA	SU	MO	TU	WE	TH	FR
07	14	21	28		SU	MO	TU	WE	TH	FR	SA

How to use this calendar:

(1) Identify in table D the key letter standing at the intersecting point of the row of the first two digits of the year shown in table A and the column of the last two digits of the year shown in table B.

(2) Locate in table D the same key letter against the row of the month referred to in table C. In table C use italicised months of January and February in the case of leap years.

(3) Locate in table F the weekday standing at the intersecting point of the row of the date in question in table E and the column of the key letter in table D. The weekday recorded thereat will be the weekday of the date in question.

In table A use Julian calendar up to October 4, 1582 and Gregorian from October 15, 1582. There were no such dates as 5, 6, ... 13, 14 in the Christian calendar in October 1582 because of correction of certain errors accumulated in the Julian style.

Bibliography

Abu Dawud:	*Sunan Abu Dawud*, (Tr. Prof. Ahmad Hasan), 1985, New Delhi
Ahmed, Mirza Bashiruddin:	*Holy Qur'an, Translation and Commentary*, 1988, Woking, England
Ali, Allamah Abdallah Yusuf:	*Holy Qur'an, Text, Translation and Commentary*, 1973, New Delhi
Ali, Dr. Hashim Amir:	*Upstream downstream Reconstruction of Islamic Chronology*, 1977, Patna
Ali, Syed Ameer:	*Short History of the Saracens*, 1977, New Delhi
	Spirit of Islam, 1976, New Delhi
Alvi, Ishaqun Nabi:	*Sirat Nabuweemen Touketi Tazadad aur uska Hal* - Articles in Burhan, May to December 1964, Delhi
Asad, Muhammad:	*Message of the Qur'an*, 1980, Gibraltar
Bedar, Dr. Abid Reza:	*Arab calendar prevalent during the lifetime of Muhammad*, 1968, Delhi
Al-Bukhari, Imam:	*Sahih Bukhari*, (Tr. Dr. Muhammad Muhsin Khan), 1984, New Delhi
Dinet & Sliman:	*The life of Muhammad, the Prophet of Allah*, 1984, Madras
Hamidullah, Dr. Muhammad:	*Muhammad Rasulullah*, 1974, Hyderabad. *Foreign Relations of Prophet Muhammad*, 1985, Hyderabad. *The Nasi', the Hijrah Calendar and the need of preparing a new concordance for the Hijrah and Gregorian Eras* - Article in The Islamic Review and Arab Affairs, February 1969, Woking, England

Hughes, Thomas Patrick:	*Dictionary of Islam*, 1979, Delhi
Hussein, Jamal N.:	*Finding the Julian Dates of the Islamic Events before Hijrah Using Computer* - Article in Islamic Culture, January 1997, Hyderabad
Hydal & Hydal:	*The Crescent*, 1985, Trinidad
Ibn Hisham:	*Siratun Nabi*, (Tr. Maulana Abdul Jalil Siddiqi), 1982, Delhi
Ibn Kathir:	*Tafsir ibn Kathir*, (Tr. Ashraf Ali Thanvi), Deoband
Ibn Sa'd:	*Kitab at-Tabaqat al-Kabir*, (Tr. S. Moinul Haq), New Delhi
Ilyas, Dr. Muhammad:	*Islamic Calendar, Times and Qiblah*, 1984, Kuala Lumpur
Khan, Maulana Habibur Rahman:	*Wiladat Khairul Naami* - Article in Burhan, April 1965, Delhi
Khan, Sir Zafrullah:	*Muhammad, Seal of Prophets*, 1980, London
Klein, F. A.:	*Religion of Islam*, 1977, New Delhi
Margoliouth, D. S.:	*Muhammad and the Rise of Islam*, 1985, New Delhi
Maududi, Abul Ala:	*Sarware Aalam*, 1979, Delhi
Mirkhond (Muhammad bin Khavendshah):	*Rauzatus Safa*, (Tr. E. Rehatsek), 1982, Delhi
Muir, Sir William:	*Life of Mahomet*, 1992, New Delhi
Muslim, Imam:	*Sahih Muslim*, (Tr. A.H. Siddiqi), 1978, New Delhi
Mustafa, Ghulam:	*Bishwanabi*, 1982, Dacca
Perceval, Caussin de:	*Arab Calendar before Islam* - Article in Islamic Culture, April 1947, Hyderabad
Rahman, Safiur:	*The Sealed Nectar*, 1996, Riyadh
Sachau, C. E.:	*Albiruni's Chronology of Ancient Nations*, 1983, Lahore

Shad, Abdur Rahman: *From Adam to Muhammad*, 1986, Delhi
Sherwani, H. K.: *The Islamic Calendar* - Article in Islamic Review, June 1956
Shibli, Maulana: *Siratun Nabi*, 1988, Azamgarh
Siddiqi, Abdul Hamid: *Life of Muhammad*, 1982, Calcutta
Siddiqi, Naeem: *Muhammad, the Benefactor of Humanity*, 1983, Delhi
Sulaiman & Salman Mansur: *Mercy of the World*, (Tr. A.J. Siddiqi), 1977, Johannesburg
At-Tabari, Ibn Jarir: *Tarikhul Umam wal-Muluk*, (Tr. Syed Muhammad Ibrahim Nadvi), 1982, Deoband
Tabrizi, Waliuddin Muhammad bin Abdallah: *Mishkatul Masabih*, (Tr. Maulana Abdul Hakim Khan), 1987, New Delhi
Tsybulsky, V. V.: *Calendars of Middle East Countries*, 1979, Moscow
Watt, W. Montgomery: *Muhammad at Madinah*, 1994, Karachi
Zakaria, Maulana Muhammad: *Stories of Sahabah*, 1986, Delhi